IGNATIUS LOYOLA.

THE
BLACK POPE.

A HISTORY OF THE JESUITS.

By M. F. CUSACK

(Formerly the Nun of Kenmare).

Author of "The Nun of Kenmare: an Autobiography," "Life inside the Church of Rome," "The Truth about Convent Life," etc., etc.

London:
MARSHALL, RUSSELL & Co., Ltd.,
6, Panyer Alley, Paternoster Row, E.C.

Brighton:
D. B. FRIEND & Co.,
77, Western Road; and 56, Church Road, Hove.

LONDON:
PRINTED BY A. M. ROBINSON AND SON, 1, LOMBARD COURT, E.C.
WORKS: DUKE STREET, BRIGHTON.

PREFACE.

THE title of this work may require some explanation. In Roman Catholic circles it is well known that the Black Pope is the term used for the General of the Jesuits. As the Pope is always robed in white, and the General in black, the contrast is obvious. But those Romanists who do not greatly love the Jesuits, and their number is not limited, use the term as indicating that the Black Pope rules the White Pope. The expression will be found in the recently published life of Cardinal Manning. As the writer had some difficulty in finding a title which would not conflict with many others used in works treating on the same subject, this one was chosen for distinction, and for its special appropriateness.

M. F. CUSACK.

Brighton,

March 26th, 1896.

INTRODUCTION.

INTRODUCTION.—Remarks on the rapid change of religious opinion since the commencement of the present century. —Advance in power and social influence of R.C.s.—They now attack Protestant dignitaries publicly without fear; formerly they were only tolerated because they were silent. —Importance of this change to the future of English speaking countries.—The influence of the Jesuit has been fatal to every country, Catholic or Protestant, where they have been allowed to exist.—They are condemned by Pope Clement XIV. as "far from being any comfort to the Holy See, or any advantage to the Christian world;" remarkable letter of Père la Chaise to Father Peter, S. J.—The Jesuits the great promoters of the changes which have been made in the creed of the Church of Rome during the last two centuries. —The predisposing causes of the Reformation.

THE marked and comparatively rapid changes of religious opinion which have characterised the 19th century will be a subject of profound interest to the historian of the future. Nor are the character of these changes less noteworthy. The Roman Catholics were a feeble folk when the century began, now they hold their own in court, and camp, on the judicial bench, and in the senate. But it was not merely that they were numerically feeble, they were the subjects of contumely and abhorrence. They were mistrusted and hated. Whence then this change? To-day, a Roman cardinal can denounce the actions of an Anglican archbishop; can question his motives, and scorn his priestly orders with scarce a note of censure. Again; whence the change?

The Jesuits, dreaded as being more papal than the Pope, and more Catholic than the College of Cardinals, were fain to remain in obscurity, at the risk of their lives, if they emerged from it. To-day the Jesuit is to all intents and purposes master of the situation. His favourite pupils decide Protestant causes, and with calm effrontery honour the head of their Church as a temporal prince before the Queen, and place him in the position which he claims to be his by divine right, as king of kings and lord of lords.

A faint breath of public disapprobation may be heard: it is but as the echo of a ringdove's note, in comparison with the shout of indignant protest which such an act would have called forth in the twenties or thirties of the present century.

If the Roman Catholic Church has advanced in England by leaps and bounds, it has been because the heads of that Church have known how to prepare the way for the leaps, by steps which were very slow, but very sure, and by ceaseless perseverance in securing advantages.

And so it has been with what, for want of a better

name, we must call Ritualism. In the early days of the century the services in St. Paul's Cathedral were performed behind the heavy organ screen, where the singers could scarcely be heard, and the few worshippers could scarcely be seen. How changed all this is now need scarcely be told.

But the influence of the Jesuit is by no means limited to that which he secures through the opportunities which he possesses of forming the character of those who are destined to be our future statesmen. With keen insight into the needs of the times, the heads of the Order make a speciality of training young men for the Press. It behoves us then to inquire whether these future editors and writers are embued with high principles of patriotism and honour, and whether they are afforded every opportunity of intellectual culture and advancement. Are they encouraged to think out the weighty problems of the age? Is the past history of their Jesuit masters, as educators, such that we can leave the future in their hands and believe that the honour of England is safe in their keeping? These are serious questions. The man who cares so little for his country as to pass them by lightly, can only blame himself if his neglect proves the ruin of his immediate posterity.

Since the fact that the Jesuit has been banished again and again from every country where he has had power cannot be denied, it is surely most important to know what are the charges made against him, and how it is that he continues to exist despite such persistent repression. What are his principles, and how far do they differ from those of his co-religionists? How is it that he has been denounced in such terms of scathing reprobation by one pope, and re-instated in all his ancient privileges by another? What shall we say of a church which so vacillates between praise and blame? What shall we say of a religious order which prides itself on being called by the name of the Saviour of mankind, and yet has made the practice of untruth a fine art, and reduced the practice of lying to a science? It may be objected that these are strong expressions. The question is, not whether the words which we use are strong or feeble, but whether they are true or false. Is it not of the gravest importance to know why a body of men, who are educating the English speaking men of the future, were denounced by the head of their own infallible Church as a Society which was "far from bringing any comfort to the Holy See, or any advantage to the Christian world?" As we shall go fully into the question of the suppression of the Jesuits by the supreme authority of the Church which they have been founded to uphold, we shall not now enter into this subject more fully. It may, however, be noted in passing that the chief points of complaint against the Society have been the same at all times, and in all countries. They have been accused of scandalous political intrigues which they have carried on for the advancement of the Order: they have been accused of teaching a lax morality, to put the accusation in its mildest form; they have been accused of quarrels amongst themselves; they have been accused of gross insubordination to ecclesiastical authority; and they have been accused of sanctioning idolatry, if they did not encourage it, amongst the heathen whom they were supposed to convert to the Christian religion. All these accusations are made in the infallible Bull of Pope Clement XIV., and in this Bull he expressly declares that he has examined all these charges, which were no new matter, as they had been brought before other popes, and that he was fully assured that they were substantiated.

The history of the Jesuits should also be studied in connection with the extraordinary influence which the Order has had in adding to the dogmas of the Church.

The dogma of the immaculate conception was admittedly their work, the new doctrine of the infallibility of the Pope, which has been the cause of so much secret revolt in the Church of Rome, is credited to them, assisted no doubt by the spiritual ambition of Pius IX.

That still further changes in the creed of the

Roman Church are imminent, there can be no question, and this is another reason why the history of the Jesuits demands special attention at the present day. Rome always feels her way for some years before the announcement of a new dogma. Efforts are made to obtain favourable opinions on the subject, so as to prepare the faithful, and to avoid the appearance of a sudden decision. Little books are issued recommending the subject, and making it appear as if the new doctrine about to be defined had always been believed in the Church: though, perhaps, if mentioned at all by theologians, it had either been reprobated, or warmly disputed. Naturally those who are anxious for preferment or ecclesiastical approval, would lend themselves to a work which would secure what they desired.

The new dogma at present incubating in the Church of Rome is the divine right of the Pope to temporal power. Statesmen who are wise enough to foresee the stupendous and far reaching effect which this dogma must have, will deserve well of their country. Some long prepared for, but apparently sudden, call will be made on the loyalty (to the Pope) of the Roman Catholic body, and then the definition will come.

In the decades which preceded the birth of Luther and Loyola, predisposing causes were at work which were destined to throw a flood of intellectual light on European nations. The conquest of Constantinople, in 1453, had scattered learned Greek professors all over the continent of Europe. The old habits of thought still existed, but new subjects of research were opened up. Such learning as there had been was confined, until now, to the priesthood, and naturally their studies were limited to a few classical authors, and to a very large field of metaphysical theology, which made that science rather an intellectual pastime than a religious study. The Humanistic movement, which revived the study of classical authors, had begun, and was not without its effect in inducing larger views of life and literature. Learning, or that which was its substitute in mediæval ages, was no longer confined to monasteries. Johannes Reuchlin and Desiderius Erasmus were the leaders of the new Humanism and the new Renaissance. New thoughts were in the air, and if all were not thinkers, all, or nearly all, were in touch with those who were. Astrological conjecture was giving place to astronomical research, and if the latter had its victims, they were the precursors in the paths of science, always watered with the tears, if not stained with the blood, of the pioneers. But it was in religion, that deepest faculty of the human soul, that the change was most keenly felt. Men were prepared for a revolt against the demand for money, in return for exemption from the penalty of sin. They could read now for themselves in the Book which records the words of Him who spoke as never man spoke, and they saw for themselves with amazed eyes, and felt with joyful hearts that the kingdom of God was within them.

The power of the Church was also seriously shaken by important social changes. Land was no longer the sole source of capital, and, therefore, was no longer, as it had been practically for the greater part, in the hands of the clergy. The dying baron who desired to assoilise his soul could give money to the Church in lieu of the broad acres which he could not take with him to the bourne whither he was reluctantly going. Justice between man and man is the offspring of knowledge, and it began to be dimly seen that justice was not all on the side of the Church. When the acquisition of land ceased to be a paramount object to the Church the acquisition of money took its place, hence the system of Jesuit theology framed to facilitate the obtaining of what was now so desirable. Hence, also, the downfall of the Society in more than one continental country, as the result of sharp practice in this matter.

Coming into active life amongst all these conflicting elements and changes, Loyola formed an association in which he preserved all the worst features of a decaying condition of society, and stereotyped all the worst evils of the past; Luther, looking to the dawn of the coming day, shouted with joy as the son of the morning, and if some trails of the darkness of the passing night from which he emerged shaded the full radiance of his glorious career, he at least cried "Excelsior!" and pressed onwards and upwards towards the noontide and the light.

MARTIN LUTHER.

THE BLACK POPE.

CHAPTER I.

THE FOUNDATION OF THE ORDER.

CONTRAST BETWEEN LUTHER AND LOYOLA.—The birth and early surroundings of Luther and Loyola.—The one uplifts the banner of light and spiritual freedom ; the other forges new chains for the enslaving of the human race—spiritually and intellectually—and transmits the worst evils of the dark ages to posterity.—The military career of Loyola.—His indifference to pain when his personal vanity was concerned. His severe wound leads to his retirement from active military service.—He reads the lives of the saints and the Virgin Mary.—He desires to become famous as a saint, as he can no longer hope to become famous as a soldier.—Contrast with Luther who reads the Bible and desires to bring all to Christ. –Loyola consecrates himself to the service of the Virgin Mary, and puts on her livery.—Luther puts on the whole armour of God.—Loyola fasts, flogs himself, and sees visions, but does not find peace ; the more he flogs himself and fasts, the more visions he sees.—Luther cries aloud "the just shall live by faith," superstitions which Luther combats and Loyola supports ; how miracles are made ; the ghost of the ironmonger.—Loyola cast into the inquisition, accused of heresy.—Spain the cradle of religious mysticism at this period.—Loyola gets into trouble by interfering with ladies of great wealth.—He goes to Paris in 1528.—He makes disciples, Peter Faber, and Francis Xavier.—He determines to devote his Order to the service of the Pope, takes vows with his disciples in Paris, 15th August, 1528.—Corrupt state of the Church at this period ; one cause of his success the

Pope eager to find any one who would restore the confidence of the people in the religious orders.—He wins the people by a show of love for poverty, and the rich by accommodating himself to their vices.—Opens a home in Rome for the mistresses of the nobles and the ecclesiastics, who had been a public scandal.—Wins the ecclesiastical authorities by the enforcement of a cruel edict against the Jews.—Obtains a Bull sanctioning his Order, 27th Feb., 1540.—How the Jesuits obtained complete control of the noble families in Rome, and knew all by their secrets.

THE close of the fifteenth century witnessed the birth of two children who were destined to make history. Luther was born in 1483. Eight years afterwards Don Innigo Lopez de Ricalde was born. How strange the mystery of human life. Who shall answer the cry of the yearning heart to know the unknowable? The one was destined to be the precursor, who proclaimed Gospel liberty to the enslaved; the other was destined to forge new chains for the souls of men, and to bind them with cords of steel. And yet, while in the dawn of life, who could have ventured to predict the future of liberator or Jesuit. For Luther, born of a humble family, an unnoticed career would have been anticipated; he might, indeed, have aspired to the cloister, for it was then the resort of the poorest and the least educated of the community. But for Loyola, the descendant of Spanish grandees, a brilliant career in court and tented field would have seemed little short of a certainty. But when the pages of life came to be unfolded for these two men, how different was the result to the anticipation.

The fame of the lowly-born Luther has echoed down the stream of time, as the champion of religious liberty, and if he was somewhat rude in his mode of denouncing error, his rudeness was as much the outcome of his earnestness and sincerity, as of the habits of the times in which he lived. As for Ignatius Loyola, he also has had his fame and his applause; but his fame has not been the fame of an enlightener of mankind, or of one who has advanced civil or religious liberty. His applauders have not been those who have loved truth and hated dissimulation. Sad indeed that the once chivalrous and knightly Loyola should have become the founder of an institution which has reduced the practice of deceit to a fine art, and taught its members how to conceal and practise evil under a semblance of virtue.

A European war was imminent (as indeed when is it not?) just at the moment when Loyola was of age to desire distinction in the field, and to uphold the war-like traditions of his family. He ambitioned the rank of general, he was a youth of impetuous desires, and naturally his aspirations lay along the line which the age had glorified. To build cathedrals and to conquer new provinces were the ambitions of the century, until the invention of the printer's noble art had opened the doors of knowledge. Cathedral building was left at that period a good deal to the colder blooded north. As for the southern, he has always been more ready for the sword than the pen or the chisel.

But the military career of Loyola had scarcely begun ere it had ended. In the year 1521 the town of Pampeluna was besieged by the French, led by Andre de Foix, Lord of Esparre. Loyola commanded the fort and determined to allow the extermination of his little band sooner than yield to the hated French. But Providence decreed that he should fail, and the shattering of his leg by a cannon ball put him *hors de combat* at once and finally. The French general treated the Spanish captain with the usual chivalry of the age and the nation. He sent his own surgeon to attend his wounded enemy, he gave him his liberty without ransom, and eventually sent him with honour to his father's castle. And here the work of the "Society of Jesus" practically commenced. The character of the founder of the Order manifested itself even in his hours of pain. He showed a grim determination to submit to any suffering which might attain the end he had in view. His leg had contracted during his illness; it must be made the right length, no matter what agony the doing of it occasioned. A projecting bone came in the way of wearing the fashionable attire of the day, and the bone must go. The bone was removed, and the most terrible instruments were applied to the leg to obtain the desired restoration to its normal condition; but the barbarous surgery of the day could do little save add pain to pain. Loyola endured all his sufferings without obtaining his desire. One thing, however, was certain—his days of chivalry were ended, his work in camp and court was done. The long illness, which he had endured with Spartan hardness, left its traces on his countenance. He could no longer play the gallant in court, or in the castles of his knightly friends. He could no longer do battle for his country. His occupation was gone. His active mind gave him no rest. Though admittedly an uneducated man, it would appear that he could read, and probably his temperament had led him to love the perusal of the romances which were the light literature of his day. He asked for books to pass the time of a long enforced convalescence, and none could be found save some legends of the saints, and a legendary life of the Virgin Mary.

What mighty effects arise from apparently accidental causes! Probably Loyola saw little difference at first between the romances and the legends, but as he read he was seized with the idea of devoting himself to the militant service of the church, as he could no longer devote himself to the military service of his country. He needed an idealised woman to replace the ladies fair, if not frail, to whom he had done his devoir in court and tented field, so Loyola now offered to the Queen of Heaven the devotion which he had previously offered to ladies, who had been saluted queens of beauty in the Court of Spain.

If we would read the history of this remarkable man aright, we must study the mental conditions in which he found himself, and the customs of the country, and the times in which he lived. Instead of placing the colours of his inamorata on his lance, or in his corslet, and challenging his fellow knights to do battle in her honour, he took the garb which, according to the religious ideas of the times, was the garb most pleasing to the lady whom he now desired to honour with especial veneration. He clothed himself in the rags of a pilgrim. He flogged his body till the blood came. He fasted until he saw visions, and the more he flogged himself the more visions he saw, and the more visions he saw the more he fasted. It was simply cause and effect. The mind weakened by the weakened body, was no longer master of his God-given intellect. He was guilty of intellectual suicide, for he deliberately deprived himself of his mental powers. No wonder if in such a state of mind the idea should have come to him of framing a rule which requires the abnegation of God's best gift to man. A general who was about to engage in an anxious and important campaign would not dream of preparing himself for it by deliberately weakening his intellectual faculties, yet this is precisely what the Spanish devotee considered to be necessary for the success of his enterprise.

Loyola, once the knight errant, had now become the Saint, according to his narrow ideas of sanctity. His relatives expostulated with him in vain. He had read the lives of the saints during his long illness, and he had determined, with that dogged determination which seems to have been the dominant feature in his character, that if he could not become famed as a knight, he would become famed as a saint. He has accomplished his desire, but how far either he, or the world at large, has benefited by his ambition, let history tell.

Yet with all this infliction of penance Loyola was not happy. It is true he had visions which must have gratified his vanity; but the visions gave no peace to his restless soul. On one occasion he lay for eight days in a trance or swoon; but his awakening did not find him any the happier. He was haunted by demons and distressed by doubts. Probably he believed in his visions, and his demoniacal apparitions were to him realities. It was an age of belief in the marvellous. The priest cannot secure power or influence with the people, unless he can show signs or supernatural manifestations. It needed not that these marvels should be genuine, so long as an ever credulous public believed them to be such. It needed not that the miracle worker should be a deliberate impostor, he needed only to believe in himself.

It should never be forgotten that the power of the priest rests solely on the credence of the people. The people cry out for a saviour, for certainty of heaven, for an assurance of exemption from the terrors of hell. Hence priestcraft can neither do without hell nor purgatory. Take away both, or either, and its power is gone. But in order to maintain a belief in the supernatural power of the priest, there must be some apparently supernatural evidence, hence these miracles, not only of the sixteenth century, but of the nineteenth. To-day we are told that St. Winefrede has given the power of speech to a woman who had not spoken for at least two years. But the case had already been diagnosed by the medical faculty as one of simple hysteria. At the period of which we write a still more wonderful miracle was reported from Paris.

A certain old ironmonger, Eustache Moubon by name, died there, not exactly in the odour of sanctity, but he was devout to the Virgin all the same, or, perhaps, all the more. It was on the night of the 6th January, 1482, when a magnificent bonfire had been commanded. Some boys bethought them that the pallet on which he lay dead would serve to help their fireworks. They accordingly seized it and threw it down in the street. It was then seized on by a vagrant, who lay down on it, hoping to secure a good night's rest. The boys soon returned with more pillage for the flames, and amazed at what they supposed to be a vision, rushed off with piercing screams, declaring that it was the ghost of the iron monger. This was sufficient to form the groundwork of a stupendous miracle. On the following day the pallet was taken in state to the Church of St. Opportune, where it remained until the year 1789, and a handsome income was made by the authorities, by whom it was exhibited as a proof of the power of the Virgin, whose statue had effected the miracle of exorcising the soul of Moubon, which had hid itself in the straw to trick the devil.

Loyola acted according to his lights. His Church taught that the doing of certain acts of bodily mortification would obtain a very high place in heaven for the doer, and that they would be very acceptable to the Virgin, if offered in her name. Furthermore, Loyola knew that canonisation was the highest honour that the Church could bestow, and that the practising of such mortifications was the sure road to canonisation. If he could no longer hope to have his name handed down in the annals of his country as a distinguished general, he might obtain the honour, as he did eventually, of having his name handed down by the Church as worthy of a place on her altars.

We are not writing a life of Ignatius Loyola, hence much of his personal history must be passed over, and only as much related as will show the character of this marvellous man who succeeded in founding an organisation which has more than once convulsed Europe by its ambitions. It can scarcely be denied, except by his submissive disciples, that he acted in direct opposition to the plain counsels of Christ, whose name he so ostentatiously assumed. Our Lord declared that His kingdom was not of this world, and by His manner of life showed that the things of time and sense were but trifles, whose only importance might be found in the use which might be made of them for the eternal interests of the users. The Jesuit, on the contrary, has always been clamorous for power and wealth, and has in consequence occupied himself both individually and collectively with the rich rather than with the poor.

Apparently Loyola became tired of his life of self-mortification, for we find that he set out for Palestine by way of Rome, in the year 1523. To follow his various wanderings during the next few years would be impossible, and is not necessary. Arrived at Jerusalem, where the Francisan Fathers held full spiritual authority, he thought he might at once commence his self-imposed mission of converting the heathen. But there were two invincible difficulties in the way—his culpable ignorance of the commonest elements of the Christianity which he proposed to teach, and his entire ignorance of the language of those whom he wished to convert. It was in vain that he assured the Provincial of the Franciscans that a miracle would be worked in his behalf; the Provincial did not believe in such miracles. Possibly also he may have accurately gauged the character of the ex-Spanish grandee, and feared a troublesome, even if ignorant rival. The result, however, whatever may have been the cause, was that Loyola at last realised that he was absolutely ignorant even of the commonest elements of theology, or literature, and with characteristic impetuosity he set about acquiring the knowledge which he needed. It is indeed difficult to determine whether Loyola most abounded in self-confidence, or in ignorance of his deficiencies.

For two weary years Loyola sat in a grammar school with mere boys, and subjected himself to their ridicule and his master's reproaches, with the same grim determination with which he had borne the torturing of his limbs, when the object to be attained was the gratification of vanity. His submission to torture from such low motives is passed over lightly in the Jesuit Schools and novitiates, while the humiliation he suffered in the pursuit of learning, is held up as a model which cannot be excelled. In the year 1526, he proceeded to Alcala, where the famous Cardinal Ximenes had founded a school, and here he combined his favourite pursuit of begging and preaching, with the study of theology and logic, but he soon abandoned the latter, as he found it too difficult for his limited intelligence. All the same, or perhaps all the more he gained notice, and attained one object which was of supreme moment. He knew that he could not carry out his projects single handed, so he left no effort unused to attract young men, whom he hoped would eventually join him. He succeeded in persuading three youths to unite with him in preaching. They knew little, if anything, more than their master, but they all agreed to wear a singular garment which at least had the advantage of marking them out as something apart from the common herd, and they also succeeded in arousing the jealousy of the priests and monks of Alcala. Rome boasts not a little of her unity of doctrine, though at least twice in each past century she has changed her creeds on points of vital importance. Rome boasts of her unity in good works, yet every life of her canonised saints gives ample evidence how the saints persecuted each other with an acrimony which those to whom they preached never attained in their secular conflicts.

Loyola was now denounced to the Inquisition by

his jealous compatriots and religious brethren. It was needful, of course, to give some appearance o' justice to the charge, and the charge was a remarkable one, in view of the mystical character of the teaching which he eventually established. He was cast into the prison of the Inquisition on the charge of being one of the Alombrados or Illuminati. The origin of this sect, or school of philosophy, is shrouded in mystery. It is, however, worthy of note that there is a very curious connection between the directions given by Ignatius Loyola in his famous "Spiritual Exercises," and the directions which were given to the Buddist novice, on his initiation into the higher mysteries of that creed, and the Alombrados or Illuminati were of distinctly Buddist origin. Von Hammer, in his History of the Assassins, a branch or development of the Illuminati, points out singular parallels between the teaching of Loyola and the Assassins. Nor can it be said that drawing attention to this parallelism is a mere Protestant prejudice, since the first charge was made by the priests of Alcala, and in the very life-time of the founder of the Jesuits. The whole subject is one which has hardly met with the consideration which it deserves, and is of grave importance in view of the recently restored power of the Jesuits in nearly every European country. Of all Christian kingdoms Spain has been the most given to a mysticism, of which St. Teresa and St. John of the Cross are eminent examples. But whether the temperament in which this mysticism was engendered and perfected was the result of climatic conditions, or of racial development, we do not profess to decide. One thing however is certain, that their peculiar forms of devotional practices closely resembled the initiatory stages of Buddism. The word Assassin is actually derived from the word Hashishin, which is again derived from Hashish, the eastern intoxicant. The Assassins ceased to be a recognised body after the Crusades, but their doctrines and some at least of their practices long survived in Spain amongst the Herbes or natives of Barbary. This accusation against Ignatius Loyola of being connected with the Illuminati, stopped his career for the time in Alcala. He was acquitted of heresy, but severely condemned for his theological ignorance, and duly warned by the Inquisitor that if he preached any longer while so ignorant of even the elements of religion he would meet with severe punishment. He was also obliged to lay aside his eccentric dress and to betake himself to another university. It may be noticed here that the peculiar teaching and practices which have again and again formed the ground of the expulsion of the Jesuits by Roman Catholics from Roman Catholic countries, had their first development in the life time of Loyola. For example, he had obtained such influence over two ladies of immense wealth in Alcala, that he induced them to leave their homes, and go forth on a begging expedition for the purpose of perfecting themselves in humility. The relatives of these ladies did not view the interference of Loyola in a favourable light, and he was again thrown into prison until his fair disciples, weary of the penance he had imposed on them, returned to their friends and resumed their place in society. Ignatius Loyola arrived in Paris in the early spring of 1528. He was accompanied by some students who had been converted to his views. His object in going to the French capital was to find a place where he could pursue his studies unobserved, and develop his plans without ecclesiastical interference. He had made the discovery, often made before and since his time, that there is no place so safe as a crowd for those who for any reason wish to pass unnoticed.

The Society of Jesuits was practically founded in Paris. Ignatius managed so far to satisfy his preceptors as to be allowed to take the degree of bachelor, and eventually of master of arts in the College of St. Barbe, but he had yet to perfect himself in theology, a matter by no means so easy as might be supposed. The complicated theology of the Roman Catholic Church, which differs so much from the simplicity of the Gospel, was the great hindrance to the success of the founder of the Jesuits. Ignatius was wise enough to know that he could not expect his disciples to render him the spiritual homage which he required, if he himself was ignorant of the science of which they naturally expected him to be a master.

But there are few things good or bad which cannot be accomplished by perseverance. Ignatius found the support, which his nascient order sorely needed, from unexpected sources. He was joined by men, who though far his superiors in intellect, and we might add in common sense, were fascinated by his schemes. Pierre le Fevre, known better as Peter Faber, a youth full of genius and imagination, became one of his disciples, and at this time also he was joined by the future glory of the Order, Francis Xavier, of Navarre. Xavier was then professor at the College of Beavais and had every reason to expect the highest ecclesiastical advancement, as well from his social position, as from his intellectual attainments. As both Faber and Xavier were held in very high estimation in the Universities of Paris their championship of Ignatius Loyola gave the tone to the Order which it needed, and without which it would probably have failed completely. The story of the conversion of St. Francis Xavier has been variously given, and at the present day it is impossible to decide between conflicting authorities, the fact that Ignatius gained this prize is the only point of importance. Strange mystery of human life. In later times there was no place where the Jesuits were so hotly denounced and so abhorred as in Paris, yet this was the cradle of the Order. Ignatius had now seven disciples, some of whom at least were of immense benefit to the new Order, if indeed his organisation deserved the name. He had no approbation except his own; so far the dignitaries of the Church whom he had approached, had dismissed him with contempt, or imprisoned him for his eccentricities and ignorance. But it seemed as if no opposition could discourage this man of iron will. On the 15th of August, 1534, Ignatius, with his seven followers, met in the crypts of a sanctuary at Montmartre, and took their vows without the permission of priest or prelate. Of the seven who had thrown in their lot with Ignatius, only one was a priest. This was Father Peter Faber. He said mass for the rest, and gave them the mutilated sacrament of the Church of Rome.

Ignatius, in his character of self-appointed superior, was the first to take the vows, and swore on the Gospels to lead a life of poverty, chastity and obedience. The rest followed his example, and thus was established an Institution, which as we shall see from undisputable evidence, has done more than any other so called religious order to ruin the peace of families, to check the growth of human progress, and to enslave the souls of men, and yet all this was done in the name of religion. Well might we paraphrase a well known aphorism, and exclaim, Oh religion, what crimes have been committed in thy name.

Spain having always been under the rule of the priesthood has always been the country of darkness, social and religious. The Spaniard, easily amused with rude pastimes, and supplied by his marvellous climate with all that he needed for food and clothing, concerned himself but little about the rest of the world. Ignatius had not heard of the course of events in Germany, nor of the stupendous religious movements which had even then begun. To him, with his narrow temperament and his stubborn will, it must have come as a tremendous shock when he learned for the first time, that men existed who were so daring, or as he would have deemed it so blasphemous, as to have condemned the Pope and rejected his authority. But France, always in the advanced guard of information, if not of knowledge, resounded with the clash of opinions, and was fully alive, whatever side individuals might take, as to the tremendous importance of this first serious blow to the spiritual power of the Papacy.

Ignatius had already intended to devote his Order in some special manner to the advancement and support of the Papal power, and here was a new, and to him all powerful motive for renewed fealty and effort. Hence, when taking his vows, he declared it to be his special intention to offer himself, and his followers, for the advancement and protection of the Church of Rome, and above all to the personal service of the Pope; he concluded his oath with the words which have since become the watch word of the Order. Would that they had been its guiding principle, instead of being used as a means of throwing a glamour of apparent piety over what is little better than a deliberate system of skilfully organised duplicity.

Ad majorem Dei gloriam, the words with which Ignatius ended his vow, was re-echoed by each of his seven disciples. To this has been added the letters, I.H.S, these initials signifying *Jesus Hominum Salvator*, Jesus the Saviour of mankind. And yet, even while these words, so true and so Scriptural, fell from the lips of the Spanish mystic, he was doing all that mortal man could do (let us hope unconsciously), to give the glory to another which he professed himself so desirous of giving to God alone.

The day which he chose for the commencement of his Order was the Feast of the Assumption of the Virgin Mary. It is true that there is not even one particle of proof of this supposed assumption; but what matter. Rome has spoken; reason is no longer to be the guide of human life. It was not until many centuries had passed that Rome established this Festival authoritatively. The motive of the Festival is not far to seek. It is self-evident that unless Mary was in heaven, she could not perform all the miracles that are attributed to her intercession. It is also self-evident that unless she had a place there almost equal to that of God, she could not exercise the omnipotence with which she is credited, hence the necessity of establishing a festival which would assure the people that not only was Mary throned in heaven, but that she held the very highest place in the celestial kingdom. The legend of the Assumption of Mary has not even the least historical foundation; but this matters very little to an infallible Church, whose dictates must be accepted at the peril of the eternal salvation of the unbeliever.

Ignatius had now actually commenced his Order. But two very important matters had been neglected. He had neither obtained the preliminary permission of a bishop, nor the final approbation of a pope. This did not concern him much, so assured was he of his own importance; but some of his followers were wiser. Ignatius now saw that the only way in which he could protect himself from the attacks of jealous religious and angry priests was to become a priest himself as soon as possible. But his health broke down again under the renewal of self-inflicted sufferings. According to his idea of religion, Christ could not save him without the help of Mary, else why take so much trouble to secure the patronage of Mary. Nor could even Mary save him without his own self-inflicted sufferings, else why had he need again and again to bring himself almost to the grave, by fasts, and vigils, and floggings. Ignatius was once more compelled to seek a southern clime, and left Paris in the spring of 1535. He took care, however, to keep his little band together, by appointing Peter Faber superior, arranging that all should meet him in Venice when their theological course should have been completed.

When the brothers re-united, according to this arrangement, their numbers had increased, for Ignatius brought a disciple with him, and the brothers brought three promising new members from Paris. It may seem strange to say it, but it is nevertheless true that one cause of the extraordinary success of the Jesuits was the awful corruption of the Church of Rome. Rome has always claimed temporal power, and desired to rule over the kings and princes of the earth. In order to accomplish this end she has left no means unused to obtain wealth, and to influence politicians. No matter what may be said of vows of poverty, if any body of men abound in wealth, they are individually, as well as collectively, rich, and all the evils divinely predicted of those who heap up to themselves riches, at once become their portion. Again and again the Church of Rome has been all but shipwrecked by those of her sons who, living in apparent conformity to the counsels of the Gospel, have actually set those counsels at defiance. It needs scarcely to point to the lives of the saints collectively for proof of this statement, but one particular instance may be given. St. Francis of Assisi, one of the saints to whom Rome points those outside her fold with unbounded confidence, commenced his career of evangelisation with the strongest denunciation of the priests of his day. With a touch of romance, inseparable, one had almost said happily, from southern temperaments, he devoted himself to his "lady and mistress, poverty." When imploring the blessing of the Pope for his new Order, he told his vision, in which he believed himself divinely appointed to save the Church from destruction by his renewal of Gospel teaching, which, according to this vision, had been well nigh abandoned. Ignatius, Francis, and almost every saint in the Roman calendar, have based their claim of the necessity of a new Order in the Church, on the evident corruption into which it had fallen, despite the efforts of those who had preceded them in the path of reform.

The people heard them gladly. This was the

secret of their success. The people, who suffer so much on earth, and who hope for so much in heaven! The people hear gladly what promises to them, either here or hereafter, something better than their life in this world. Even those who from temperament, or piety, envy the rich the least, are willing to hear of poverty which they are assured shall purchase wealth where alone wealth shall be abiding, of humiliation which shall secure honour, where honour will be everlasting. We do not say that Ignatius or Francis, or others who aspired to be the spiritual rulers of their people, deliberately played the *rôle* of deceivers, when they adapted themselves to the needs and desires of the poor, but that they did so adapt themselves is a fact which cannot be questioned.

As the efforts of Ignatius had been so far successful, he won the toleration, if not the admiration, of his kinsfolk. It is wonderful how success enobles a cause. He was "a rising man," and his world appreciated him accordingly. But Ignatius was either too wise or too sincere in his idea of Christian poverty to accept from his own family the hospitality they now offered. He won the hearts of the people, and after all it is the people who make success, by refusing to live the life of the noble, and choosing the life of the poor. He stooped to conquer. If he had then thrown in his lot with the rich and the noble, the poor would have abandoned him; but by winning the applause of the people he gained the ear of the rich. He and his followers were to be found with the sick and the leper, and this was sufficient to win for him the mighty voice of the populace.

Ignatius Loyola was gifted with the worldly wisdom which has pre-eminently characterised his Order. He found means to win over Caraffa, afterwards Pope Paul IV., and then Archbishop of Theate. Caraffa gave him letters of recommendation to the Pope, of which Ignatius made Xavier, Leynes, and Faber the bearers. They were welcomed far more warmly than could have been expected, they received the papal blessing, and permission for the ordination of all those who had not yet been ordained, in consequence of their ignorance of theology; but what cannot a pope do? Further the Pope gave a considerable sum of money towards the expenses of the proposed mission to Palestine. But once more the plans of the ex-chevalier were defeated by circumstances. A war had broken out between the Venetian Republic and the Ottoman Powers, and travelling was out of the question.

Again Ignatius gave himself and his followers to the congenial occupation of preaching. They ascended rude platforms, and with much noise and gesticulation invited men to what they called repentance. As the brothers were for the most part, absolutely ignorant of the language of the country, the work was carried on principally by shouts and gesticulations. Noise always attracts, if it does not impress, a multitude, and it is said that this preaching, if such it could be called, was not without effect.

Ignatius now began again to make arrangements for the more specific settlement of his Order. He had many difficulties, but difficulties only stimulated him to further efforts. There were some men of considerable ability, as well as of more than ordinary worldly wisdom amongst his followers, and they saw clearly that in order to succeed they must offer the Pope and the world something entirely new. It was now finally decided that the Order should exist only for the service of the Pope, and under his immediate direction, for the service of the Church. But it is not to be supposed that the other religious Orders, the principal of which were then the Dominicans and the Franciscans, were willing to allow a new body of men to deprive them of their prestige, or perquisites. These Orders raised a mighty outcry, and as it was always safe to show one's zeal by accusing others of heresy, the accusation was made that Ignatius and his followers were far from being what they professed to be, and that they were actually in league with the Reformers now so active in Germany. The charge was obviously absurd;

but such is human credulity that it often happens the more absurd the slander, the more readily it is believed. But Ignatius again triumphed, and triumphed finally.

There was a terrible famine in Rome at this time, and this afforded another opportunity for the advancement of his Order. Ignatius, always alive to the tone of public opinion, saw, and used, his opportunity. He convinced the rich of his piety by his fervent appeals for money for the poor, and he convinced the poor of his regard for their interests by bestowing on them at least some of the wealth which he obtained from the rich. He also obtained great honour from all classes for his zeal for the conversion of the Jews. His method was not original. He obtained a decree from Pope Paul III., then reigning, that the Jews should not be allowed the services of a physician, no matter how serious might be their danger, unless they first accepted the ministrations of a priest. This mode of obtaining conversions proved very efficacious, and Ignatius was honoured accordingly. Thus the Society of Jesus inaugurated its career of unchristian diplomacy. Ignatius knew perfectly that such "conversions" were writ in sand. The next move of the diplomatic Jesuit was to secure the influence of the ladies of Rome. This was not difficult. His Order was new, and he must have been gifted with some special fascination of manner, which his knightly training had enhanced.

We have already spoken of the terrible state of society at this period, and naturally, Rome being the chief ecclesiastical city, the corruption was greatest at the fountain head. Priests and people were alike sunk in the deepest debauchery. Women of nameless character made even the churches their haunt, and the place where they exhibited their meretricious charms. Luther was calling attention with trumpet tongue to the fearful condition of the city where the Pope reigned supreme, as temporal, as well as spiritual king. If he tolerated, and by tolerating encouraged such evils, how could the Church be called holy? Paul III. was aroused at last. He assembled his cardinals; but the only remedy which they could suggest was to drive all the women of doubtful character out of Rome, and obviously, it was much easier to suggest this remedy than to apply it.

But here again Ignatius saw his opportunity, and came to the rescue. He secured large sums of money from ladies of rank, whose own husbands and confessors had been probably the chief sources of the downfall of these unhappy women, and with this in hand, he proceeded to establish a home for all whom he could induce to enter it. His success was great indeed, but his plans were laid with his usual consummate skill. He carefully avoided anything that might seem degrading to these unfortunate women. He called the house which he had prepared for them a Home, and made it such. There were no restrictions, and no vows. The house was soon filled with penitents, or those who at least appeared to be such. Many, no doubt, were utterly weary of their miserable life, and thankful to find a refuge where they could live without cost to themselves, and in comparative luxury. Ignatius got the credit of having accomplished a wonderful reform, and was honoured accordingly.

In August, 1539, Ignatius asked the approbation of the Pope for the rules of his new Order. It is the rule in the Roman Catholic Church, when anyone desires to found a new religious order, that they should first obtain the permission of their immediate ecclesiastical superior. This approval having been obtained, the work goes on tentatively for a time; eventually, if it has shown good prospect of success, it is approved by the Pope. It need scarcely be said that all this cannot be accomplished without a very large expenditure of money, in order to obtain the goodwill of the cardinals, and other officials, not, of course, as a bribe, but for "expenses." The expenses are very considerable; but then success is secured in proportion to the outlay. Further, it is a curious fact that Rome never canonises a saint without an immense disbursement on the part of those who are interested. Some saintly personages remain uncanonised because either their relatives or their Order had not sufficient capital to invest in the necessary preliminaries. A curious question therefore arises as to the precise value of the canonisation of saints, and how far their power in heaven is proportioned to the honours paid to them on earth. Nor can it be said that this is a mere Protestant calumny. It is a Roman Catholic fact. The Roman Catholic Church teaches that masses are the one great means of delivering souls from purgatory. Now masses either are, or are not, necessary to obtain this most important end. If they are necessary why is it that the poor, who have no money, cannot have masses, while the more or less wicked rich have thousands of masses, and ought to escape from their penal abode at once ?

When the Pope had read the documents containing the rules of the new Order, he exclaimed, *Digitus Dei hic est !* Yet another Pope, not so many centuries later, condemned the whole scheme as an infamy, and practically the handy work of the devil. Which infallible Pope was the true prophet ? But Loyola was by no means satisfied with a mere verbal approbation. " Words, mere words," he cried, " words may be denied and explained away." He therefore bent all his energies to secure a written approbation. After some dispute and difficulty, and after considerable opposition from at least one of the cardinals who were appointed to investigate the matter, Ignatius obtained his desire. On the 27th of September, 1540, Pope Paul III. issued a special Bull commencing, *Regimini æilitantis ecclesiæ*, in which he established the Order, henceforth known as the Jesuits.

There were two reasons why this Order was established with so little difficulty. In the first place the German Reformers were already winning souls from the forms and ceremonies of the Church, to the eternal freedom of the Gospel. The cardinals, and Roman theologians, were not without fear lest the whole fabric should fall to the ground. They are always quite as much politicians as prelates, and were, as Roman cardinals always are, very keen for the things of this world, and very wise in their generation. Here were men, whose very *raison d'être* was to save the Church from the overwhelming danger with which it was threatened, and who by no means blinded themselves to that danger. One of the principal sources of danger was the dissolute habits of the religious Orders. These men promised to live chaste and holy lives so that their example could be pointed out to detractors. But there was another, and a very powerful motive for this ready acquiescence. It will be remembered that

Ignatius had provided a house of refuge for such of the courtesans of Rome and the neighbourhood as chose to avail themselves of it. These women were by no means the off-scouring of the populace, many of them were cast off mistresses of ecclesiastical dignitaries and nobles. The Jesuit Fathers were, of course, their confessors. Need it be said that these confessors knew the private history of hundreds, if not of thousands of prelates and princes, and that men who dared not have their secret lives exposed were very prompt to serve those who, if opposed, would soon find very pious reasons for exposing them.

We have not space here, nor is it necessary, to give the Statutes of this Society at length. We shall only call attention to one or two important points. We then propose to glance for a moment at the work which was being accomplished at this very time by Luther and his followers. While Ignatius was calling on his disciples to place themselves under the banner of Mary, Luther was proclaiming in stentorian tones that Christ alone can save us, and that the just shall live by faith. Look not to saint or angel, to man or woman for your salvation, look to Christ and to Christ only. Do not believe in churches which become corrupt by the weight of their inherent fallibility, look to Christ, the Rock and Foundation Stone of the true Church, and He will never fail you. Ignatius demanded an abject and degrading obedience from his followers; Luther would have obedience to none but to Christ his Master.

The chief obligations of the rule of Ignatius are easily distinguished. His rule has not changed with changing times or circumstances, as the rules of other Orders have done. This period of European history was a transition period for religious orders, and Ignatius saw his opportunity. The religious Orders which had suited the manner of life in previous centuries became, by degrees, less and less fitting for advancing civilisation. Men had begun to think, men had begun as a necessary consequence to criticise; they no longer took their opinions from a dominant priesthood as a child takes its mother's milk. They asked was this or that regulation best for the general good? was this or that doctrine consonant with reason? The question came to be openly asked by many, What has Christ said? It was no longer universally asked, What has Rome said? Rome, while declaring herself infallible and unchangable has proved her fallibility by many changes, and her mutability by alterations, both in creed and discipline, of the most important character. For example, she has quietly, but none the less completely, changed the whole character of her religious institutions in order to accommodate herself to the times. The establishment of the Jesuits was her first departure in this direction.

The world moved, and the Church moved with the world. Changes were rife everywhere, and the heads of the Church found that their own special interests would be seriously imperilled if they did not move also. But this by no means implied that the Church encouraged the march of intellect. The modifications which were made did not allow more freedom, they simply changed the form of restraint. New bonds were forged to suit new times. The religious Orders had lost all credit with the people. As long as they observed their primitive rule and lived in the poverty which they vowed to observe, it was all very well, at least in the eyes of the poor. They were pleased and consoled to see that poverty was honoured as a religious virtue. If practising poverty could be the means of saving the soul of the friar, it must also benefit the serf. But when the friar ceased to practise poverty, or even to show much respect for it, all was changed. And when the friar, who vowed temperance, was often seen in a condition which would have been punished with severity if his cloth had not protected him, the poor man was not slow to denounce the injustice.

Further, the friar was vowed to chastity, and here also he failed, till at last ribald songs were sung, or said, which held men up to public scorn, and not without cause, who had once been revered as the angels of the earth. The friars, as a class, were ignorant, and far too secure in their own estimation of their position to trouble themselves about learning. But when men began to think, they expected to be helped by those to whom they once looked up as the sole depositories of learning, and when they failed respect was lost and doubt began. Wandering friars, who neither taught nor prayed, soon became of little account. The enclosed monasteries had decreased in numbers, and the popes no longer encouraged them. It needed new rules, and a new form of so called religious life for the new conditions of society. Ignatius had realised these new conditions and established new rules. The new rules declared that the propagation of the faith and the promulgation of Christianity, which in that age meant the same thing, were to be the primary objects of the Jesuits. The methods by which they were to be carried out were preaching, hearing confessions, and educating the young. An admirable programme for the end in view. The young were to be trained to believe that in the Church, and in the Church alone, salvation was to be found. At an impressionable age they naturally became as wax in the hands of their superiors, and provided they did not revolt in after life, would remain the humble servants of their early teachers. But that the Jesuit pupil did revolt, we shall see eventually. A boy may be made to believe, while he is a boy, that he will fulfil the high destinies of his manhood by continuing this submission; but when he arrives at man's estate he wants something more than mere assertion before he will be ready to place all the affairs of life under clerical control.

The control which the confessional gave to the Jesuit will be considered elsewhere. Ignatius might have established his colleges and educated youth in vain, if he had not made plans fraught with a marvellous and foreseeing wisdom for retaining the prizes which he had secured. The iniquities of the confessional have been justly made again and again the subject of public exposure and denunciation; but the direction which is given in the confessional, and its far reaching results, is a subject which deserves more attention than it has received. To the consideration of this point we shall return later. In the meantime let us glance at the work of the Reformation. Luther and Loyola both visit Rome; but with what different results! When Loyola commences his career of human policy and craft, he uses the sins and follies of his fellow men and women for his own advancement. Luther has but one thought, the greater glory of God and the advancement of His kingdom. He needed not to frame rules or compose spiritual exercises, to court cardinals or fallen women; his rule was the Bible, God's charter of eternal life; and his spiritual exercise was prayer to the one and only Mediator between God and man.

CHAPTER II.

LUTHER—AND SOME OF THE CAUSES OF THE GERMAN REFORMATION—WHICH THE JESUITS WERE FOUNDED TO COMBAT.

THE JESUITS FOUNDED TO COMBAT THE DANGERS TO ROME OF THE GERMAN REFORMATION.—How Luther evangelised. —He sings for his daily bread in the streets of Eisenach. Hardships of his early life.—Frau Cotta befriends him.—Germany more independent of Rome than Spain, and has more light.—Angry disputes between the religious Orders on articles of faith.—The Dominicans and Franciscans quarrel about the immaculate conception.—The Dominicans get up an apparition to uphold their side, how they were found out and defeated.—The exposure greatly helps the cause of the Reformation.—Luther tried by the cruel calumnies of some Christian people.—His pathetic complaint.—His appeal to posterity for justice.—His dying words.

THE name of Luther is familiar as a household word. There are few who do not know something of his simple history. His parents were poor and his friends were few. If his words sometimes offend the sensibilities of the 19th century, we should remember that he had a work to do in the 16th, which required some very plain speaking. Besides, at this period blunt and even coarse speech was used in the ordinary affairs of life. If

Luther is blamed for expressions which shock us, we may at least do him the justice to remember that he was brought up in a Church which had ever set its face determinately against education in the highest sense of the word. Neither honied phrases, nor that liberality which is so often made a cloak for cowardice, would have served the cause for which he fought, or the work which he had to do.

Ignatius Loyola had not even thought of his Order, or seen his visions, when the hungry little lad Luther was singing for his daily bread in the streets of Eisenach. His early life was one of hardship and much suffering. The times were hard. The severities of the Inquisition had made men callous and brutal to each other. If the Church considered cruelty a virtue, why should the populace resent the infliction of pain? The tyrannies of the nobles had also their evil effect on human life, and on the formation of character. A word, and a blow, and often the blow without the word was the common rule of life. But there were tender hearts for all the hardness of the times, and Frau Cotta was one of the gentle ones who loved mercy and practised peace. Luther had a voice of some power and sweetness, and sang from time to time at her door. The good Frau, who had no children of her own, was touched by the boy's poverty, and became his friend. The lad who sang himself into her heart eventually became a priest. His father was strongly opposed to this step, and no wonder. The name of priest and monk had long been a term of reproach because of the evil lives of so many of those who bore it.

The Wycliffite movement in England had been rather a revolt against the wickedness in the high places of the Church, than doctrinal. In Germany the revolt began in the same way, but ended in the discovery that what men did depended on what men believed. By their fruits ye shall know them. The clergy, too, were very much more concerned with what touched their material interests than with what touched their faith. Nor has this ceased to be true, for when Ireland manifested a determination to resist the political interference of the Pope and showed her displeasure by the reduction of payments to the ecclesiastical treasury she was at once conciliated.

The custom of writing in Latin, which was universal during the middle ages, greatly facilitated the transmission of thought, and information as to movements religious or secular. Hence Huss was thoroughly familiar with the writings of Wycliffe and made them his text books when teaching in the University of Prague. It was a noted fact that licentious living was far more common amongst the religious orders than amongst the secular priests.

Hence the success of Ignatius Loyola in founding a new and professedly reformed rule. Men who still clung to the ancient faith, and who could not deny existing evils were ready to aid any plan which promised amendment. The quarrels between the two great religious orders was another source of scandal, yet serious as they were, they seem insignificant when compared with the intestine disputes and scandals which eventually developed amongst the Jesuits themselves.

It was no wonder then that Luther's plain thinking and pious father, should have objected strongly to his becoming a priest. A public scandal in the shape of a quarrel between Dominicans and Franciscans, which has been very fully recorded by contemporary historians, had nearly as great an effect in shaking the power of the Roman Catholic Church, as the sale of indulgences.

The facts of history are so strongly against the Church of Rome, that she has found it necessary to omit or minimise these facts in the histories which she places in the hands of the young. She would fain have all men believe that her faith has never changed, and when it is pointed out that she has continually added new articles to her creed, she replies, that these new articles have always been believed. History attests that the very reverse has been the case. There is scarcely an article of the creed of Rome which has not been hotly, and even acrimoniously, disputed for centuries by members of that Church. This has been especially the case with regard to the doctrine of the so called immaculate conception of Mary. The great mediæval orders, the Franciscan, and the Dominican, were rivals for the support of the people, and for the honours of the theological schools. Between these religious bodies, the war of opinion raged with a fury which could scarcely be credited by those who are not familiar with the subject. An appeal to Scripture was of course never thought of, there was not a word in the Bible which could be turned to account, even by the most dexterous metaphysical theologian. St. Thomas might write learned essays on the number of angels who could exist on the point of a needle, but for the doctrine of the immaculate conception of her who had declared that she rejoiced in God her Saviour, there was so little that could be pressed into the service, that the Franciscans were driven to supply a miracle. Sebastian Franck gives the story at great length in his "Chronica," published in 1531. We can only give the briefest abridgment here, but the affair is too characteristic of the times, and the consequences were too important, to omit all notice of it.

Miracles come in sometimes very opportunely, the Dominicans, who had always opposed the doctrine of the immaculate conception, were losing ground on that account. They were reproached with want of devotion to the Virgin, which practically is the greatest crime of which a Roman Catholic can be guilty. The Franciscans, on the contrary, were lauded for their piety and zeal, much to their satisfaction. Something had to be done to help the lessening *prestige* of the order of Friars Preachers. And something was done. A miracle was carefully arranged and carried out, with precautions which ought to have secured success. What makes the matter most revolting is, that the miracle was not the result of either the fraud or the imagination of a single and perhaps scarcely responsible individual; on the contrary, it was planned and authorised in a secret Chapter of the Order, held at Wimpfen, in 1506.

Nurnburg and Frankfort were first proposed as suitable places for carrying out the pious fraud, but eventually Berne was selected; as the inhabitants of the other places were believed to be rather too much inclined to make careful investigations before accepting evidence. The victim selected was a young novice who had just entered the convent, and who was full of zeal, and more likely to believe than to question anything apparently supernatural. Mysterious noises were made in his cell at night, and he was led to suppose that he had been visited by a spirit. Between fright, and gratification that he should have been selected by heaven for such favours, he was soon in just the state of mind to believe anything. The prior appeared to him in the form of a spirit, and told him that he (the spirit) needed prayers, that he should ask to have eight masses read in the chapel of St. John, and that the friars should also scourge themselves during this period.

The vision, according to pre-arrangement, was made the subject of sermons in the Dominican Church, the preacher declaring that suffering souls never came to ask help from the Franciscans, whom he described in the coarse and violent terms characteristic of the theological disputes of the day. The prior placed relics in the cell of the favoured youth, sprinkled holy water, and went through the usual Roman Catholic forms of protecting him from bad spirits, and encouraging the good. The spirits continued their visits. The confessor of the unfortunate youth gave him a letter addressed to the Virgin Mary, which contained questions on the disputed theological points, and desired him to implore the Queen of Heaven for a reply. The reply came as was to be expected, and in order to make the miracle more convincing, it was found in the tabernacle, with the host where it had been placed "miraculously." Further, the novice was told by the Virgin to ask the Pope (Julius II.) to order a festival in honour of her having been born in original sin. If this had been done the Church would have been so bound to this doctrine, that it would have been impossible, if indeed anything is impossible to infallibility, to have proclaimed her immaculate conception hereafter. It was now considered time to bring the novice forward publicly as an inspired person. So far all had gone well. He was deprived of his senses, by some draught which the monks gave him, and while in a state of apparent trance, they made the marks of the wounds of Christ on his hands and feet, a form ardently coveted by Roman Catholic visionaries. This was another triumph over their Franciscan brethren, for no male saint had ever received the stigmata except St. Francis of Assisi.

The novice, who seems to have acted so far in good faith, began to find out, through the carelessness of his deceivers, who were now sure of their success, that he had been made their tool. They tried to poison him, they tried to starve him, they tried to bribe him, but all was in vain. Rumours got about, as rumours will, and there were loud cries for ecclesiastical intervention. The matter was referred to Rome. Rome appointed a commission of inquiry, but the good burghers of Berne were not quite so credulous as the monks had hoped, and they had not quite as much faith in ecclesiastical investigation of ecclesiastical cases as might have been expected. They demanded that eight of their own councillors should be joined with the ecclesiastical commissioners, with the result that four of the monks were sentenced to death, and were burned alive in the market place at Berne, according to the barbarous custom of the times.

Nor was this a solitary example of the state of the monastic institutions of the age of Loyola; other and similar cases might be recorded, but enough has been said to show how the people were prepared for revolt. It has, unfortunately, been too much the habit with controversialists of all denominations, to attack the character of those from whom they have differed. Of course, one who has held such a prominent position as Luther could not escape. Even his parents were made the subject of attack, yet they were simple and God fearing people. If they were not anxious to see their son a member of a religious order, facts such as that which we have just related might plead their excuse, even with members of the Church in which they lived and died. But Luther's father was guilty of what was then considered a serious crime. He refused to obey the demand of the priest who attended him on his death-bed, and who tried to make him leave all, or nearly all, his little property to the ever grasping church instead of to his children, who sorely needed it.

We find a marked difference between the views with which Luther and Loyola studied for the priesthood. Ignatius desired only just as much knowledge even of theology as would enable him to obtain the dignity to which he aspired. Indeed, so great was his ignorance, and so self-evident his inability to learn, that he never could have received orders, even in that lax age, if his want of the necessary qualifications had not been dispensed with. Luther had many advantages in his educational career. He lived in Germany, where the Inquisition had not the power which it had in Spain, and where, consequently, learning was encouraged rather than forbidden. He found a superior in the Augustinian Monastery at Erfurth in the person of the Vicar-General of the Order, John von Staupitz, who entered into his spiritual difficulties and exhorted him to study the Scriptures. How little either the master or the pupil anticipated the result! But the chains which bound Luther to his Church were broken slowly. It is indeed difficult for those who have not had personal experience of the Church of Rome to realise what a tremendous force of spiritual strength is required to forsake this strange religion. To those who never have suffered it is in vain to speak. It needs a Christ-like sympathy to feel for and with others at any time, but above all in circumstances which are foreign to our personal experience.

It is true that Rome has forbidden the reading of the Bible in language too plain, and by authority too strong to be questioned. It is also true that under certain conditions Rome relaxes her rule. It is also true that every monk, nun, and priest is obliged to read portions of the Bible daily, when saying the Office. But whether a small portion of the Bible or the whole Bible is read matters little in the end, for, small or large, what is read must be read with the eyes of the Church, and explained as required by the Church. Hence the Bible is practically a sealed book to the Roman Catholic. This is a point which is scarcely understood, either by those who think that Roman Catholics are never allowed to see a Bible, or by those who think that they can use it freely. The words used by our Lord to the Jews exactly describe this condition of things in the Church of Rome: "Making the word of God of none effect through your tradition, which ye have delivered" (Mark vii. 13). The mere mechanical reading of the Bible can avail little, and the mere mechanical reading of part of the Bible is all that Rome allows.

There is no doubt that Luther felt very keenly the false accusations which were brought against him, not only by his enemies, but even by those who ought to have been his warmest supporters. The unity of Rome has always been its strength. The dis-union of Christians has been the greatest hindrance to the spread of the Gospel. As the end of time draws nearer may we not hope that Christians will draw nearer to each other, and to their coming Lord.

There are few things more touching than the appeal which Luther makes to posterity for the justice which was denied to him even by some of his Christian contemporaries. He says: "I am yet alive, and I write books, and I preach sermons, and read public lectures every day, and yet virulent minded men, adversaries and false brethren, allege my own doctrines against me, and represent me as saying what I do not say, and as believing what I do not believe. If they do this while I am alive, and while I look on and hear it, what will they do when I am dead. But how is it possible for me to stop all the mouths of the evil speakers, especially of those who set themselves to pervert my words." No doubt Luther must have often felt that it was indeed hard for him to suffer from both sides: from the Roman Catholics against whose errors he was fighting so earnestly, and from those professing Christians, who, through jealousy or ignorance, were ever ready to attack him. Surely the path of an earnest reformer is ever one of pain. It should be said, however, that the best and noblest men of his day were his defenders, but this did not lessen the guilt of those who added to his already heavy burdens. Erasmus has left it on record that the better any man was the more he appreciated the writings of Luther. In the same letter, which is addressed to Archbishop Albert, he says: "that he (Luther) was accounted a good man even by his enemies, and that the best men were least offended by his writings." Even the Roman Catholic historian Lingard admits that Luther's morals were unexceptional. He says: "He (Staupitz) selected a young friar of his own order, Martin Luther, a man of an ardent mind, and unimpeached morals, and of strong prejudices against the Church of Rome." Luther's last words have been placed on record, and with these words we shall conclude this part of our subject.

"O my Father, God of our Lord Jesus Christ, the Father of all consolation, I thank Thee for having revealed to me Thy well beloved Son, in whom I believe, whom I have preached and acknowledged, loved and celebrated, and whom the Pope and the impious persecute. I commend to Thee my soul. O Jesus Christ my Lord, I am quitting this earthly body, I am leaving this life, but I know that I shall abide eternally with Thee."

And so Luther was gathered to his fathers, and rests in the unchanging peace of God. Rome could no more threaten him with its thunders, nor could the mistrust and unkindness of false friends vex his tender heart. And his work follows him. It is still the same because it is Divine. And those who worked with him and those who worked against him know now that his teaching was the teaching of the Spirit, and that with him was the grace of the Father, the Son, and the Holy Ghost.

CHAPTER III.

THE FOUNDATION OF THE ORDER—THE FOURTH VOW THE REAL OBJECT—THE IDEA OF FOUNDING A UNIVERSAL MONARCHY WITH THE POPE, NOMINALLY, THE GENERAL OF THE JESUITS PRACTICALLY, AT THE HEAD.

THE FOUNDATION OF THE ORDER OF JESUITS. — The service of the pope their avowed object; remarkable clause in their Constitutions on this subject; the vow of obedience to the pope not what it seems; it secures great honour and many advantages to the Jesuits, but is practically useless to the pope; no Jesuit is permitted to obey the pope unless he is ordered to do so by the General.—Practically the pope is obliged to obey the General.—Proof of this.—The General takes the place of God, and of the individual conscience towards those under him.—The Jesuit forbidden to listen to the voice of conscience.—Proof of this from the Rule.—Reasons why R. C. bishops are often unwilling to have Jesuits in their diocese.—How bishops are sometimes outwitted by them.—The Jesuits are the only religious order which has been condemned and dissolved by a pope.—The comparison between the obedience required from a soldier and from a Jesuit not well founded.—Extraordinary privileges given by some popes to the Jesuits; the popes have tied their own hands; has this been a case of hypnotism? the Jesuits allowed to make priests of persons who have not been born in lawful wedlock, etc. though this is strictly forbidden to others.—Allowed to say mass in time of interdict; these permissions give them great power; can require the secular power to enforce their excommunications, and to punish those who may oppose them in any way; unlimited spiritual and temporal power of the General. — Jesuits obliged to report on public affairs to the General.—Ignatius' wonderful diplomacy.

ON Easter Day in the year 1541, Ignatius Loyola attained the summit of his ambition and was elected general of his Order. That he should be the first general was a foregone conclusion. There were then only five members of the Society in Rome, but as all had been pre-arranged those who were absent had sent in their votes, so that delay or confusion was avoided. Before we enter further on the history of the Order, we must carefully study its constitutions, its rules and the objects of its founder. It should be noted first that the Jesuits are the only religious order in the Church of Rome—and these orders are very numerous—which has lain under the ban of the Pope, or which has been expelled from any country because of its interference in politics. Hence we may expect to find that to obtain political power forms a main feature in the plans of the Society.

A sketch, rather than a detailed statement, of the proposed objects of the new Society was drawn up by Loyola and submitted to Pope Paul III.: it was confirmed by him on the 27th September, 1540. At a later period the constitutions were greatly enlarged, but the substance remained the same. This rule required the taking of the three vows, poverty, chastity, and obedience. These vows are required in all religious orders. But the fourth vow was the real object and distinguishing mark of the new Order. By this vow every Jesuit is bound to the service of the Pope in the most solemn manner. It must have been no little inducement to the popes of that day to sanction the plans of Ignatius, when they could no longer depend on the services of the older orders, for as we have shown in the last chapter, they were fast decaying under the weight of their own corruption.

There are some remarkable points in this remarkable document. First, we find the following direction: "He (the Jesuit) should always have God before his eyes, or more correctly, the aim of our Society and our rule, which is the sole way to God." This sentence so carefully framed, is the key-note to the whole system of the Jesuit. It is self-evident that no mere man could come forward and demand on his own responsibility the abject and absolute obedience which Ignatius exacted from his disciples. It is because Ignatius claimed to represent God, not as a mere figure of speech, but literally and actually, that he claimed to be obeyed as God. No other claim would have supported his exactions; and that claim once admitted, there could be no limit to the demands on the obedience of the disciple. When once it is believed that Divine authority, and the claim is nothing short of a claim to Divine authority, is bestowed on any individual, that individual takes the place of God, and becomes the god of the person who admits the claim. It is certainly difficult to believe how any human being gifted with ordinary common sense could think that a fellow mortal like himself could possess such power, but we have to do with facts, and not with conjectures. It is a fact that thousands have believed and do believe that a mortal like themselves has such power, and exercises it by Divine right. It is quite clear that there are many circumstances in human life in which we may have a difficulty in deciding which of two courses is the better or most pleasing to God, but the Jesuit has no such difficulty, he has no choice, for his superior takes the place of God and decides for him. Hence also the demand which is made on the Jesuit for absolute and unasking obedience in the smallest as well as in the most important matters.

When God speaks there can be no question as to the duty of obedience, but these men claim to speak as God, and with an equal if not almost a superior authority. We use the expression superior authority advisedly, because with the Jesuit the voice of the superior must always over-rule the voice of God in the individual conscience. It is this which makes the rule of the Jesuit at once so dangerous and so unchristian. The Jesuit is taught and believes, that he commits a deadly sin if he allows himself to question for one moment the command of his superior, because the superior represents God, hence he must stifle promptly the voice which tells him that this or that is contrary to the law of God, and he must do an unholy violence to the voice of God's spirit within him. The words which we have quoted are very remarkable, and framed with an almost diabolical ingenuity. The novice, indeed, must always "have God before his eyes." So far the pious and unsuspicious might think there could be nothing but good, but the qualifying clause which follows over-rides this, and shows the real aim of Ignatius.

The next point to be noted is the vow of obedience to the Pope, and here the remarkable cunning of Ignatius is apparent. After much expression of the readiness which should characterise each member of the Order to obey the Pope, and to go wherever he might command, a clause is inserted which limits this obedience, and renders it practically a vow of obedience to the Society. No member of the Society shall have a right to enter into communications, either with the "chair of Rome" or any other ecclesiastical authority as an individual; all must be arranged through the General. Hence this much vaunted vow of obedience to the Pope, simply resolves itself into a promise to obey the Pope if the General of the Jesuits approves of what the

Pope has commanded. The tremendous power which this places in the hands of the Society is self-evident. It is a practical illustration of the old story of the bundle of sticks. The Pope cannot use one or any number of Jesuits for his own ends; if he requires the services of the Order he must ask it of the General, and he must accept these services as the General pleases. Hence the Pope must submit to the Society and keep on terms with it as a society, while the Society poses before the Catholic world as the humble servant of the Pope. The clause which limits the power of the Pope is thus worded: "The power of the General shall be so unlimited that should he deem it necessary for the honour of God, he shall even be able to send back, or in other directions, those who have come direct from the Popes."

Thus by the rules of the Order which have been approved by many Popes, the Popes actually placed themselves under the feet of the Jesuit. The name given in reproach to this Society, or rather to the head of the Society, of the Black Pope, is singularly appropriate, and the complications which such arrangements involve is unique in the history of the world's religions. It has been said already that no member of the Order can accept any ecclesiastical position whatsoever, even at the command of the Pope, without the permission of the

General, which permission is rarely given. The object of this rule is apparent. A Jesuit bishop in virtue of his ecclesiastical standing, would be the superior of his General; other members of the Order might attach themselves to him, or obtain his assistance in difficulties with their superiors. This could not be tolerated for a moment, hence every rule is framed with marvellous skill to secure the abject submission of the individual, and to prevent in advance even the least opening for relaxation.

The obedience which is exacted in a lesser or greater degree from individuals in Roman Catholic religious communities has been compared to that which is required from a soldier and has been justified by this comparison. But you cannot compare things which are not equal. There can be no comparison whatsoever between the obedience required from the Jesuit and the obedience of a soldier, which is simply an external obedience and limited to time and place. In the case of the obedience of a monk or nun, the circumstances are altogether different. The monk or nun is obliged to obey under all circumstances, and the obedience of the monk or nun is a spiritual obedience.

The soldier may criticise the actions of his superior officer, if his criticisms are not such as to interfere with the exterior obedience required from him, and on occasion he may represent to higher authority his objection or suggestion. He is not bound to internal agreement with his officers, though for the time being he is obliged to obey their lawful commands; far less is he told that obedience can be exacted from him, under pain of eternal damnation. It is the spiritual element in the obedience required in the church of Rome which makes it a bondage too heavy to be born by all but those who can believe that a mere man has the authority of the Eternal God.

The Jesuit once bound by his vow is bound for ever. No Pope may sign his release. No Jesuit may confess to any priest who is not a member of his order. It is not altogether unusual for a member of one religious order in the church of Rome to pass to another order. Many difficulties are put in his way, but still such change is made from time to time, especially, or perhaps exclusively, when the monk or nun wishes to go from a lower to a higher order — the higher order being in all cases the more strict as to discipline. But in the case of the Jesuit this is not permitted, with the exception of the Carthusian Order, the vow of perpetual silence observed there being the cause of the permission, as the Jesuit would have no opportunity of exposing evils, or grievances, which he may have experienced in his former life.

But one of the most important and diplomatic

rules of the Order is the one which forbids the interference of any ecclesiastical authority whatsoever in the affairs of the Jesuits. The bishop of every Roman Catholic diocese is practically the Pope of the various religious orders in his diocese, but over the Jesuit he has no control whatsoever. He dare not enter the Jesuit monastery except as an invited guest. The Jesuit has no need to ask his permission to say mass, or to hear confessions. All the personal and jealously guarded powers of the bishop are of no account whatsoever. Hence it is that the Jesuit often finds it so difficult to obtain a place in any diocese. A bishop can generally prevent the Jesuits from establishing themselves in his diocese, but once established he cannot expel them. An impecunious bishop may accept a very liberal consideration for permission to found a college under Jesuit management in his pastoral precincts, but the impecunious bishop generally finds that while there have been two parties to the contract, when the contract is once signed, only one party benefits.

Hence the dislike which has been manifested even openly by many bishops to this Order. Another privilege which was granted to the Society was that of being allowed to say mass during an interdict, a privilege which was of immense importance to the Jesuits in the middle ages. All the ordinary rules of the Roman Catholic Church were, in fact, dispensed in their favour. Bishops were ordered to ordain anyone who might be presented to them by the fathers, without further examination or ceremony. The Church and the services of the Church were placed at their disposal, and none dare gainsay them, while they only gave in return the very doubtful benefit of establishing colleges, when they took care to secure for themselves all the best pupils in the district. They were to pay no taxes or dues, but were permitted to take all they could get, and to keep all they got, other ecclesiastical privileges or laws to the contrary being suspended in their favour. All donations of land, or money, or houses are at once their property, and the Pope binds himself to this at the time of the grant without knowledge of what is granted. Truly the Spanish knight was by no means deficient in worldly wisdom.

The amount of exceptions and favours granted to this Order by the infallible bulls of infallible popes is something which can hardly be understood by those who are not familiar with the intricacies of Roman Catholic canon law and observance. One most important permission was that which allowed the Jesuits to receive into their order those who might be the offspring of adultery or incest. It is a strict rule, on the whole faithfully observed in the Roman Church, that no person can be ordained priest who has not been born in lawful wedlock, the reason being the high character attributed to the priestly office, nor could anyone be ordained who has any notable physical deficiency. But for the Jesuit all this was dispensed, nor can there be any doubt that just as Ignatius Loyola saw the immense gain to be secured when he opened a house for the mistresses of the Roman nobles and ecclesiastics, he saw also that the illegitimate offspring of the Jesuits' *clientèle* would prove an immense source of income to his Order. The progenitor of such offspring would gladly give considerable amounts of money, or grants of houses or lands, to have their children thus provided for, and no questions asked.

But the great means through which Loyola expected to gain power was the education of youth. Hence he obtained permission and authorisations, which all tended to strengthen his hands in this direction. His Order was empowered to send professors to any university, and to give lectures there no matter what objection might be made by the existing authorities. Not content with all these advantages, his keen knowledge of human nature and extraordinary worldly wisdom quickened his perceptions, and he soon perceived that these favours would excite both jealousy and a perfectly natural opposition. This was also provided for in advance, just as he provided in advance the authority of the Pope to accept donations, no matter how large, of which the Pope knew nothing All persons whatsoever were commanded to refrain from hindering, harassing, or disturbing his Society, under penalty of excommunication, and the Jesuits were empowered to call in the aid of the secular power to support them in opposing and silencing such of their Roman Catholic brethren as might interfere with their plans. The placing of such authority in the hand of any body of men was tantamount to giving them all power both in heaven and on earth. They could close the gates of heaven with a word by excommunicating those who opposed them, no matter whether justly or unjustly, and they could use the power of the earthly sword to exterminate, and compel obedience to their commands.

Ignatius certainly knew how to make the best of both worlds for the advancement of his Order. There is a manuscript collection of the sayings of Ignatius, which is well authenticated. Both the Bollandists, and the Jesuit author of the life of the saint, have quoted from it. In this collection it is stated that Ignatius, when conversing with Polanco, his confidential secretary, said: "In those who had offered themselves (to join the Society) he had looked less to purely natural goodness, than to firmness of character and ability for business."

His disciples have followed his example. Further, he declared emphatically, according to the same reliable authority, that however valuable the connections or qualifications of a candidate might be, he would not avail himself of his services unless he discerned in him a character which could be moulded to strict obedience. If Ignatius Loyola knew how to make rules for his order, he knew also how to choose those who would obey these rules.

It is often, and not unnaturally, supposed that theological propositions which may be used or endorsed by members of the Society of Jesuits are simply the opinion of the individual. This is a serious mistake. No individual opinions are allowed in the Society, nor, indeed, in the Church of Rome. No Jesuit dare write or publish any book which has not the full and free imprimatur of his superiors. No Roman Catholic can persevere in the publication of books, or in the assertion of opinions, which have been condemned by the Church, and even at the present day Rome is not slow to silence authors, or to condemn those of whom she does not approve.

In such a Society it was absolutely necessary that a system of espionage should be arranged and carried out systematically. Ignatius laid down the lines for this system, and trusted to human nature to do the rest. No Jesuit novice (and the novitiate lasts for many years) can receive visits from his friends, unless a superior is present, a curious commentary on the supposed happiness and freedom of the religious life. No Jesuit can read a letter or write a letter without the express permission of his superiors. To ask such a permission is an obvious humiliation ; hence the end is attained, for few will voluntarily place themselves in such a position. Besides, this rule cuts off all possibility of free intercourse or of expression of unhappiness. After a time letters to friends or relatives are gradually discontinued, neither side caring to write what must be carefully inspected, and the individual stands alone. The same rule is observed in every convent and monastery. It may be asked, why do men or women submit to such unnatural restraints. The answer is simple, and will be easily understood by those who have the happy faculty of entering into mental conditions which differ from their own. The Jesuit novice believes that this sacrifice will be acceptable to God, and he enters on his career under the firm conviction that it is pleasing to God, and that the more he "conquers nature" the higher will be his place in heaven.

The power placed in the hands of the General is practically unlimited, but in order to exercise this power he must be fully informed of all that passes in every house of the Order, and in each individual soul. The Pope exercises a somewhat similar power, with this exception, that the Pope is not so minutely informed. But in the case of the Pope, while the affairs of the Church in all countries are reported to him, the reports go into the hands of the cardinals and others appointed to make digests for his use. In the case of the General, all must come directly into his hands, though he is allowed to employ confidential secretaries who aspire to his exalted position, and therefore protect the interests of the Order *con amore.*

The Jesuit Order has been always the determined opponent of the Freemasons, yet they are themselves a secret organisation practically independent of the Church, whose powers and far reaching effect exceed all that the most ambitious Freemason could desire. The superiors and rectors of all Jesuit houses are obliged to report every week to the Provincial of their province. This report is not confined to an account of the internal economy of their respective convents. They are obliged to report specially as to the exterior work of the Society in their locality, and many a good Protestant would find his character well analysed in these reports, while the statesman, whether Catholic or Protestant, Liberal or Conservative, would see that many an action in which he supposed that he had been a free agent, had been secretly suggested through channels which he had never suspected. Evidence will be given later on this point when treating of the interference of the Jesuits in politics. The Provincial makes up his report from these reports for the General once a month, but so complete and complicated is the plan to secure knowledge of places, persons, and motives, not merely as regards members of the Order, but as regards each person of the least note in the various towns or neighbourhoods, that the inferior officers of the Society are also required to report once in three months to the General, in addition to the weekly report which they make to their local superiors.

But on every check there is a counter check. Superiors, rectors, and, most important, also the masters of novices, are required to send a report to the General every three months. Thus each report can be compared, and accurate results obtained. Arrangements are made also in case the affairs reported refer to persons outside the Order, that these reports shall be so worded, that while they are perfectly clear to the General and his immediate *entourage*, they would convey no information to others into whose hands they might fall. It may be well to say here that these statements are not the mere assertions of ignorant or prejudiced writers. The "Institutes" or authorised rules of the Jesuit Order, were published at Prague in 1757, and contain not only the rules of the Order as authorised by the various popes who approved them, but also the decrees of general congregations. Everything is provided for, nothing has been left to chance, or future arrangement, even the possibility of the defection of the General himself is foreseen, and arrangements made to provide for such a contingency. The General is also under a certain supervision. He is not allowed to travel alone; he is provided with assistants, without whom he cannot act in certain cases, but his restrictions are few, and practically he has the absolute power of an autocrat. He can receive or dismiss at pleasure, he can promote or degrade his subjects as he thinks fit, without giving account to anyone whosoever. Furthermore, he has the most extraordinary and absolute dispensing powers, as regards the rule, and the observance of the rule. Certainly Loyola believed in autocracy, though the Society, as a body, accommodates itself to every or any mode of government in the various countries where it exists.

St. Charles Borromeo, the well known Roman Catholic saint and doctor of the Church, has made some notable observations on this subject. He says: "The superiors often do not admit the best subjects, while admitting with open arms those who are skilled in sciences, though they may be often destitute of piety or devotion." This, however, was strictly in accord with the instructions given by their founder.

The Jesuit is not permitted to take his full and final vows until he has attained the age of forty-five. As a consequence there are few fully professed members of the Order. There may have been more than one reason for this rule, the longer the practical novitiate the more formed the habit of obedience would become. The spiritual elevation on which the few and select Fathers are placed, would make them an object of envy to those beneath them, and there is something in human nature which leads men to value what they do not possess and to strive for its attainment, but when the object is possessed and the desire attained there will be a relaxation of their efforts.

Besides the rigorous regulation as to age, the rule requires that thirty-one years shall have been passed in the Order before the final vows are taken, so that a Jesuit who had not entered the novitiate at a very early age, might be far older than the years specified before he could take the final vows. In the meantime he is simply the bond slave of the General, who may dismiss him at will, or retain him at pleasure. He must become a corpse in the hands of his superior, the original words of the rule are *"ac si cadœver esset."*

When God desired to punish Nebuchadnezzar, He deprived him of his reason, and he had his dwelling with the wild asses, but when Solomon chose an understanding heart as the highest gift which God could give him, he was commended by eternal wisdom for his choice, but these men cast aside the divinest gift which God can bestow, and glory in their self-inflicted degradation.

The proud distinction chosen by Loyola of being the founder of the "Society of Jesus," was part of a well arranged plan. There can be no question that the primary, if not the sole object of the Spanish monk, was to counteract the effects of the German Reformation, and he actually established a college in Rome which he called the German College, in which Germans were especially trained with the view of returning to their own country to reclaim those who had followed the Reformers, the keen insight of Ignatius enabling him to realise that those who were natives of Germany would obtain a hearing sooner than those who might neither understand the language nor the customs of the country. It may be said here that in the original papal bull which authorised the establishment of the Order, the number to be received was limited to sixty. Ignatius probably smiled at the restriction, well aware that unlimited leave to act as he pleased was a foregone conclusion, and would necessarily be given in a very short period. In this bull, promulgated on the 27th of September, 1540, the founders associated with Ignatius are named as the "ten dear sons, Ignatius de Loyola and Peter Faber, and James Laynez, as well as Claude le Jay and Paschal Brouet and Francis Xavier, with Alphonse Salmeron and Simon Rodriguez, John Codure, and Nicolas de Bobadilla."

Not only at first, but from time to time during the lifetime of Loyola, objections were made to the name which he gave to his Order. But while on some other points Ignatius stooped to conquer, on this point he remained immovable. If he had not extraordinary foresight, he may have had some larger knowledge than his disciples of the doctrines then taught by the German reformers, and have believed that the prominent use of the name of Jesus would enable his followers to secure a hearing when all other means failed. To have had, and to have carried out such an idea, was altogether consonant with the whole plan of the Society, and others besides Ignatius have made unholy use of the sacred name of the Saviour of mankind. One of his earliest and most trusted disciples, Father Michael Torres, implored him to yield this point, but he refused with characteristic determination. His

Order was to be a company of soldiers, under the nominal command of Jesus Christ, but Christ was represented to his army by the general for the time being. He distinctly refused to allow his spiritual children to be called or in any way represented as a monastic body. They were the Pope's soldiers, who nevertheless on occasion commanded the Pope. Orlandini, the official historian of the Order, says that the term *Societas* was chosen expressly because it was the best rendering of the Spanish word *Compania*, the technical expression for a company of soldiers under the command of a captain. This use of the name of Jesus was made a subject of special complaint by the French clergy, and the Sorbonne protested, but protested in vain, against the presumption of any religious body in arrogating to itself the special headship and approbation of the Saviour.

Some very remarkable circumstances occurred when the title was under dispute in Rome, during the generalship of Acquaviva, and after the death of Loyola.

In the month of August, 1590, Sixtus V. intimated officially that the Order would not be allowed to continue if the name by which it had been known hitherto was not promptly changed. But such were the constitutions of the Order, as fully authorised by a previous Pope, that even the Pope himself could not make the change, the General was therefore compelled to act. So determined was the Pope that Acquaviva was prepared to yield. He drafted a document enforcing the required change, but scarcely had it reached the hands of the Pope for approval and inspection, when he died suddenly. Sixtus was succeeded by Cardinal Castagna, who ascended the pontifical throne under the title of Urban VII. It was expected that he would be even more uncompromising than his predecessor, but he survived his elevation to the chair of Peter only eleven days. His successor, Gregory XIV., was a warm friend of the Jesuits, and the remarkable death roll was closed. This Pope added notably to the already vast powers of the Order, and empowered the General to dismiss any one from it without even the semblance of a trial.

The words *ad majorem Dei gloriam,* which is the motto of the Order, were also imposed by the founder. The novices were taught that whatever benefited the Order promoted the glory of God, that they could only learn from their superiors what would be most for the benefit of the Order, and for the glory of God. It is quite certain that the glory of God and the glory of the Society were convertible terms in the mind of Ignatius Loyola.

CHAPTER IV.

The Making of the Jesuit.

The Making of the Jesuit.—The motives which induce men to submit to such discipline; the object of Loyola was the success of the Order at any price; proof of this.—How novices are secured and selected; gradual influence used to persuade them to join the Order.—Boys easily impressed by the praise and attention of their elders.—They do not suspect that they have been chosen, so carefully is all arranged; the effect of honours paid to three youthful canonised Jesuits.—The ambition fired by reports of the glory of the Order, and its power everywhere; a novice may one day be confessor to a king, or a pope, and rule the destinies of the world; the use made of the Spiritual Exercises; sermons preached to excite the imagination; spiritual terror produced; impossibility of forming a calm judgment under such circumstances; close resemblance between the Spiritual Exercises and the Eleusinian mysteries.—Ignatius imprisoned by ecclesiastical authorities at Alcala in 1526, on the charge of being one of the Illuminati; the Jesuit novice and the Buddhist novice; strange rites; politics controlled and affairs of state regulated in the interests of the Order; secular priests jealous of the power which the Jesuit Director has over women of rank and public men.—How the Jesuit novice is hardened for his work.

WHEN the extraordinary rules which govern the order of Jesuits have been studied, even in the barest outline, and their peculiar characteristics understood in some degree, the question may be asked naturally, what motive could induce those who are still in the vigour of manhood, if not in the very buoyancy of youth, to bind themselves to such a mode of life? In studying such subjects we can best succeed in obtaining the explanation which we desire, by realising that whether we approve or disapprove, thousands of our fellow beings sincerely believe what we disbelieve and what we consider morally wrong. They act on principles, and from motives, which are altogether foreign to us even if they are not absolutely repugnant. We must try to understand the motives which influence them, and look at them from their point of view, if we would know why they think as they do, and why that which is so repugnant to us seems to them an act of the highest virtue.

A long and exceptionally intimate acquaintance with the deepest feelings of those who have held the most widely opposite views on religious questions must certainly lead to toleration. But toleration is something very different from condoning evil. Unfortunately for the cause of truth, there are, and no doubt always will be, a certain class who are not capable of considering any subject from any standpoint but their own, hence they rarely win souls from error; and such persons naturally misjudge those who have larger and more Christian views.

We who rejoice in the liberty with which Christ

has made us free, may find it difficult to understand the bondage of evil; but this bondage has been the unhappy birthright of thousands, who believe in it, and glory in it as we do in our freedom. It requires, then, no common faith and love to reach such souls, and we can do so best by giving them credit for their sincerity, while we strive with all patience and charity to lead them into the light.

When studying the characteristics of the Order we should remember that like all other institutions it is composed of units, and that each unit is equally necessary to the formation of the whole body. We shall therefore take a unit and follow the line of thought and indicate the motives which induce a youth to enter such institutions. When we come to treat of the Jesuit colleges and their mode of instruction, whether religious or secular, we shall find on their own authority that the heads of these colleges make use of a system of espionage, which they have elevated to a fine art. One object of this is to secure for themselves those of their pupils who give the best promise of being useful members of the Order. Here we have at once one reason why the Jesuit devotes himself to the education of youth. We have already mentioned the special qualifications which the founder of the Order considered most necessary for those whom he desired to join his institute. Talent was to be preferred to piety, or moral qualifications, and the permission which he obtained to receive and even to advance to the priesthood, those who for moral reasons were universally rejected by other orders, is an evidence that his object was success at any price.'

The youths thus selected received special attention, both in regard to their studies, and their conduct. The parents of these youths were never informed, until the last moment, what had been arranged for their sons. The boys themselves were kept in ignorance, until some supreme moment in their religious training, when it became necessary that they should assent to the suggestions of their confessor. If they had known the object in view too soon, they might have been induced to offer some opposition by those of their companions who were less devout, or less amenable to discipline. If they had known that they were being trained for a certain end, they might have resented the training. The Jesuit masters have all the advantage on their side, and their pupils for all practical purposes are at their mercy. In all such cases the first object would be to impress the mind of the youth with the great honour which was conferred on those who were chosen by the Society. The young are easily fired with ambition by hearing of the deeds of heroes, especially when the hero is highly commended by those to whom they naturally look up with respect.

The youth begins to think how glorious it would be if he too might one day be spoken of as this hero has been, and thus the first idea germinates.

Let it be added to this that the youth who are under Jesuit training are inspired with even more devotion to the Church than the *alumni* of other Catholic Colleges. To belong to the Church is to be sure of salvation, to belong to the Society of Jesuits, is to secure a most exalted place in heaven. It is an army, and youth burns to do battle in what he firmly believes to be so good a cause. It is an army where he is told that the rewards are always sure, and the distinctions depend on the valour of the individual. He is fired with the ambition to destroy heresy, and to conquer the world for the Church. He is not yet told anything of the means whereby this apparently glorious end is to be attained.

The time approaches for his first communion, and all around is made subservient to the impression which such an event is desired to make. The Jesuit saints and their doings are brought prominently forward for his consideration and admiration. Indeed, the Jesuits have been astute enough to secure the canonisation of some of their very youthful, but long deceased members, so that schools and educational institutions are placed under their patronage. The canonised youths Aloysius and Stanislaus, have a monopoly of clients amongst the young, and lately a certain blessed Berchmans has been added to the list. Novenas, or nine days of successive prayer, are said to these deceased heroes of the Order. Altars are erected in their honour, and decked on their feast days with the choicest flowers and the most costly ornaments. Who shall say but one day this youth may have such honours paid to him also!

The desired end is helped by a little word from a father, a master, a professor, which has been so carefully pre-arranged as to seem quite accidental. It is the old story of the constant dropping of water. But the drops are dropped very cautiously, not one too many, nor one too few. Now let it be remembered that the youth believes in his Church with an intensity of belief which is difficult for the non-Catholic to realise. He is told certain things, and he believes them to be true, and he has no opportunity of hearing the other side of the question, and indeed he does not believe that there is another side. Rome has spoken; his Jesuit masters tell him what to believe, and he believes accordingly. Later we shall show that history, for example, is taught according to Rome and not according to fact, and that all students, whether intended for the Order or for the world, are carefully prevented from having access to any book, pamphlet, or paper, the reading of which might lead them to question what they are taught. There is only one side of any question, literary, metaphysical, social or political, for the Roman Catholic, and that is the Roman Catholic side. The habit having been so well formed in youth of believing what is told them, and the warnings being so terrible as to the dangers of listening for a moment to the opposite side of any question, that later in life, when there is comparative mental freedom which might be availed of for obtaining information, such information is not desired, because it has been so impressed on the mind in youth that there is no other side except what is false and dangerous.

At last the time arrives when the youth must make his choice between a world which he has been told is full of snares for his destruction, and a state wherein he is assured he will be absolutely certain of heaven. Once more let it be remembered how his earliest years have been impressed and moulded, how sure he is that his teachers are infallible, and that they actually represent God. It is difficult to tell which is strongest, the vividness of Roman Catholic belief or the certainty of the Roman Catholic that his Church is the one Church founded by Christ Jesus. All that is needed now is to deepen impressions already made, and to excite the youth to make a definite and final choice. To attain this end what are called the spiritual exercises are brought into use, and these exercises are the final touch which is given in the making of the Jesuit.

The spiritual exercises are simple enough in themselves. They consist of a series of meditations on sacred subjects. With the exception of those, and they are few, which deal with worship of Mary and the saints, any Christian might read them without perceiving evil. Apparently their only object is to lead the soul to a greater love of God, and a greater zeal for His service. These exercises are used in all convents, at what are called "retreats," which take place once at least every year. They are used also in Jesuit, and, indeed, in all Roman Catholic Colleges both by the priests and the students. The general use of these exercises has done not a little to help the Society, and to spread it. Devout persons naturally wish to have their retreats given to them by members of the Society, as they are supposed to be experts in the use of their own formulas.

The spiritual exercises may be gone through in nine days, or they may be so arranged as to occupy a month. They may be used either publicly or privately. There are three exercises for each day, but, as we have said, the words used are simple, and give but little idea of the effect produced when a preacher who has been trained to make them his text preaches them to an absorbed audience.

It is the accessories which produce the effect.

First, a profound silence is required. It is considered a serious fault if even a word is spoken during the time in which the exercises are being used, not only while the preacher is expounding them, but at any time. Only those who have had personal experience of a retreat can have the least idea of the terrible effect of this enforced silence. Day after day, and at every hour of the day, and night, there is a silence so profound that the falling of the smallest article, or the shutting of a door or window so as to be heard, is forbidden, and penance inflicted. The nervous tension produces in some minds a feeling akin to madness; but the desired effect is obtained. The mind is no longer able to take a clear view of duty, it becomes so enfeebled by its surroundings that it is impossible to think sanely, or calmly. Every mental faculty is strained; how then can a decision be made deliberately. Spiritual terror is the chief factor in the exercises, and the silence and gloom of all around enhances the terror.

In the meditation on hell each individual is required to picture hell to himself, with all its horrors, and if he honestly does what is required, he reduces himself to a pitiable state of mind. When the retreat is given in public the trained Jesuit preacher knows how to pile up the agony with words and gestures, until some of his auditors burst into sobs of anguish, or even shriek aloud in this

8

artificially produced terror. When the imagination is thus worked up anything will be promised which affords a hope of escape from such a future, and here the Jesuit's opportunity comes in. The novice master, to whom alone the novices are permitted to speak, goes round to those in whom he is especially interested, and finds them only too thankful to relieve an overstrained mind, and often a promise is given and taken, when the hapless individual is utterly unfit to decide a matter of such supreme moment. But it is all for the good of the Church and the Order—perhaps we should rather reverse the words —and the end justifies the means.

Those who are unacquainted with the realities of Roman Catholic convent life, are often under the impression that all those who enter convents or monasteries, are reluctant victims. If it is realised that they believe in the existence of all the terrors of which they are told, it will be seen that there is motive enough for their decision. It is indeed difficult for those who know that Christ saves fully and freely to realise the state of mind of those who do not believe, and who think that they can escape an eternity of torment by their own efforts.

But the spiritual exercises of Ignatius are by no means so original as may be supposed. It is impossible now to discover whether he had or had not any knowledge of the manner in which the heathen were initiated into the Eleusiman mysteries, but it is more than probable that he was not unacquainted with Oriental mysticism. In the year 1526 while Loyola was in the town of Alcala where Cardinal Ximenes had established a high school, he was arrested by the Inquisition, and cast into prison on a charge of being one of the Illuminati. There is no doubt that there were many disciples of secret and occult Eastern sects in Spain at this period.

The account given in "Rollins' Ancient History" of the introduction of novices into the Eleusiman discipleship is strangely like the initiatory exercises of a Jesuit novitiate. The principle at least is the same. Spiritual terror is the means used to impress the votary. When the time of their initiation arrives they are brought into the temple, and to inspire them with greater reverence and terror, the ceremony was performed in the night. Wonderful things took place on this occasion. Visions were seen and voices heard of an extraordinary kind. A sudden splendour dispelled the darkness of the place, and disappearing immediately, added new horrors to the gloom. Apparitions, claps of thunder, earthquakes, heightened the terror and amazement, whilst the person to be admitted, overwhelmed with dread, and sweating through fear, listened with trembling to the reading of a mysterious volume, if, indeed, in such a condition he was capable of hearing at all. In this case the mind was impressed through the senses, in the case of the Jesuit and Buddhist novice they make their own sensation, and the bodily faculties are impressed through the mind. The Jesuit novice is commanded to smell the stenches, to see the tortures, and to feel the pains of the damned, and he who best carries out this self-impressed illusion is considered the most fitting subject for the Order. In the case of the Buddhist the method is somewhat more spiritual.

The Buddhist novice who performed his spiritual exercises long centuries before the Ignatian method was in use, proceeded thus:—Five states of "Yama" or purifications and meditations had to be passed through before the novice could obtain holy wisdom, or union of the soul with the supreme God. First, the Chela, or novice, must spend some time in purifications and fasting, and then he comes into the presence of his teacher or master, who is to help him, as the Jesuit novice master assists the Jesuit novice in the process of advancement in the science of Divine things. A patron saint is selected, for the heathen theology has its saints, generally the spirits of ancestors to whom worship is rendered in kind, as well as verbally.

In the Church of Rome the offerings in kind, which are usually made to the chosen saint, are given in kind to the priest, or other representative of the authority of the Church; in the Eastern worship of the departed the offerings in kind are burned, as it is supposed that they will thus reach the personality for whom they are intended, through the medium of fire. The idea is curious. The ignorant heathen, having seen that any substance which is placed in fire disappears rapidly, concludes that the fire has absorbed the substance of what is offered, and that this, whether food, or clothing, or other gift, will be presented to the person in whose honour it is offered in another world by the Fire God. The Indian novice is taught to look on his teacher or master as an incarnation of his god. He must worship at his feet, and present to him the same offerings as he would to Krishna (see "Vishnu Purana," by Wilson, the Orientalist, p. 652). His master is at once his guide and his god. He accepts the voice of the master as the voice of God. Thus the teaching of Rome has been anticipated by the teaching of the followers of the gods of old. Nor is it necessary to account for this similarity of religious teaching by crediting the later teachers with actual imitation. Men who are ignorant of Gospel truth have manifested a similar fashion of worshipping in all ages; and visible signs and symbols have been used as a medium of honouring or communicating with the invisible and unknown God.

Of the two systems, however, the more ancient

has in some respects a greater spirituality. In the spiritual exercises of the Buddhist novice he must endeavour to abstract himself from all outward things by silence, by closing all the approaches of the senses. The eyes must be closed, the ears must be filled with some substance which will prevent the entrance of sound, the very breathing must be suspended. When he is fully abstracted from all the things of time and sense, then, and then only, may he hope for heavenly communications. So also must the Jesuit novice withdraw himself even from the usual course of his sufficiently secluded life. He is removed into a new sphere. Even his former routine of spiritual duties are changed. All must be silent as the grave, and he must lay aside even his holiest occupations. He also must place himself abjectly at the feet of his master, to learn from him the further abandonments of himself to which he is now called.

When the Buddhist novice has altogether abstracted himself from all outward things, he is desired to conjure up the image of his god; it is true that the symbols and form under which he is taught to represent this deity are gross and materialistic, but the same may truly be said of the images of saints which are placed before the Roman Catholic youth for their veneration. But the anthromorphism of the Buddhist is but a step in passing to the realisation of the abstract and purely spiritual deity whom he learns to adore, while the Roman Catholic is always required to venerate exterior forms, and to adore exterior symbols. But there is this important difference: the Eastern novice was taught to use these material things as a means to attain a state of complete abstraction from everything earthly, whereas the Jesuit novice, even if he may attain eventually to a condition of spiritual ecstasy, continues to use the things of sense. We are told, in the life of Madame Guion, that she fasted and prayed and scourged herself in vain, until a Jesuit, more enlightened than his brethren, told her she was searching from without what could only be found within.

There is a certain satisfaction to the natural man in doing some exterior work which he hopes may secure his welfare hereafter. The visible is nearer to us than the invisible. What we see and what we feel is more real to us than what others have seen, or what others have felt. Hence the special adaptability of the spiritual exercises of Ignatius to the natural man. The individual who is engaged in this work is withdrawn, as we have said, from all exterior distraction in order that all his faculties and all his senses may be occupied in the one object of realising the subjects proposed to him. It is not sufficient that he shall listen to the words in which the preacher describes the torments of hell —torments which are supposed to assail every sense, and to torture each with an agony devised specially for the purpose.

The listener is at last left in the dimness of an artificially created solitude, to work up the scene which has been described in such a manner as to make him imagine that he already feels the whips and scorpions and the burning fiery instruments with which he will be punished for ever and ever.

But the spiritual exercises were not all words. Ignatius had taught and had practised the gospel of salvation by works. Once it is believed that we can save ourselves, or at least that we can merit salvation, by personal suffering, there is no limit except the limit of human endurance, which can be put to self-sacrifice. But it often happens that those who have practised the most degrading humiliations to obtain the grace of humility have found a source of pride even in these humiliations. The temptation to spiritual pride in the Roman Catholic Church is proportioned to the honour which that Church pays to those who practise voluntary humiliations. And this is the case above all in the cloister. Here ambition is limited, and has but one outlet. It is true that a few may ambition advancement in position, and desire the higher places. For the rest, they know well that the prizes are few indeed, and the difficulty of attaining them is very great; but the poorest and the most ignorant have not only a chance, but the best chance of advancing themselves to that high position of sanctity which must eventually secure them honour, even if that honour is sometimes manifested in pitiful exhibitions of envy and jealousy.

Indeed, to secure the very high honour of being considered a saint, the very first step is to practise, in season and out of season, acts of extraordinary humility, or perhaps we should say, acts which in conventual life are supposed to be acts of extraordinary humility. Humility is a relative term, and humiliations vary accordingly. Then there are two kinds of humiliations: first, the humiliations which are part of the convent rule, as, for example, kissing the floor when reproved by a superior, or performing a penance prescribed by rule in the refectory; and second, the penances or humiliations which are voluntary. These are the penances which obtain credit of the highest kind. A good *religieuse* is one who observes well and carefully the ordinary routine of the convent; a saint is one who, besides observing this rule, does a great many other things which to the uninitiated seem more or less absurd.

It was perhaps natural that some soul who had

so followed the instructions of the guide of his retreat as to have counted the blows received by Christ in the scourging, and "seen" the blood which flowed from His stripes, should at last be so overcome by this realised scene as to desire to bear himself what Christ had borne. It is certain, however, that in all religions, and at all times of the world's history, men have sought to propitiate their gods by personal sufferings, and there is little difference, either in the motive or the act, between the scourgings which the Roman Catholic saint inflicts on himself or others, and the piercing of the flesh with hooks of the Hindoo fakir. *

Nor need it be assumed that this seeking for honour through humiliations is done deliberately. Pride is one of the most subtle of sins, and the

* A sketch was published some years since of a young English lady, a member of one of the oldest Roman Catholic families of this country, which gave an account of her novitiate in a French convent of the most austere order. Amongst other things, it is related of her that on one occasion she was so overcome by her meditation on the scourging of Christ, that she induced a companion novice to go with her to the chapel, where she was to scourge her until she fainted. The attempt was frustrated by some means, probably by the watchfulness of the mistress of novices, who would not have allowed a young and very delicate English girl to undertake austerities which would have been permitted to one of a different nationality.

pride which apes humility has passed into a proverb. The monk or the nun who practises humiliations with a remote view of future exaltation, may have scarcely realised the temptation, and would resent the imputation of such a motive with an indignation not altogether feigned. We have considered the spiritual exercises of Ignatius Loyola principally with regard to their effect on, and use by the Jesuit novices, but these exercises are intended for the use of Roman Catholics of all classes. Many editions of this work have been published by the Jesuits, and to the uninitiated reader they may seem as we have said elsewhere, simply a good guide to a higher spiritual life. But the real object of these exercises consists in what they are made to mean when expanded or used as a text-book by a trained priest.

In the edition published by Cardinal Wiseman, he calls attention to the necessity of a director for those who wish to avail themselves of the full benefit to be gained from them. He says, "The essential element of a spiritual retreat is direction. In the Catholic Church no one is allowed to trust himself in spiritual matters." Elsewhere he says, "Let no one think of undertaking these holy exercises without the guidance of a prudent and holy director." It is a fundamental axiom in the Church of Rome that every one must be guided in all things spiritual and temporal by the Church.

But as the Church is an abstraction, and only general—though very well defined lines of conduct are laid down for the guidance of the children of the Church—it becomes necessary that all who desire "perfection" should apply to some one individual for the personal guidance which is of precept, if not of obligation.

It is here that the tremendous power of the Church makes itself felt. It is through this "direction" that statesmen are compelled to act, not for the benefit of the country to which they belong, but for the benefit of the Church, which controls them. It is here that matters of the most secret nature are discussed and decided. It is here that alliances of marriage are arranged, and political treaties are agreed on. That we do not over state the case will be shown later. It is even advised that the confessor and the director should not be the same person, and the reason for this is obvious. A good Roman Catholic is supposed to go to confession frequently, and may have to change his confessor often. But the case of direction is different. Direction is not needed at every moment, letters can pass between the directed and the director, and at regular and not infrequent interviews, particular orders can be given by the director and general principles laid down for the guidance of the individual.

The great power of the Jesuit has been obtained

and preserved through the director. To have a Jesuit director is fashionable, and the Jesuit has succeeded in persuading the world of Catholics that he is an expert in this matter, as indeed he is. As it is of the utmost importance that the General should be kept informed of every important public affair in every country, and in every cabinet, it is obvious that he can obtain the information through the fathers who hold the position of directors to Roman Catholic politicians; hence the efforts which are made by the Order to secure for themselves the direction of Roman Catholics who hold a prominent place in politics or society. Hence the jealousy with which they are regarded by other religious Orders, and by the secular priests.

The Jesuit novice has also his director, but the one object of his spiritual guide is everywhere the same—to impress on him the glory and honour of becoming a member of an institute, which has not only kings and princes, but even popes and cardinals at its feet. But while the neophyte is dazzled with the glory which is offered to him, he is at the same time well impressed that the only way to secure and preserve this glory, is obedience. It is the first and the last lesson of his spiritual life. His training on this one point is terribly severe. But the end pointed out to him is glorious. He may some day have kings and princes kneeling at his feet, and have the power to direct the destinies of nations. He may regulate the policy and frame the laws even for nations which are not of his own faith, through the members of his Church who now take their places in the councils of Protestant nations. If the process of the "making of a Jesuit" is hard to flesh and blood, he is reminded that he aspires to belong to the only body of men in the world who can boast of almost universal domination, who wield a sword with the hilt in the hand of their General in Rome and the point everywhere. He is not required to practise great austerities, for this was scarcely part of the Ignatian plan. Indeed, Ignatius is credited with having had a special care as to providing for the bodily requirements of his disciples, and the anecdote of how he purchased lampreys in Rome when the price was prohibitory for all but the most wealthy, is read from time to time in the Jesuit refectory with unction, and heard with suppressed murmurs of approval.

At the commencement of the Order, Ignatius was obliged to receive older men into his novitiate, but he desired only the young. With them there could be less question of obedience; when the director of their retreat described the misery of the lost in blood-curdling accents they would not be so likely to recall a time when they believed that "a certain mitigation of punishment, a certain happiness, might be possible even in hell."* It is necessary that these aspirants to so exalted a position should be hardened, and hardened with the hardness of steel. At any moment they might be called upon to exercise the most terrible cruelties on others, or to bear the most terrible cruelties themselves; not indeed that these sufferings would be necessarily physical, but there are mental sufferings which cut as deep into the soul as the lash of the most cruel discipline cuts into the quivering flesh of the body.

Obedience is the one end of all this training—unasking, unthinking, unreasoning obedience.

It is more than unwise to underestimate the strength of an attacking army, or to express contempt for the ability or plans of the leader of an opposing force. What may seem to us the merest folly, is to others heavenly wisdom. We cannot expect to convince if we do not understand the point of view of the individual whom we desire to convert. We cannot expect the hearty co-operation of those who dislike, even if they do not fear, the Jesuits' system, if we either mis-state its working, or understate the motive power by which it is governed. It is true that the Jesuit, like all Catholics, has his Pantheon of divinities, but he believes in them as firmly as the Christian believes in God, and he also

* See notes at end of volume.

believes in God. It is true that the Jesuit has his General to whom he gives the obedience of a slave, but the Jesuit believes his General to be as God, so that if the dead voice of God, so to say, in Scripture, seems to conflict with the living voice of God which comes through the General, the authority of the living voice must prevail.

It cannot be too clearly understood that religion, or we may say a certain view of religion, lies at the root of the whole matter. It cannot be too clearly understood that the whole system would fall to the ground at once, if the obedience of the Jesuit was claimed on merely human grounds. A number of men may agree to obey a fellow man, for a limited time, as soldiers obey their generals in war. But though attempts have been made by Roman Catholic theologians to compare the two kinds of obedience, there is actually the greatest possible difference. We have alluded to this matter before, but its importance may justify us in returning to the subject.

The obedience of the soldier is an obedience of convenience, the obedience of the Jesuit is claimed to be an evidence of the highest religious virtue. The soldier is not obliged to internal obedience, he may criticise the actions and motives of his General within certain common sense limits. The Jesuit is taught that an internal criticism is quite as much an act of deadly sin as an openly expressed murmur.

The soldier can appeal to higher authority, and to public opinion if he considers himself wronged, but the hapless Jesuit is allowed no appeal, even to the Pope; to appeal is to suppose it possible that the superior may have erred, and to admit such a supposition, would be to open the door to a freedom, however limited, which the Jesuit cannot allow to his subjects.

Although the General of the Jesuits is the head of the Order, religiously as well as in all matters of discipline, it will be observed how powerfully his authority is strengthened by the vow required from every Jesuit, of personal service to the Pope. If a Jesuit perchance rebelled or doubted, he can at once be told that it is quite as much against the individual Pope he rebels as against the individual superior, and what Catholic, while he retains even a spark of faith, would try to rebel against his God on earth! That these men should have succeeded as they have succeded is matter of little wonder, when they have been governed by such a code of laws, that they should have failed, and have been driven forth with contumely from Catholic countries, proves that after all the skill which organised was but human, and that the ends which it strove to attain were not for the benefit of humanity.

CHAPTER V.

The Jesuit as an Educator.

The Jesuit as an Educator.—Great importance of this subject.—Jesuit education fashionable ; important revelations on this subject by a distinguished R. C. priest, and two R. C. gentlemen of position.—The Rev. Lord Petre, M. Gleize, and Count Paul Von Hoensbraech, remarkable similarity between their statements and experience.—M. Gleize's description of a Retreat for boys in preparation for their first Communion ; use of spiritual terror ; stories told to frighten the boys by the Director ; story of the Freemason.—Story of a lad who went to a theatre and appeared to the priest to say he was damned ; the cries, shouts and gesticulations of the father intensify the effect.—After such sermons M. Gleize obtains extra supplies of holy water before going to bed ; the effect of this teaching wears off in after life, and indifference to all religion is the result ; hence many of the present evils of French society. — Contemptuous remarks about women in the Spiritual Exercises ; the Jesuit not having wife or lawful offspring cannot be fit to educate those who, in the future, will probably have the duty of caring for a wife and bring up a family ; how the boys practise receiving the wafer before their first Communion.—The boys treated like criminals at their time for recreation ; watched at every moment, not allowed even a passing word of private conversation with each other ; forced to play rough games to prevent free intercourse ; system of humiliating and harassing espionage ; all personal friendship carefully prevented ; the education of boys carried out on the same principle as the novitiate ; the Jesuits do not educate in the highest sense of the word, they merely impart information, which their pupils must receive without discussion and without explanation.—A Jesuit college is the grave of thought.—All the class books written by the fathers.—All are spiritually peptonised.—M. Gleize gives some notable examples of this method of teaching history.

THERE are few subjects which command so much attention at the present day, as that of the education of the rising generation, and this is as it should be. The future of the nation depends on the education of the present, hence, any contribution towards the better understanding of methods of training for the young cannot fail to interest—we had almost said the parents of to-day, but the march of intellect has advanced so far that we might say the children of to-day. The Jesuits are the educators of the Roman Catholic Church *par excellence.* To have been educated by the Jesuits is to have a hall mark, which passes in all catholic circles as one of no ordinary value. And since so many of our politicians, and especially of our Press men, are educated by Jesuits, it is desirable to ascertain the nature and the value of the education which they impart, and what have been the results intellectually and morally of their method of education.

Before proceeding further with this important subject, it may be well to correct an erroneous impression which prevails extensively. Some persons suppose that the Jesuits are, somehow, different from other Roman Catholics, and if they are offered evidence of teaching which even the most indifferent cannot approve, they suppose that this teaching is something quite different from the authorised teaching of the Church of Rome. This misapprehension is serious in its consequences. The Jesuits are as much under the control of the Roman Catholic Church, as any other Roman Catholics, and they dare not, and do not, teach any theology, moral or dogmatic, which is not fully approved by their Church. The Roman Catholic Church, therefore, and the Pope, especially since the definition of his personal infallibility, is responsible for all that they teach, and for all that they do collectively. Any work published by a Jesuit must first obtain the approbation of his immediate superiors, it must then have the approbation of the General of the Order after it has been examined by the theologians of his immediate *entourage*, appointed for the purpose. Lastly, such a work must have the approbation of the Pope, which is given, directly or indirectly, through the Sacred Congregation of the Inquisition, which if it has not power to burn heretics at the present day, can, and does forbid the circulation of books which are not orthodox according to Rome. It is important that this point should be clearly understood, so that there can be no mistake as to the authority when quotations

LUTHER SINGING FOR FRAU COTTA.

are made from the works which the Jesuits use in their schools and colleges.

There are three ways by which we can ascertain the kind of instruction which the Jesuits give to their pupils, and what kind of moral and intellectual training they receive. First, we can ascertain this from their published and authorised writings. However secret the Jesuits may have been in regard to their private affairs, it has not been possible for them to conceal their books of moral theology. As this chapter is concerned with the training of youth, we do not touch the question of dogmatic theology here. Next, we can judge of their educational methods from the narratives of reliable historians, and, indeed, from historians of their own Order. Lastly, we can avail ourselves of the published criticisms of Roman Catholics who have been educated by Jesuits, without even referring to such Roman Catholics, or Jesuit students, as have left the Roman Catholic Church. Our statements will be taken principally from the published works of the late Rev. Lord Petre, who lived and died a devoted Catholic, and from the remarkable narrative of M. Lucien Gleize, "Chez les Jesuites," recently published in Paris, and from the narratives on this subject recently published in Germany by Count Paul von Hoensbrœch. As these gentlemen are persons of well known social position, and of unquestionable integrity, the exact correspondence of their testimony gives it considerable weight.

M. Gleize tells us that he spent twelve years with the Jesuits, and was educated by them, hence, he had every opportunity of studying the system. In commencing his preface he says: "*Deja bien de livres furent ecrit pour ou contre les Jesuites, surtout contre. C'est livre n' est ecrit ni pour, ni contre; il est ecrit sur les Jesuites.*"

The youth who is trained in the Jesuit college must necessarily be trained in the principles of his masters. He will learn what they can teach, and no more. He will believe what they say with the confiding innocence of youth, and with the additional confidence of the Roman Catholic in his appointed teachers. We have spoken in the preceding chapter of the spiritual exercises used as a means of forming character and deciding vocations. These exercises are intended for all conditions of men and women, and are used even for children in a modified form. But while the youth, who is so far advanced as to be allowed or invited to consider his vocation to the Order, may be given the exercises in private, the youth who is not destined for the religious state is not expected to meditate alone. Retreats are organised several times in the year for the students in general, and the exercises are preached to them with more or less eloquence by one of the fathers.

M. Gleize has given us very full information on this important subject. Before we give extracts from his work, it may be well, however, to note some apparently trifling, but nevertheless very important differences between the spiritual exercises as published in this country, and the spiritual exercises as published in France. There are no trifles in Jesuit programmes. In the English edition additional exercises are added in honour of the "Blessed Virgin Mary, Mother of God;" and in these new doctrines, such as that of the immaculate conception, unheard of in the time of Ignatius Loyola, are introduced. Surely there could not be a greater evidence of the changeable creed of Rome, if indeed the suppression of the Jesuits by one infallible Pope and their restoration by another is not sufficient to prove it. Another curious and significant alteration in the exercises is made in the edition used in England.

At page 267 of the latest English edition we find the following: "Satan with his weak, but obstinate character, may be compared, when he attacks us, to a woman daring to contend with her husband. Let her husband oppose her firmly" (in the French edition, which professes to be an exact translation of the original Spanish, the word used is "man,") "she soon lays aside her war-like mood, and quickly leaves the field to him. On the contrary, let her see in him any timidity or inclination to fly or give way, she becomes audacious, insolent, cruel as a fury." In the original there is not a word about a husband, the words used being "*un homme*," but in either case it is a gratuitous insult to the female sex, and how can those who thus hold a wife up to scorn, and compare her to the devil, be fitted to form the characters of the future husbands of this or any country? And, indeed, it is in the formation of character that the Jesuit so specially fails. His pupils become a weak replica of himself. If they are not bound to the abject obedience of the Jesuit, they are taught that this abject obedience is the highest perfection, and they are compelled to an obedience which is degrading to their coming manhood. But on this and kindred subjects we give the evidence of those who speak from personal experience.

Another important authority on the subject of Jesuit training of the youth confided to their charge, is that of the late Rev. Lord Petre. He published four pamphlets in the years 1877 and 1878. The value and importance of these documents cannot be over estimated, first, because of Lord Petre's social position, next, because of the value of any information he gives, as he has made a speciality of the subject, and lastly, because of his well known loyalty to the Church to which he and his noble family have belonged for centuries.

We shall first deal with the statements of the French writer, also a devoted Romanist; the singular agreement of the two authorities cannot fail to strike the least observant reader.

In commencing his narrative of personal experiences, M. Gleize says: "*Ce que Jesuite veut, Dieu le veut.*" But it does not necessarily follow that what succeeds is Divine. The Jesuit does not act without foresight or consideration, nor does he abandon his designs at the first discouragement. He commands success, but he leaves nothing undone to secure it.

M. Gleize took the initiative himself at the early age of ten, in the affair of his education. He had been a pupil in an ecclesiastical seminary, but he ambitioned the distinction of being a pupil of this famous Order. It was "*comme il faut,*" he tells us, and something of which the parents of the pupils could boast. The abbe who governed the seminary in which he had received his education so far, did not quite approve the change; but the boy had his way, with results which he has faithfully recorded.

The Jesuits made two rules with regard to the admission of pupils, and kept them. No boy would be received who had been previously in any public school. No boy would be received of bourgeois origin, or whose parents were not people of wealth and good social position. Thus at the expense of the present they secured the future—the Jesuit can always afford to wait. In order to keep their pupils from contact with the common herd, they chose recreation days which would not allow their pupils to mix freely with the pupils of other institutions; they arranged even for the conveyance of their pupils to and from their school in their own omnibus. Everything was done to separate the elect from the common herd, and to give distinction to their pupils. They understand human nature, even while they profess to despise it. M. Gleize enters into the most minute details of his personal experience, "Chez les Jesuites;" but we shall only uote what he has to say of the religious education which he received, and the literary course through which he passed.

Spiritual terror was the one and marked feature of the spiritual instruction. "We heard of nothing but the hideousness of sin, and the terrible penalties with which God punished those who offended Him. The great occasion for enforcing these lessons was the retreat, which was of absolute obligation for these, one might say babies, in preparation for their first communion. This day of days on which this event was to take place, was made to stand out in the memory by observances of piety and pleasure which it was expected would for ever impress the mind."

Yet with all Rome's precautions and efforts, the first communion is the last in the vast majority of cases. The youth, once freed from the imposing restraints of the college or seminary, rushes eagerly on the career of pleasure hitherto denied, even in its most innocent form, and though he may retain his fear of hell, and send for the priest when he is dying, he keeps as far from him as possible while he lives. "We were completely isolated from the other pupils during our retreat. We passed from mass to sermon, and from sermon to meditation, from meditation to spiritual reading." These men, however well intentioned, had forgotten their own boyhood, with its joys and its freedoms; they would make their pupils monks in miniature, and ecclesiastics in practice, when they should have been taught that the yoke of the Lord is easy, and His burden light.

The service of benediction, litanies, the recital of the rosary, were, so to say, the only recreations allowed, and this for boys not yet in their teens, and scarcely out of the nursery. It is little wonder that religion became utterly distasteful to them, and that spiritual terror was needed to enforce the lessons which were given, with so little discretion. But the astute fathers looked rather to the future than to the present. They wished to leave such impressions of fear on the minds of their pupils as would prevent them in the future from even listening to any arguments, or reading any literature contrary to that which is permitted by the Church. In acting thus, they believed that they were consulting the highest interests of those who were confided to their charge.

The boys were duly impressed, but M. Gleize declares that when he attempted an apostleship in his own family, as the result of the retreat, he was considerably discouraged. His first attempt at mission work was made on the family *chef*, whom he suspected of not being as devout as he should be. He tried to impress this functionary with the fear of eternal torments, and the terrors of hell fire. But the *chef* assured him that God knew too well all he suffered from fire in this world to inflict further torment of a similar nature in the next. This repulse so discouraged the young missionary, that he abandoned the *rôle* of preacher for all time to come. Still, he remained impressed, or rather terrified. Narratives were introduced by the conductor of the retreat in order to further emphasise his exhortations. Of course these narratives were believed literally, as it was intended that they should be.

These lads of ten or twelve were told of a youth who forgot all the good instructions which he had received, and went one evening to a theatre; swift indeed was the retribution which followed. The next day he was found dead in his bed. But this was not the least part of the horror. He appeared to one of his companions the following night, damned, and in a state of the most horrible torments. "The father," says M. Gleize, "exhausted himself in describing the torment of the lost." Every narrative was commenced with the assurance that he had known the unhappy subject personally. Who could disbelieve him? Certainly not his youthful and terrified audience. To doubt would have been a sin of which they at least could not have been guilty, especially at such a time. The preacher even descended to cries and shouts and grimaces, the better to terrify his trembling hearers. As for M. Gleize, he took care to provide himself with additional supplies of holy water and relics after such discourses. But these fears could not stand the test of experience. The boys eventually became men; they went to theatres, and their friends went to theatres, and no serious retribution followed. Naturally they reasoned, if the fathers terrified us so needlessly in this matter, why should we respect their teaching in other matters?

But there were also sermons on the joys of heaven and the certainty of attaining to these joys for the obedient, especially for those who remained under the direction of the good fathers, and who did not stray into forbidden paths of literature or enter lyceums or colleges which were under the direction of government. "At one moment we were sure of being lost, the next moment we were equally sure of being saved." But there were exceptions when there was no possibility of redemption. But there was one course which must end in our eternal damnation if we were so unhappy as to enter on it. The spiritual director of these boys had a horror of Freemasonry which amounted to a mania. In season and out of season he impressed on his charges the dreadful consequences of having any connection whatsoever with persons already past redemption. He shuddered, he groaned, he cried, he shouted, in order to impress what he believed to be the truth. He described the horrible stenches which would proceed from the damned, he desired his charges to place their hands for a moment over the flame of a candle that they might feel in a faint degree the agony which these unhappy persons would suffer for all eternity, and to enforce further his lessons he narrated certain facts which of themselves should have been sufficient to terrify the most hardened.

One of these narratives is recorded in the work from which we quote. A young man so far forgot all the lessons of his youth as to join the Freemasons. But happily for him there was one religious duty which he performed in secret and never abandoned. He recited one Hail Mary every night before he retired to rest. This proved his salvation; Christ may forsake us, but Mary never, she is the all merciful mother. She touched his heart at last, and he determined to forsake the Freemasons. But he knew that if he did so in France, they would certainly assassinate him, so he fled for his life to America. It was in vain; the very moment he landed he was assassinated. The good priest shuddered as he related the terrible tragedy, and his little hearers trembled also, and promised that they would never be united to men who could be guilty of such dreadful deeds. Indeed such was the horror which this Jesuit father professed to have of the Freemasons, that he declared he would far rather see the devil than see a Freemason. Either the father was wilfully and deliberately deceiving his pupils, or he was so ignorant of the world as to be utterly unfit to educate. His pupils could scarcely continue to respect him when they knew later that Freemasons do not assassinate those who withdraw from their membership.

M. Gleize describes the days of his first communion, for which all these elaborate preparations had been made. His experience has been the experience of many. The receiving of the "host" was the end for which all this preparation was made, and naturally the over wrought imagination of these little lads, led them to expect some wonderful effect when the supreme moment had arrived. They had been taught that they were to receive their God, and with all the trusting faith of youth they believed what was told them. On the eve of the great day they had to practise receiving the Sacrament. They were expressly forbidden either to eat the holy wafer, or to swallow it immediately. It should be moistened slowly in the mouth, and then swallowed with supreme reverence. Even in the merest particle there was a God. M. Gleize relates how he envied one boy, who, when they were practising, succeeded in swallowing the wafer "like a priest." Afterwards it appeared that he had obtained some unconsecrated wafers and practised on them.

But all this preparation ended in dismal failure of emotion at the moment when religious ecstasy was most desired and expected. "Notwithstanding my fervour and my faith, I was terribly disillusioned. I had anticipated something more mysterious, something more consoling; I thought that my soul would have been wrapped in ecstasy. After I had received the communion I found myself just as I had been before the great event, and I found within me a longing desire which had not been satisfied."

Weakening the mind by exciting the imagination, and subduing the will by fear, such are the means employed by these religious educators to attach children to the faith.

The constant observance of religious exercises cuts up the day to a formidable degree. A short prayer was said at the commencement of every change of employment. This might be suitable for those who had resolved to lead a religious life, and who could arrange their time as they pleased, but for boys or other young persons, the result is not always what their instructors desire. We have indeed known of painful results from the long practise of this incessant devotion. It leads in some cases to a scrupulosity which is mentally dangerous. When those who have been accustomed to such practices of piety for many years during the most impressionable period of their lives, return to their homes, where it would be impossible to continue the signing with the cross, and saying prayers, however short, at every stroke of the clock, and at other frequent intervals, they either omit these practices altogether, and, weary of a mechanical devotion, cease to pray, or they fall into spiritual despair because they cannot do what is evidently impossible. They cannot understand if it was so serious a matter to omit these practices in the convent or college how they can be justified in omitting them at home. Between the desire to do what they have been taught to consider so essential in order to please God, or rather, to secure their salvation, and the plain fact that such practices cannot be continued, or even remembered without considerable effort, they begin to lose all hope of doing what they once believed to be essential, and fall into indifference, if not into vice, or become morbid and live in a state of despair which sometimes ends in religious mania.

A spiritual lecture was read every evening. "This lecture was always the life of some saint, and was spiritual only in name." Twice during the mass the boys sang canticles which were set to airs which they heard afterwards on the stage.

But the Jesuit arrangements for recreation, which indeed are much the same as those in use in all Roman Catholic educational establishments, were the special subjects of M. Gleize's reprehension. Active games were insisted on for two reasons, first because it prevented anything like private conversation, which is dreaded above all things in such places: next, because the exercise was obligatory, and regulated by the superiors, it naturally became very distasteful to the boys, and in the higher classes especially they refused to amuse themselves to order, unless actually compelled to do so. Boys who complained were told that they were wanting in the "proper spirit" of obedience, and treated as *mauvais sujets*. Thus bad feeling was being constantly engendered between the pupils and the masters, than which nothing could have been more conducive of evil results in the future.

"I do not wish to draw a comparison between the games and recreations customary in secular colleges: I only desire to show the difference in their methods. Secular colleges encourage physical exercises for the greater good of their pupils. They wish to establish an equilibrium between their mental and animal being. The Jesuits, on the contrary, care nothing for the body, their principal object is to prevent any kind of free intercourse between their pupils. But what an antiquated idea of training for their future life. It may be considered necessary to enforce a rule of the strictest silence in religious houses, where to pass even the most cursory remark of criticism on the rule or observances is considered an unpardonable crime. But boys will think, and will talk, even under restrictions which will silence their seniors who are vowed for ever to a life of obedience, and if the thinking is not permitted, or rather if the expression of thought is not permitted in youth, the flames of the volcano may be covered over for the time, but sooner or later they will escape with a force which will destroy the restraints of the past and seriously imperil the future."

With regard to literary education of the Jesuit pupil, M. Gleize is explicit and condemnatory. He writes without passion, and with an evident desire to do justice not only to the Jesuit, but what is quite as important, to the public. It has been unfortunate for the cause of truth, which is the only cause worth consideration, that so many who have written on the Jesuits have written as partisans. Every one who does not agree with their bitter denunciations is a "Jesuit in disguise;" they do not want truth, they want denunciation, than which nothing is easier, and nothing less satisfactory to men who think. They cannot see any side of any question except their own, and their own is narrow with the narrowness of a feeble intellect. They denounce the Jesuit because he denies to others the intellectual and spiritual liberty which they profess to admire, yet they are quite as narrow as he is and they have an inquisition of their own, in which they martyr as far as they are able, those who do not agree with their particular opinions. Men who think and who are capable of judging, but who have not time or opportunity for personal investigation, have been at the mercy of these controversialists and have either supposed that the individual Jesuit is little short of a demon incarnate, or that he is a much calumniated man.

He is but the victim of his fate and circumstances, but the wise will ask, What does he teach ; what is his real object ? and will pause before they commit the destinies of their country or the youth of to-day to those who, however sincere, are bound by a system which denies all liberty, intellectual and moral.

In the commencement of this chapter on the literary training given by the Jesuit, M. Gleize relates an anecdote worth recording. Even Jesuit colleges are examined on occasion by the bishop of the diocese where they are situated, such examination being permitted not as a right but as a diplomatic courtesy. Mgr. de Mazenod, bishop of Marseilles, on one occasion was the examiner in a Jesuit college. One of the pupils proved so stupid and deficient, that he could no longer restrain his impatience. The rector observed what was passing and whispered to his Eminence, " He is not very bright; but he is very pious." To whom His Grace replied: " Yes, yes, but the piety will vanish ,and the stupidity will remain." The general opinion (of devout Roman Catholics) is, that the Jesuits are the best educators in the world. If, says M. Gleize, we understand by education simply the imparting of prepared knowledge, this may be true. But if we understand by education drawing out the latent faculties of the mind, and assisting the student to think for himself and to cultivate his intellect, the Jesuit does not educate; he merely teaches.

The simple fact is that the Jesuit dare not educate. He dare not because he is a Roman Catholic, and Rome does not permit education in its highest sense ; still less can he educate as a Jesuit, because the rule of his Order is, if possible, still more opposed to the imparting of knowledge than the rule of any other teaching Order in the Church of Rome. This may appear mere assertion, and mere assertions are worth little ; but we proceed to give proofs which can scarcely be disputed. The subject is certainly one which no thoughtful mind will lay aside without careful and attentive consideration. The writer knew of a case in Ireland where the bishop, who as usual sat beside the superior of the convent, during a public examination, seemed lost in admiration. The superioress not unnaturally supposed that he appreciated the answers of the children which were indeed wonderful. But the bishop was not so easily deceived as the admiring friends and audience of relatives. He was asked what had especially attracted his attention, and replied, not without a gracious smile, "I am amazed at the wonderful memory of the monitress who is examining." He had discovered early in the proceedings, that the questions and answers which were supposed to be improvised at the moment, were simply learned by heart. The answers so learned were easily given by the child to whom the interrogation was put, but the effort of memory on the part of the monitress was marvellous, as she had to remember all the questions, not only in their exact sequence, but also which child should be asked the question to which she had learned the reply.

To the Jesuit there is nothing which is not "of faith." There can be no liberty of thought, hence there can be no intellectual liberty, and by liberty we do not mean licence. The Jesuit impresses on his pupils that there are certain fixed and immutable rules of literary and philosophical belief, from which no departure is possible, and that it would be the height of presumption to form any independent personal opinion on any subject whatsoever. The Jesuit college is the grave of thought. Here the high and glorious inspirations of youth are strangled at their birth. It is true that such inspirations are not always well founded, but if they are not permitted free course how can youth learn wisdom by experience, as the first step to larger judgments, when the impressions of youth have been corrected by time and increased knowledge. The frame of mind which would lead even to scientific discovery is sternly repressed. All books for study are religiously peptonised, so that they may be assimilated without digestion. There is no chance for an expanding intellect, for expansion is unnecessary when there is nothing more to be known. Ridicule, the most potent factor in discouraging the young, is freely used if any attempt at originality of thought is manifested. It is the business of the student to learn what is set before him, and to believe in history and science, as well as in religion, what he is taught, and nothing more. What the fathers do not teach him is either not worth knowing or dangerous. All the books used in Jesuit colleges are prepared by the fathers. There are two reasons for this. The fathers can write their history and philosophy so as to suit the views which they hold on these subjects, and they add very largely to their income by the sale of their own books.

If the necessities of the times had not compelled them to another course, the Jesuits would have continued to give the same education to-day, which their predecessors gave in the 17th century. Another serious disadvantage of Jesuit education is the use which is made of Latin which is not always classical, as a medium of instruction and communication. For this there are also reasons—the Jesuit always has his reasons. For the Jesuit we do not deny that these reasons are good, but the important question remains, Are these reasons good for the education of the youth of to-day? In the Jesuit colleges Latin is spoken everywhere, and used in every study. No doubt this facilitates condensing information, and by condensing it, limits it. But there is yet another and important reason for the constant use of the Latin tongue. Latin is not merely the language of the Church in an ecclesiastical sense, it is also, with rare exceptions, the usual medium of ecclesiastical communication. All Papal pronouncements are written in Latin. All communications with the Roman Curia are written in Latin. When a bishop makes his visit *ad limini*, he spends some time conning over his syntax before he sets out on his voyage. The popes and the cardinals who reside in Rome, with very rare exceptions, do not understand any language but Italian, and the English and other bishops with rare exceptions, do not speak Italian. It is a curious fact that the men who dictate the policy and politics and license the books for foreign countries, do not know one word of the language in which they are written. Everything must be translated into Latin or Italian for their decision or revision. It is still more curious that men of intelligence and education submit to the continuance of such a system, especially when they are not members of the Church which pronounces its fiats on their public and private proceedings.

In the French Jesuit colleges Latin is the ordinary medium of conversation, and the boys are furnished with phrase books, in which they may find all that is necessary for the very limited intercourse which they are allowed with each other, even in their games. The Jesuit, however, rarely attempts to teach science. Masters are usually employed to teach the boys these departments, but all the same the books used must have the Jesuit imprint, and the mystic letters A.M.D.G.' The professor of algebra in the college where M. Gleize was educated, told his pupils they should learn by heart, for as they really understood nothing they would be sure to make a serious mistake if they altered or added a word. It was, he observes, a singular way of teaching mathematics.

The Jesuits discourage the study of the exact sciences, and not without reason. They fear that a mind trained to accept nothing which cannot be proved to demonstration, may at last turn on the church, and refuse to believe what is not logically proved. The mathematician accustomed to accept nothing which is not proved, and to discuss and weigh every argument, may one day apply this method of analysis to religious questions, with a result which would be fatal. The Order has a specialist for each study, who prepares the book on each subject. Père Sengler prepares the grammars of the dead languages. Père Gazeau writes the ancient and modern histories. Père Mestre undertakes the study of general literature. The A.M.D.G. which is found on every title page indicates that the book is written for the greater glory of God, and as the greater glory of the Society is a convertible term, orthodoxy is assured.

It need scarcely be said that a carefully expurgated history, is not a history likely to benefit young men who would eventually be called on to play their part in the world's story. Distorted views of facts, and perverted representations of character, would leave them helpless victims to prejudice, when they most needed reliable information. Even though many Frenchmen who have received their education from ecclesiastics have practically abandoned their Church, they can never recover lost time, and such education as they have received has not prepared them to make the best use of their freedom. The prejudices of early education are rarely, if ever, overcome, no matter what may be the intellectual freedoms of later life. All the more reason why the present generation should leave nothing undone to bequeath a glorious heritage of intellectual liberty to those who are coming after us. The only liberty which Rome allows to her children is the liberty to agree with her, and the liberty which she so loudly demands at the present day from the world at large, is liberty to take away our liberty. Rome is the only religion in the world which asks liberty in order to enforce restraint. It is difficult for those who have not studied the subject to understand it, but if the literary history of the Church of Rome is carefully read, and if her explicit teaching on such subjects was understood, it would be quite sufficient to open the eyes of all who are not either indifferent, or wilfully blind.

"The History of France," A.M.D.G., revised, corrected, and completed by the Rev. P. Gazeau, of the Company of Jesus, was the title of the work on French history, which was the class book of the college. It was written for the youthful students in order that they might know all that was considered good for them to know, as regarded certain historical events, and that they might be taught to think as their masters thought on every event connected with the history of their country. Can it be a matter of surprise if the youth so educated should become incapable of judging for himself, or of understanding the real interest of his native land. At each social cataclysm in France —and they have not been few—the pious Catholic lifts up his hands in sincere amazement, and wonders how such events can come to pass! But what else can be expected from men who at the most important period of their lives have been trained to think independent intellectual effort a sin, unless, indeed, it is an intellectual effort to remember what they have been taught, and to believe that all else is false and vain. When the necessity for personal decision comes to such men, they either lean weakly on the feeble reed of the advice of a "director," whose mind is as narrow as their own, or they break from all restraint and rush headlong on the first course of action which seems to promise good, or to relieve them from the burden of personal responsibility which they have not been trained to bear.

The Jesuit professor of history did not believe in the conversion of the world by peaceable means, but rather by the sword and the torture. Providence always intervened for the Church of his affections, and when Providence was too plainly against him, he had reasons to show that it was not at least the fault of the Church. When he is obliged to record the miserable failure of the second crusades, he explains it by saying that the wickedness of the soldiers was extreme, and that the eastern Christians were no better than the infidel whom they desired to exterminate. In this we find he ignored the fact that these bad Christians were devout Roman Catholics, "*de quoi expliquer la conduite de Dieu sur cette Croisade;*" but he has no explanation to give of the failure, of the lamentable failure, of the Crusades of St. Louis. Everything connected with the Reformation is of course grossly misrepresented; pride and a desire for a licentious life was, according to him, the one motive of the "pretended Reformers." Luther secured success by assuring the

German and other princes that they should have all the ecclesiastical spoils. But the Jesuit father does not tell his pupils how it happened that men who had been under the exclusive teaching of his Church for centuries became so opposed to it. As for the massacre of St. Bartholomew, it was a mere nothing; it was an affair of state. We shall see later that it was entirely an affair of the Jesuits.

As for the revocation of the edict of Nantes, Louis XIV. only desired to bring the heretics back to the fold of the Church. The new edict, he says, caused "general rejoicing," and was received with enthusiasm. Not one word of the fatal and cruel dragonnades, but he admits that about 70,000 Protestants were compelled to emigrate. As for the Albigenses, he declares that Innocent III. desired ardently to save the Christian faith from danger, and that, in consequence, many towns where these dangerous people lived were put to the sword, and the inhabitants were destroyed. He depicts in the most vivid colours the terrible fate of kings who rebelled against the Church, and describes with holy unction the awful consequences of the excommunication of those who would not obey the Pope in temporal as well as spiritual affairs. Even the very dishes from which they ate, and the vessels from which they drank, were passed through the fire before they could be used by others, and thus spiritually antisepticated. The kings of France, according to this history, were all more or less religious, generally more. When dying, their sole concern was for the religious future of their country, as, for example, the only care of Louis XIV. when dying was that he feared "the ravages which Jansenism would accomplish in the Church and in society."

Enough has been said on this subject, though too much could not be said to impress thinking men and women with the danger of entrusting education to those who are none the less false and fanatical in their teaching because they are unquestionably sincere. A man who is blind either by nature or from circumstances, is scarcely the person to whom one would entrust the care of a youth about to travel in a new country; it would not minimise the danger if the blind guide believed that he, and he alone, possessed sight. Of general literature as little was taught as possible. Books which might enlarge the mind were strictly excluded, and a sort of *pot pourri* of safe extracts was provided by a father who taught this department. Information was given in the form of question and answer, and the study either intentionally or otherwise was made as uninteresting as possible. To permit a boy the range of a well selected library, such as every English public school possesses, would have been looked upon as a suggestion from an emissary of the evil one.

"The Jesuit's dream of a perfect college," says M. Gleize, "is of one where there would be a crowd of young men who would listen only to their masters, speak only to their masters, think only as their masters, and have no intercourse with their companions except such as should be altogether unavoidable." In fact, they desire naturally to have the college a replica of the novitiate, and the world outside, if indeed it must exist at all, is looked on as a necessary evil to be availed of for the use of the Church. There is, however, one notable difference between the discipline of the Jesuit colleges in France and those in England. The Rev. Lord Petre, of whose narrative we shall make much use later, accuses the English Jesuit fathers of inflicting the most cruel corporal punishments on their pupils. M. Gleize, on the contrary, declares that corporal punishments are unknown in French Jesuit colleges.

There is one point on which the Jesuits deplore that their educational efforts have not the success which they deserved. Their pupils have no enthusiasm, either for the Order, or for the spread of the faith. They may remain members of the Church so far as to frequent the sacraments on stated occasions, to marry with the rites of the Church, to attend mass occasionally on Sundays, and even to send their sons to Jesuit colleges, but here the matter ends. They are passive, they never become apostles, they may become opponents. But the Jesuit has only his own system of education to thank for this.

In every Roman Catholic school and college there are confraternities, and the ambition to become a member of one of these confraternities is the earliest desire instilled. The youngest boys are placed in the confraternity of the Holy Angels. Later they are removed, if considered worthy, to the confraternity of the Children of Mary. The desire ot religious distinction, which is so carefully fostered, often becomes a source of serious evil, since even the walls of a convent cannot change human nature, or exclude the passions of jealousy or ambition. Nor is an ambition less strong because its end is spiritual, nor is the jealousy less bitter because the object desired is presumably pious. But, in addition to these ordinary confraternities, to belong to which a boy or girl is taught by those whose opinions he most respects to believe to be the highest honour, there are also confraternities special to each religious Order. The Jesuits recommend three saints to the imitation of the youth confided to their care: St. Aloysius, St. Stanislaus, and later blessed Berkmans.

To belong to the confraternity of these saints is considered the greatest privilege possible, and the honour is coveted accordingly. But these youths are also presented to the Jesuit pupil as the object of his imitation. Now, if all the pupils of a Jesuit college were to enter the Jesuit novitiate eventually, to emulate the sanctified dirt, or the intellectual idiotcy of a saint, might harm no one but the imitator. But these saints, who obtained all their honours because they renounced the world in a very practical manner, are certainly not persons who should be recommended to the young for imitation, unless they propose to live out of the world. Yet in season and out of season, the virtues and above all the passive obedience of these holy youths are brought forward and praised. If the Jesuit father, in the making of the future man of the world, impresses on him that to become like a corpse in the hands of his spiritual director, is the very highest end of man, he certainly should not be surprised if the advice he gives so persistently is followed; if the man takes the impression of the seal which is placed on him, and retains it in placid indifference like a piece of wax, or if in the burning heat of the world's strife and life, the wax is rudely melted, and, far from retaining any of the original impression, becomes a flaming torch searching for a liberty which has been so unjustly denied.

CHAPTER VI.

AN ENGLISH JESUIT COLLEGE.

AN ENGLISH JESUIT COLLEGE.—Rev. Lord Petre's account of his experience in the English Jesuit College of Stonyhurst. He says English R. C. colleges are far from friendly to each other.—He gives the reason of this plainly.—Only for their unity in religious belief, there would be frequent and open quarrels ; they are unfit to educate because education is not their first object ; carrying out the rules of their Order comes first ; after that the interests of their pupils.—Grave injustice of sending young and inexperienced Jesuits to teach, because it is part of their rule to do so without regard to their qualifications.—Boys sacrificed for the sake of the training of the Jesuit novice.—Those who have the courage to speak are denounced as "disloyal" to the church. — Count Hoensbræch on this subject ; the secular Press denounces any one who attempts an exposure.—Lord Petre complains of the religious teaching in Jesuit colleges, and says it is "parrotted"—no trouble taken to teach intelligently; contrasts R. C. and Protestant colleges to the great advantage of the latter.—Stonyhurst boys under supervision day and night ; this produces many evils ; is fatal to the formation of a self-reliant character.—No real recreation permitted ; the boys not allowed to walk even for a moment arm in arm, to shake hands, or to touch each other ; must walk like criminals in threes or be absolutely silent ; list of the officers masters, and subjects studied at Stonyhurst ; very few books allowed for general reading, and these few are "mercilessly expurgated."

IN Lord Petre's account of his experience of a Jesuit college, he enters more into the formation of character under Jesuit training, than into the subject of intellectual training. The one subject is scarcely less important than the other. It is commonly supposed, particularly by those who are too lazy to think, that Rome has changed in some mysterious way, and Rome is no doubt quite content that this idea should prevail. So long as those who might be active to reform suppose that there is no need of reform, evils can continue without disturbance. It is supposed that Rome has in some way been influenced by the larger views of the 19th century, but where is the proof of this supposition ?

There is something infinitely pathetic in Lord Petre's allusions to his love for his church. For him there is but one church, but one ark of safety, for the whole world. But he cannot help seeing her evils, or rather—for he would scarcely call those things which he so strongly deplores evils—he would have the blots removed from her fair face. How noble this man is and how grand is his love for truth, and desire for the triumph and advancement of the cause so dear to him, even at any sacrifice of his personal feelings or interests. In one of his pamphlets he compares the Benedictine method of teaching and training, which he considers all important, with the methods of the Jesuit.

But he says, "though the public are dissatisfied, the religious orders will never agree." There are too many pecuniary interests mixed up in this question, and though the religious orders possess enormous wealth, they will not pay teachers to impart knowledge of which they are deficient themselves. They spend money on buildings, which may be an ornament to their particular order, but something more is wanted at the present day than mere material work. One cannot but think of Lourdes and the millions of money hoarded by the Fathers of the grotto, when the poor parish priest, the founder of the shrine, could not get sufficient to build a modest and much needed parish church.

Strange as it will seem to some, Lord Petre comments strongly on the failure of Roman Catholic schools to impart a good religious education. Catholic boys show a marked poverty of results, and what they do learn is "parrotted." This statement corresponds with the statements of M. Gleize as to the education given in French Jesuit colleges. The system of espionage as practised in Jesuit colleges is spoken of by him with stern reprobation. He says, "Espionage is yearly,—we speak advisedly, irritating our boys out of all balance of intellect and out of all dignity of character. Where this distortion of supervision is practised, it would seem that Catholic boys must be supposed to come to school so degraded and brutalised, so inferior in purity and rectitude to their Protestant fellows, that they must be treated as meditating the worst kind of evil, at every hour of the day or night.

"There have been many who have come from the peace of tender and gentle homes, and who have found themselves cast suddenly into a world where suspicion, reserve, the extinction of the natural affections, severe and frequent punishments, have rudely displaced paternal advice and maternal gentleness, and under the oppression of an asceticism for which quaint is a term too mild, many have learnt why it is in countries not our own, the character of the priesthood has already become odious and abhorrent to the feelings of boys, ere yet they were in full possession of their reason.

"Under such a discipline many beside myself have become 'desperate by too quick a sense of a constant infelicity.' There have I noted the hardening and souring of childhood's sweetness. There have I seen in its working a process all too apt to foster the growth of artificial and constrained habits in some, of rebellious protest and decay of self-respect in others, of a senseless and uncultured Spartanism in very many, of development more or less distorted in all.

Whose mind can expand when its path is cut between adamantine rocks? Whose aims should be definite, when his natural and laudable objects are beset with clouds of suspicion and mistrust? Whose purpose shall find time to concentrate itself upon natural objects, when its whole energy is focussed on avoidance of trumped up moral dangers which, had they never been suggested to him, would by the grace of God never have been seen, or felt, or known?" These are indeed strong words, and coming from such a source, they demand the earnest and careful consideration of those who would place the education of English youth in the hands of Roman Catholic teachers, whether lay or clerical.

Lord Petre thought that more could be done to improve or rather to form the character of a boy by general care and religious advice, than by the compulsion which the system of espionage involves. He would have youth trained to the love of virtue and to high and lofty ideas which they should put in practice while young, thus forming habits for the future. He says, "I think we do not come near Eton, Rugby, Cheltenham, Wellington and some other non-Catholic schools in these particulars, viz., in scholarship, secondly, and much more in composition, thirdly in expansion of mind, earnestness of purpose, definiteness of aim."

Lord Petre compares the English public school

system with the Jesuit system, and very much prefers the former. He says, "Catholic boys are wanting in definiteness of aim, and earnestness of purpose," all personal manifestation of character is sternly repressed. There can be no special aim of life, boys are obliged every hour of the day and even of the night to move about like automatons; yet he is not without a glimpse of the cause of the evils which he deplores, though naturally he does not see far enough. He does not realise that the religion which he so much loves is the actual cause of the evils which he so honestly deplores. He pays the usual and almost fulsome compliments to the ecclesiastical authorities of his church; but he does not see, or if he sees, he considers it either prudent or loyal to conceal the self-evident fact, that the bishops of his Church could remedy all these evils if they pleased to do so.

But in the case of Jesuit education, he certainly has the courage of his opinions. It is a matter of no little importance, when the education of the youth of this country is being placed more and more in the hands of Roman Catholic ecclesiastics, that we should show on such high and indisputable authority, what are the characteristics of that education. On two points his condemnation of the Jesuit system is emphatic and clear, and as one who received his entire school education at Stonyhurst, he speaks with authority. He says, "The theory and practice which I found in acceptance at Stonyhurst were, at no hour of the day or of the night should boys be away from the eye of a master. Stonyhurst College consisted in my day of a community of some twenty-five Jesuits, and 'exclusive of Hodder,' a school of some hundred and seventy boys—perhaps more, perhaps less.

"The community consists of the following:—

THE HIGHER LINE.

1. The Rector.	6. The Prefect of Studies.
2. The Minister.	7. The Prefect of Philosophers.
3. The Sub-Minister.	8. The Master of Rhetoric.
4. The Procurator.	9. The Master of Poetry.
5. The Spiritual Father.	10. The Master of Syntax.

THE LOWER LINE.

11. The Master of Grammar.	15. The First Prefect.
12. The Master of Rudiments.	16. The Second Prefect.
13. The Master of Figures.	17. The Third Prefect.
14. The Master of Higher Elements.	18. The Fourth or Supply Prefect.

19. The Sub-Prefect of Philosophers.

Several other resident Jesuits, and several other lay Brothers.

"The rector is the head of the whole establishment, but his office cannot be compared to that of a head-master, as it comprises two distinct sets of duties. He is, first of all, a religious superior, having under him a religious community, bound by vows to obey him."

Father Petre, to give him his religious title, saw plainly the incompatibility of the monastic life with secular teaching. The combining of the two is a relic of the middle ages, and an anachronism.

"The rector does not teach, but he occasionally sees the boys individually, but on matters of business, rather than with a view of exercising moral influence over them; he conducts all, or nearly all the correspondence with the parents. He is invariably a priest: he is sometimes a scholar.

"2. The minister, 3. the sub-minister, 4. the procurator, are concerned with the temporal affairs of the house, with the commissariat, not being concerned with either spiritual, moral, or intellectual discipline. All three of these officers are priests.

"5. The spiritual father. He is a confessor; his relation with the boys is theoretically very close, practically it may not be so. As far as my personal experience has extended, I have not found generally, that the spiritual father has usually been chosen with reference to his breadth of sympathy with boys, in their eccentricities, troubles, moods, and difficulties, but rather with reference to the vehemence of his personal piety, his zeal for and devotion to the special ascetic spirit of St. Ignatius.

"As a rule, perhaps, the spiritual father may be said not to be successful in gaining the confidence of any boys, excepting those of a decidedly devotional turn.

The spiritual father does not teach. The prefect of studies is charged with the complete management of the intellectual work of the school. He is a priest; he is not in any way concerned with the boys out of school. He is always a sound scholar, but is in a great degree bound to conduct the studies according to the tradition common to Jesuit schools throughout the world, and which is of ancient origin."

This method of teaching is also especially condemned by M. Gleize.

"Into the merits or demerits of that tradition, I do not hold myself competent to enter. The prefect of studies has under him a staff of masters, who are all Jesuits, and for the most part, junior ecclesiastics. Elements is the lowest class or school, which contains two classes. Elements is usually a very large class. It is entrusted to the almost entire control and care of a young Jesuit, generally a man of two and twenty or three and twenty. He has had no previous experience of teaching. He teaches nearly all subjects to his boys.

"In the schools conducted by monks, the professors must necessarily be drawn from the narrow limits of the Order, and are generally young scholastics, who are appointed to teach, not because they have any special taste or talent for it, but simply because they are scholastics, and take to teaching as a matter of course, as part of their training. If at the end of the year, one is found to be notoriously incapable, doubtless he is removed. But what, meanwhile, has become of the victims of the experiment, the twenty or thirty boys he had to care for? They have passed another year of their lives, and it will be well if it has only been wasted.

"If by chance a body of professors has been found who display an aptitude for their work, it will not avail the students long, for as scholastics they must be called away to other and more pressing duties. So the weary round goes on, continual experiments are made on the boys, and masters are formed, and if some good material is wasted, if some young lives are spoiled in the process—why, then it is a part of the system.

"The master who begins with elements, if tolerably successful, rises in the following year with his boys to figures, thence to rudiments, and so on until he reaches rhetoric, when he prepares the rest of his class for the London University Matriculation Examination. He has worked hard day and night for seven years, and as a chief result (intellectually) some of his pupils pass their examination with more or less credit.

"His career as a schoolmaster is at an end, he goes to study theology for four years, during which time he is ordained priest, and, in the majority of instances, he then takes joint charge of a parish, or is sent abroad on the mission. There are, of course, occasional exceptions to the rule. Meanwhile his place is always supplied from below by a constant stream of junior members of the Society of Jesus.

"I have now to describe the prefects. These are three gentlemen called respectively first, second, and third. The first is usually a priest, the other two are junior ecclesiastics. It is the business of the prefects to keep their boys at all times under their eyes. This duty is conscientiously performed, and is assisted by the fact that during play time boys are confined within a square of gravel surrounded by railings. A boy is not permitted, except under the most exceptional circumstances, to leave this square of gravel during his recreation time. The entrance to it is guarded always by one and generally by three prefects.

"There were three play-rooms, in two of which were billiard tables, and a bagatelle table in the third; these rooms were dirty and ill-ventilated; there was a reading-room for the 'higher line' older boys. All novels were strictly forbidden, and books were mercilessly expurgated. The infliction ot corporal punishment was frequent and severe, and administered not by the masters but by the prefects.

"Everything in the system they work is so thoroughly mechanical, and the fear of anything like 'particular friendship' or favouritism is so strong, that it is difficult indeed for them to do more than energetically and conscientiously act by their card. They are much overworked. It must be further considered that the lower masters and the lower prefects are not priests, but quite incipient ecclesiastics, and very young, whereas intercourse with matured piety and virtue, combined with some experience of life under varied aspects, may be thought for boys manifestly desirable.

"The boys now have a good cricket ground and play football.

"Baths were very rare, and cleanliness and tidiness were not the prominent characteristic of the boys.

"The boys were not allowed to walk in couples, they were liable to arbitrary separation on the part of the prefects. There is a special fear of 'particular friendships' in the school of which I am speaking. This fear amounts almost to superstition, and is of obvious foreign origin.

"Any kind of demonstration of affection was regarded with marked suspicion. In all these matters we were surrounded by a close atmosphere of suspicion. There were no monitors; big boys were occasionally put in charge of little boys—but always watched by a prefect.

"They rose at 5.30, and were watched washing and dressing by prefects, while strict silence was enjoined;

at 6.30 to Mass, which lasted forty minutes; chapel over, into the class-room, prepared lesson alone and silently; at 7.45 breakfast—strict silence; 8 o'clock lessons, morning school which lasted until ten. Play until 10.30, school until 12 o'clock—dinner 12.30, strict silence. Play until 2.36, lessons until 4.30, when bread and beer were served in the refectory. At 5 o'clock chapel, back to school-room for 'night studies;' 7 o'clock supper, recreation until 8.30, back to chapel for night prayers. In all the coming and going, all the roads were sentinelled as usual. The last sentinel was the spiritual father, who was posted outside the chapel door. Fifteen minutes allowed for undressing. The rule of silence was enforced in the dormitories with a jealous strictness which could not be exceeded. The prefects remained on guard until the boys were well asleep. Then two of them retired, but by turns each one maintained the watch throughout the night armed with a dark lantern. There was also another night watchman. Vigilance was Stonyhurst's predominant characteristic.

"There were a very large number of foreigners at Stonyhurst, mostly Spaniards, West Indians, or Spanish Americans. The college is decidedly cosmopolitan; so, I believe, are most of the Jesuit colleges in England. Added to this it remains to notice the 'philosophers.' They were a body of some thirty or thirty-five young gentlemen, who lived in a separate part of the house, and have altogether superior accommodation to the boys. It is also open to students at some of our colleges—*e.g.*, Stonyhurst—to follow the course of philosophy. This is a three years' course of logic, metaphysics, and ethics, with natural science. At the same time they have the opportunity of learning Italian and German, and perfecting themselves in French.

"At present there are at Stonyhurst thirty-two ecclesiastical students of philosophy and thirty-two lay philosophers.

"Even still and at all Jesuit schools it is considered necessary that up to the age of seventeen or eighteen a boy should be always under the eye of a master by day and by night. If such discipline be for the advantage of the Catholic youth of England let it stand, if not, the sooner it is modified the better.*"

Father Petre points out very plainly the serious difficulties in the way of improving Roman Catholic education, especially as conducted by the Jesuits. His points may be summarised briefly:—All Roman Catholic education of the middle and higher classes is conducted exclusively by the clergy. The clergy are naturally jealous of each other's success, but as Rome never permits any of her family quarrels to

* The Rev. Lord Petre's pamphlets were published in 1878.

come before the public, and has sufficient control of the Protestant Press to have silence preserved, she is safe from public censure. But all the educating clergy agree on one point, and this unanimity is their strength, they are determined to keep education in their own hands, and make a close corporation which excludes even the Roman Catholic laity.

It is therefore impossible that Roman Catholic educational institutions can be improved or reformed from without, " because no college under the charge of religious could, even if they would, submit to a system of inspection and interference from without. Though the public (Roman Catholic) are dissatisfied, the different religious orders will never unite, nor make any change, nor will they pay qualified lay teachers." But there is yet another difficulty in the way of reform in monastic or quasi-monastic teaching institutions. The rule of each order is jealously guarded by the priests, and as the rule must always be the first consideration, the benefit of the pupil takes second place. That this is true, and that its serious inconvenience is felt, and even resented by the Roman Catholic bishops who take a larger view of affairs, may be seen from a touching letter of the late Cardinal Wiseman's, which is published in the biography of Cardinal Manning. Cardinal Manning also protested, but protested in vain, against the selfishness of the religious orders, who would not make the least sacrifice for educational or other work, the requirements of their Rule being their plea for refusal. Of this plea the Cardinal makes very little account. It may be added, however, that whenever there is question of getting a further grant from government for Roman Catholic schools or colleges, there is a unanimous silence on these points. But the thinking public should pause before consenting to place education in the hands of those who are reprehensibly incapable of doing justice to their pupils, above all when this incapacity is deplored by Rome herself.

It has been admitted by a leading Catholic journal that "the condition of the Catholic youth of what are called the higher classes is such as to warrant the belief that there exists, either in our domestic or collegiate and public education, some grave defects which need a remedy."

Another and valuable source of information as to the training in Jesuits' colleges has been given to the public lately in Germany. Count Paul Von Hoensbruck has published his reasons for leaving the Jesuits and his experience while with them. He notes especially how their system of training destroys the individuality of those who are subjected to it, but this is precisely what the training is intended to do. The mechanical routine, never varying from day to day, the perpetual silence, the severe and frequent repression, and the continual introspection soon kills the personal vitality, and the "cadaver" takes the place of the living and sentient being.

Not one action of the day is left to the free will. The Jesuit novice cannot take a drink of water, he cannot use a pen, or paper, he cannot go from one room to another, without first asking and obtaining permission from his immediate superior. How can men who have been and are subjected to this system of intellectual slavery have the nobility of character to educate youth for a world where he must think and act for himself, not only in domestic affairs, but in the most momentous subjects of the day.

In 1878 the late Lord Petre published another pamphlet in two parts, on the "Position and prospects of Catholic liberal education." As the whole system of Catholic education is sharply, though respectfully criticised, it need scarcely be said that the edition was soon bought up by those who had an interest in suppressing it. To the present generation it is absolutely unknown, but the information which it contains is none the less important. To-day, indeed, it is of possibly more value, since the so called liberality of public men and politicians has placed the education of a vast number of English youth in the hands of men whom some of their co-religionists have declared absolutely incompetent to conduct it.

It may be thought that the state of affairs here described, is now past, and that Roman Catholic education has advanced with the times.

The recently published life of Cardinal Manning which has aroused such a storm in Roman Catholic circles, gives undeniable evidence to the contrary. Men who were daring enough to say that Dr. Newman's spirit "must be crushed," were not the men to uphold or desire liberal education. Hence we find Ward and Manning so determinately opposed to anything like higher culture. Rome dare not allow discussion or investigation. She decides every subject for her followers, and when she has the power to do so, she removes, by destroying or mutilating it, all the literature which might supply facts or inferences which would tell against her claims. We have already shown how history is "peptonised" for the Roman Catholic youth in Jesuit Colleges. How can men, who in their youth have been deprived of all that is necessary for the formation of a just judgment on the most important affairs, be able to judge fairly of any subject, literary or religious?

Attempts are made from time to time to attract the attention, to gain the admiration of the public for the Jesuit college at Stonyhurst. An article written with this object has been lately published in the *Pall Mall Magazine.* But though the writer does not say a word of criticism, there is quite sufficient statement of fact to show that there has been no advance since Lord Petre's opinions were published. The writer frankly admits that "an average public school boy would feel like a fish out of water," in the playgrounds.

Every school time is begun and ended with prayer. There is a three days' retreat at the commencement of each session. The masters, as in the time of Lord Petre, are appointed to teach because it is a part of their religious training, without any regard for their fitness for such an important duty. Their inclination is never consulted, but a Jesuit is supposed not to have any inclination.

A great effort is made to produce a show of distinguished men who have been educated at Stonyhurst, but the result is a dismal failure. One general, unknown to fame; one admiral, who looks like a Jesuit out for a holiday, and doubtful whether he should enjoy himself or not; the editor of a comic paper, which is going fast to decay, because he dare not admit a joke not approved by the Church, and the Church is particular as to what shall be said in this direction, for all roads lead to Rome, and Rome leads to the inquisition; to-day this does not mean the stake, but there are social inquisitions, all the same. An astronomer of no special note, and who would scarcely have been mentioned in any scientific journal, if the public at present was not so specially bent on complimenting Rome. Last, though not least, we find the name of the naturalist Waterton. He may be considered a star of great magnitude in the Roman Catholic church, but what has he contributed to science in comparison with what he might have done if he had been a free man? Of him an amusing story is told of how he could hoist a Jesuit father with his own petard.

Waterton proved incorrigible in the matter of breaking bounds, and gave the prefects many a chase in consequence. On one occasion, when hotly pursued by the authorities, he managed to double back, and ran to the friendly shelter of one of the farm servants, who promptly covered him with litter in the pig sty. Waterton has himself related the story, which concludes thus:—

"The man had hardly complied with my request when in bounced the prefect by the same gate through which I had entered. 'Have you seen Charles Waterton?' said he, quite out of breath.

"My trusty guardian answered, in a tone of voice which would have deceived anybody, 'Sir, I have not spoken a word to Charles Waterton these three days, to the best of my knowledge.' Upon this the prefect, having lost all scent of me, gave up the pursuit and went his way. When he had disappeared, I stole out of cover as strongly perfumed as was old

Falstaff when they had turned him out of the buck-basket."

The anecdote is amusing, but it is far from amusing to know that English boys should be subjected to moral training which teaches them how to be expert deceivers.

It is to the credit of our poor humanity that there are men, some of whom at least are better than their creed.

As regards the intellectual training at Stonyhurst and elsewhere, Lord Petre complains sadly that while enormous sums of money are spent on buildings and halls, nothing will be expended on securing the services of lay teachers who have been properly educated for their work. But such teachers could not be found easily in the Roman Catholic church, as witness the difficulties of the late Cardinal Newman in Dublin, and of Cardinal Manning in London. In each case it was found necessary to fall back on converts who had received their education at Oxford, before entering the Roman Catholic church.

All Roman Catholics who have written on the subject of education have either implied, or said expressly, that the religious orders in their Church are selfish and exclusive, and will not allow strangers, even of their own faith, to be admitted to their cloisters. The late Cardinal Wiseman complained bitterly, that though "religious" asked freely for dispensation from Rome in matters which concerned their own comfort, they would neither ask nor take dispensations, which would have enabled them to do more good, to do work which was urgently needed for the Church.

The present writer knew of a case in Ireland, where the sisters absolutely refused to receive broken meat and other food from a nobleman's house in their neighbourhood, because it would have given them too much trouble to distribute it to the poor.

A book of Rules for the Jesuits was printed in Rome with the approbation of the General in 1607.

We give some extracts from this, as showing the spirit of the Order.

RULE 5.—You must not read prohibited books without leave, nor meddle with anything which does not concern you.

RULE 6.—You must learn to be very ready in the language of the country where you dwell, or may be ordered to dwell.

RULE 7.—While residing in any college, your chests, boxes and trunks, and your chamber doors, must never be locked; you must not sleep at night with your chamber window open, nor lay naked, nor go out of your chamber undressed.

RULE 13.—You must not complain of one superior to another.

RULE 17.—No brother must go into the office or chamber of another without leave.

RULE 18.—While two of the order are in one chamber the door must be open.

RULE 20.—You must not hold discourse or have any correspondence by letter with any person, without your superior's leave.

RULE 21.—No person must hold idle talk, or discover without what is done within the college or house.

RULE 24.—No person must go out without leave, and telling why he goes out, he must write his name down and tell the door-keeper where he goes to, he must return before night, and give notice to his superior on his return.

RULE 25.—When on a journey, you must always lodge at a Jesuit college, if there is one in the place, and while there, must pay the same obedience to the superior as unto your own.

RULE 28.—You must divest yourself of all worldly, irregular love towards your parents, relations and friends, and of all worldly affairs.

RULE 29.—You must renounce entirely your own will, and embrace and follow the cross of Christ; you must aspire to humility, perfection and every virtue.

RULE 32.—You are diligently to aspire to true obedience, and never contradict whatever your superior commands you.

A series of special rules follow for each office.

THE RULES FOR THE PROVOSTS OR RECTORS.

(Of which Rules there are eighteen.)

RULE 2.—You must impose common penance on those who fail in, or are wanting in their duties, or punish them publicly, either by making them eat under the table, or in making them kiss the others' feet, or by praying in the refectory or by fasting.

RULE 13.—You must hold a conference twice a week on cases of conscience at which every priest in the house must assist.

RULE 18.—You must not permit any Jesuit to go out of your college or house without a companion with him.

THE RULES FOR THE MASTERS OF NOVICES.

(Of which Rules there are fourteen.)

RULE 5.—You are to appoint each novice a companion by whom he may be improved.

RULE 7.—You are to be careful that no novice shall speak to any of his relations without your leave, nor even these without some person being present, for which end you must not suffer any novice to be in any office by which they have any intercourse with strangers, such as purveyor, porter.

THE RULE FOR THE MONITORS.

There are only three rules for them, which are as follows:—

RULE 1.—As monitor or admonisher, you are

obliged to put the superior in mind whenever he has failed in his office; but you must represent this with humility and respect, with the advice of the council, and not let any other person know what is done upon such an occasion.

RULE 2.—If after several admonitions the superior remains incorrigible, you must then acquaint the higher powers.

RULE 3.—You must have a seal for the letters sent to the superior.

THE RULES FOR PRIESTS.

(There are six of these.)

RULE 2.—You must be very expedient in cases of conscience, and diligent in hearing confessions.

RULE 4.—When you confess a female, there must be a third person as an eye witness, though not so near as to hear what is said.

RULE 6.—You must admonish all your sick patients to make their will, but you must not be present when they are making it. In everything else you must observe the general rule.

THE RULE FOR THE PREACHERS.

(Twelve Rules are given.)

RULE 7.—When sent on mission, or to preach afar off, you must, if able, go on foot, live upon alms, and lodge in religious houses, and also keep a memorandum of the most pious and devout people in each place that you come to.

RULE 8.—You must not only preach, etc., . . . but seek to make all men your friends.

RULE 10.—You must write every week to acquaint your superior what progress you have made in your mission.

THE RULES FOR THE LIBRARIAN.

(Four Rules.)

Rule 1 states: You must always have by you the "Index Expurgatorius," and not keep any forbidden books.

RULES FOR THE PORTER.

(Six Rules.)

RULE 2.—You must not permit any person to go out without the superior's leave.

RULE 3.—You must deliver to the superior every letter you receive for any person in the house or college; and you must not let any person in who comes out of the country, without the superior being first acquainted.

RULE 5.—You must every night lock the doors and give the keys to the provost or regent.

Rules are given for the wardrobe keeper, house steward, cook and purveyor.

THE RULES FOR THE WATCHMAN.

It states that he must wake every individual; if they do not get up he must report them to the superior.

Four Rules are given of which in Rule 4 it states:

RULE 4. –At night you must visit every chamber, and ring or knock to advertise each person to examine his conscience. A quarter of an hour after, you must ring the bell for them to go to rest; and in another quarter of an hour you must go to every chamber to see if the light is extinguished, if not you must acquaint the superior.

THE RULE CONCERNING THE WRITING OF LETTERS.

RULE 1.—The superior or regent of each house or college must write every week to the Provincial (and also to those of the house who are sent to preach on mission) acquainting him with every affair of consequence that regards the Society.

RULE 2.—He must also write every three months to the General.

RULE 3.—The Provincial must write every month to the General, and also to the provost, regents, and those who are sent on any business of the province.

RULE 4.—The General is to write every two months to the provincials, but only twice a year to the regents, etc., unless some affair of consequence obliges him to write oftener.

RULE 5.—That no letter may be lost or miscarry, several copies must be wrote of each, and they must also be copied into a letter book.

RULE 6.—Every secret order or affair must be written in characters or cypher.

RULE 7.—The letters which are written by the General at Rome must be read and carefully preserved in the house or college to which they are sent.

THE MASSACRE OF ST. BARTHOLOMEW.

CHAPTER VII.

Life In a French Jesuit College.

Life in a French Jesuit College.—The narrative of M. Dziewicki.—His retreat.—Choice of a state of life.—How made.—Mistaken ideas of perfection.—God made us to live in the world, and not to fly from it.—The novitiate at Pau.—Early rising.—How the day is spent in a French Jesuit novitiate.—How the tempers of the novices are tried.—Penances.—Stern rules about silence.—Every human feeling crushed under an iron discipline.—The Jesuit idea of Christian perfection.—The *Tourtier Rodriguez*.—All studies carefully prescribed.—Obedience.—Dinner.—Well fed.—The lapidarium or stoning; how performed.—Bad results of Jesuit training; it excites all the worst passions of the young novice; makes him a good Jesuit, but not a good man.—The *silentum majus*.—Watching and prying.—The trials of recreation.

A SHORT description of life in a French Jesuit college may prove interesting, above all as it is taken from a narrative of personal experience. There is but little difference in the mode of life, save what comes of unavoidable necessity, and from differences of national customs and climate. The rule of the Jesuits is wooden and unalterable.

M. Dziewicki commences his narrative with an account of his retreat. As an account of a retreat has been already given, it is omitted here, but we may again remark on the want of common sense in making the time of retreat one for deciding the future, for the conditions under which a retreat is made are by no means those which would enable a clear and wise decision to be made. The object of the retreat apparently is to make a choice between the service of God, and the service of the world. But Christ drew no hard and fast line, to say so reverently, between the service of God and the service of humanity. His disciples were ever exhorted to be in the world but not of it. To declare the world which God has made for His creature to live in to be an accursed place, where there is nothing but danger to the soul, is not true in fact or in religion.

We should certainly pray and pray with all earnestness, when we desire to be guided by God in the choice of a state of life, but to work ourselves up deliberately into a condition of spiritual exaltation or depression is not the way to strengthen the judgment. Hence it is that so many "vocations" which are decided in this fashion prove defective, and a cause of much after misery.

Pau may be taken as a type of French houses of the Order, from which type they never recede very far. It may now be worth while to follow step by step, a day passed in the novitiate.

A brother rises a few minutes before four o'clock

in the morning, dresses hastily, rings the bell, and passes through all the rooms, saying in each: *Benedicamus Domino!* to which *Deo Gratias!* having been answered, he lights a candle placed over night for him, and passes on. The moment the bell rings, you hear a series of jumps on the floor; some dress more, some less quickly, but all, hearing the voice of God in the bell, instantly obey. And should the visitor, who passes through the rooms a quarter of an hour after, find anybody still in bed, it would certainly be a case of illness. They throw away the water in which they have washed down a sink, "*walking on tip toe.*" The reason for this peculiarity is that the master of the novices thought that one of the best means to inculcate silence. It was a rule often broken.

As soon as the rapid toilet of the novices is over they hurry down to the oratory to visit the Holy Sacrament and say their morning prayers. If not ready by 4.25, they must not go in for fear of disturbing the others. During this service not a movement is permitted, even when bitten by fleas—very common in the South of France. This immovability amounts almost to torture.

After these prayers, they proceed to make their beds; every bed untidily arranged is liable to be pulled down. Every thing is done to try the temper of the novices, although the bed is perfectly well made it is pulled down to get him to make it again. Sometimes secret orders are given, and he is set upon and teased for trifles by five or six novices in office. In other cases, when he is too weakly and sensitively attached to the master, the latter treats him for months together with affected coldness, never finds time to speak with him and so on. Every weak point of every character is soon found out, and war waged against it in different ways; if it be serious, and no progress be visible after some time, the novice receives notice to quit.

Mass is heard at six. The novices remain kneeling all the morning, except from the Gospel to the sanctus bell, during which they stand. Their attitude is the following: head slightly bent forward, neither to the right nor to the left; eyes cast down; body straight as an arrow, hands folded in each other. By the bye, this attitude they are required, or rather counselled, to keep at all times, as far as possible, except, for instance, when either hands or eyes are required for useful purposes.

These may be looked upon as miserable minutiæ, reducing every Jesuit to the state of a machine, grinding every particle of individuality out of him, and unworthy of Loyola's genius. These practices, particularly the rules of modesty, appeared extremely important to St. Ignatius, and he paid more attention to them than to many other matters, seemingly of greater importance. His ideal was *Jesuita alter Jesus*, and therefore he wished the Jesuits to imitate the exterior of Jesus as far as they could. He laid down those rules according to the ideal that he himself had formed. After mass, from 6.30 to 7.30, the novices repair to their rooms in order to read their commentary on the Holy Scriptures. At 7.30, they go to breakfast—an excellent meal. At a quarter to eight, the bell calls all hands upstairs; the novices, standing in two lines in the passage, await orders of the director of manual work, from whom, as from the hand of God, they are to accept whatever he tells them to do.

For three-quarters of an hour, the novices are all busily engaged; some working in the garden, some drawing the wine in the cellar, some in the sacristy and oratory waxing the floors; some in the lecture-room, making disciplines, chains and rosaries; others helping in the refectory or the kitchen. But 9.30 has struck and the bell rings. At once, leaving the bottle of wine half filled, a link of a chain half formed, or a weed half pulled out, all the novices, with the admonitor at their head, speed to the garden with Rodriguez' treatise, "*On Christian Perfection.*" The admonitor threads the alleys of the garden, and all follow close behind him in single file, like a flock of geese, or convicts, walking faster or more slowly according to his pace, turning when he turns, and taking care at the same time to read Rodriguez and not to tread on the heels of those before him. This exercise called Tourner Rodriguez, though ridiculous enough in outward seeming, is not without its motive; it is done for exercise of the body.

From nine to ten is a lecture upon spiritual subjects, being in general an explanation of the rules of the Society, given by a master. Then one novice is required to give an abstract of what was said at the last lecture. After this the master drops his voice, says a short prayer, and goes out; the lecture is ended. Then follows the repetition of the conference, a most strange scene. Groups of novices are formed by threes or fours, as the admonitor tells them off; a novice in each gives an account of what has been said. Each novice raises his voice to be heard above the others. The lecture-room seems a Bedlam.

A visit to the oratory follows; the novices again proceed in single file to the garden, there to get by heart a few verses of Scripture. St. Ignatius prescribed all studies in the novitiate except an exercise of memory, to prevent that faculty from rusting by disuse. That all studies are carefully prescribed in the novitiate I know very well.

M. Dziewicki says: If a novice leaves a room, "he must inform the 'ancient' of the room where he has been—The term 'ancient' does not imply advanced in years. It is the custom in all Roman Catholic convents and colleges to ask permissions of the brother or sister who has been the longest time in the convent, and whoever is the eldest present is so asked, when the regular superior is absent. The object is to teach the practice ot humility. If no one was in the room when he left it, he must say on his return where he has been."

Eleven o'clock strikes, it is the hour for the pronunciation class. A novice presides over this exercise. From the beginning, Loyola accustoms them to obey those who are not above them in station or age, in order that later on in life, old fathers may reverence a young superior quite as much as an aged one, and not inquire whether the rector is a professed father, or only a coadjutor.

At a quarter to twelve o'clock, "examination of consciences," reflection and silent, of his conduct by each novice.

At twelve the midday bell—dinner—a good meal with a pint of wine a head, a book read during the time.

In the evening at supper is read a history of Jesuit fathers' experiences called "Mènologe," adventures of missionaries, such as Father Anquita, full of the miracles he worked. "We find Father Anquita thaumaturgising (if I may use the expression); he left certain provisions under the care of two jaguars, they watched them some weeks. He walked under the water, he caused a roast pigeon to come to life and fly away. For my own part," says Dziewicki, "I think one should never admit any such facts—whether miracles, spiritualistic phenomena, or assertions about thought transference—until it becomes unreasonable not to believe them."

Dinner being ended, the Holy Sacrament is visited again in order to prepare for the most difficult exercise of the day; the recreation. Why I call it the most difficult exercise is evident enough, for an almost impossible combination of virtues is required to pass it correctly; the multitude of virtues—charity, modesty, cordiality, gaiety, self-collection, piety, and I know not how many besides—required for a recreation to be properly passed has in most cases an unsuccessful result. The difficulty is much increased by the fact that one is never allowed to choose one's companions; to do so would be a most flagrant breach of fraternal charity. Except on festivals, bands of three or four novices are made by the admonitor, and he is instructed beforehand by the master to put the most contrary characters together, on purpose that their tempers may be tried.

The exercise of "modesty" or of charity which ought regularly to take place once a week instead of conference. A novice designated by the master goes down on his knees, in the middle of the room, and listens to whatever may be said against him. All such as are questioned, are bound in conscience to state whatever defect they have noticed in his conduct. Such as, our brother makes too much noise in eating, he talks too loud. This form of penance is practised in some way or other in all convents and colleges. But it has been much modified of late years, except in the Jesuit novitiates on account of the serious heartburnings and anger to which it gave rise. In some convents it is called the *lapidarium* or stoning, and is supposed to be performed in honour of the stoning of Christ by the Jews. The words of censure addressed to the novice by those around being the substitution for stones. It may be added that most of these practices of humiliation are carried out in the colleges where priests are trained.

The present writer heard an amusing story from a priest who had been educated in Maynooth, about the use of the expression *Benedicamus Domino.* A new night porter had been placed in the dormitories. There was then a professor named Donohue, who was for some reason very unpopular. Some of the students, who were after all boys suffering from this drastic system of repression of every natural feeling and enjoyment of youth, thought it a good opportunity to get even with the obnoxious professor. They went to the new porter and told him that the professor was very particular about the pronunciation of Latin, and that when he came to call the *Benedicamus Domino* he must say it very plainly or he would be very angry indeed. But they taught him to say *maledicamus Donohue* which he did with great and grave emphasis to the no small delight of the conspirators.

Little remains to be said about the afternoon. After the visit to the chapel, by which "recreation" ends, as it began, there is once a week an exercise of "tones." The "tones" are a short sermon; it is learnt by heart and recited, and from being badly delivered they often occasion laughter among the novices.

On other days instead of tones, a novice had to explain a chapter of catechism to the others as if they were children, and question them in the same way. They had to answer as children, and they certainly did—a worse class could hardly be found in all Christendon. Such laziness, such insubordination, such utter recklessness of reproof and punishment! It was, however, a little overdone; for children, even the worst, are never as bad as that.

By the bye, I may here say a few words about an analogous exercise practised during the third probation by the young priests who are preparing themselves for active service in the Society. It is the exercise of confession. But here the novices have their part assigned to them beforehand, and have come well prepared; one as a nun, with no end of scruples and peccadilloes of her own; another as a devotee laden with the sins of others; another as a trooper, rough and ready, hearty and frank. A man kneels down; he is a Voltairean workman, come to dispute; he is followed by an innkeeper, whose gains are not always of the most honourable sort, and then there comes a monk with an unintelligible confession, having something he does not wish to tell, and fears to leave untold. When all these have been counselled, rebuked and shriven, one after another, then comes the criticism—the most important part. Evidently, though highly comical and more amusing than many a comedy, this exercise is of much use to Catholic priests.

After catechism, half an hour of manual labour—half an hour of writing or French grammar—a quarter of an hour of private reading of the "Imitation of Christ"—half an hour over the life of a saint, then a second meditation. Then out in the garden to say their beads. At seven o'clock, supper, which consists of meat, vegetables, wine and dessert; at half past seven to a quarter past eight, recreation, then silence, "*silentum majus*," begins, only to end after breakfast the next day. The Litany of the Saints is the evening prayer, said by a resident priest, the whole community being present: at a quarter to nine the examination of conscience, and at nine, bed.

Recreation among Jesuits is not companionship, or the unbending of the overstrung bow, or friendship or even hilarity or outdoor sports, such as football or cricket; they, of all youths, amuse themselves sadly, for with them before they can play they require such a multitude of virtues, such as charity, modesty, cordiality, gaiety, self-collection, piety, and M. Dziewicki says, "I know not how many more virtues are necessary to pass through the most trying test of the day, a blameless recreation."

No lad in a Jesuit college is allowed to choose his own companion, nor are they ever permitted to walk singly, three or four youths are chosen by the admonitor, and especially selected that they may correct each other's failings; a sad, pious mystic with a lad overflowing with fun, an ignorant lad with one fond of studying, a stupid lout with a highly cultivated intellect; and what makes an atmosphere of cautious reserve among them the more marked is, that each lad is expected to act as a spy upon his companions, and repeat every jest, or thoughtless word, or still more each too thoughtful remark, all of which they consider it a duty to report to the admonitor. Therefore, as each youth is among watchful enemies, silence is golden, for each lad is ever in danger of being dismissed as unsuitable to the Society, that Society, which, to most of them, is their only home and protector on earth, for the novices, with few exceptions, are very poor.

During recreation, they are not allowed to talk

about each other in private conversation, but once a week, as we have stated, they have an opportunity of exercising the gift of criticism to its greatest extent, and for serious faults, if they existed, the system of secret denunciation is enjoined, under pain of expulsion. The system of watching and prying exists in all and every order of monks and nuns, and it is by that, and also by confession, these communities are kept in some outward order, but the spite, hatred, envy and secret detestation of each other in which they, with few exceptions, live, is the outcome of this continual tale bearing, which places the higher and nobler natures at the mercy of the most slanderous and the most base.

We have given the experience of M. Dziewicki in full, for it is these young men, who have undergone this irrational training, who in very few years after become the schoolmasters of the upper classes of all Romanist countries, and the Jesuit confessors of a vast number of women and girls. In the Jesuit schools they always have young masters of classes, called "Regents," who are only a few years older than the pupils themselves, and this is one reason that thoughtful, liberal minds on the continent have given for the degeneracy of the Latin races; with such masters, trained by such a bad system, what can be hoped for the pupils!

This early training will not make learned or wise

men, but it does make artful flatterers of infinite courtesy and patience, ready and accustomed to make use of the folly and credulity of their fellow creatures, and to do so with such tact that they are invariably forgiven.

It is said that the world belongs to people of good manners, and while they are becoming rapidly extinct in all other classes, they are always to be found among the Jesuit priesthood, it is one of the great features of the "Matchless Organisation."

CHAPTER VIII.

CAN THE JESUIT BE A LOYAL SUBJECT?—THE JESUITS IN CANADA.

CAN A JESUIT BE A LOYAL SUBJECT?—Erroneous idea that Jesuits are different from other Roman Catholics.—Jesuit teaching on submission to civil authority. — Cardinal Manning; his loyal statements. — England, Rome's last refuge.—She tries to obtain civil power.—Extracts from catechism, and Roman Catholic authors.—Roman Catholic "Emancipation."—Infallibility of the Pope.—When first made article of faith.—Lord Fingall's remarks at Dublin Convention.—English Roman Catholics who are not ultramontane. — The "Catholic Committee." — The "Irish Remonstrance." — "Protestation" published by Roman Catholics in 1789.—Pope Gregory XIII.'s Bull in 1577.—Pope Innocent X. sends a Nuncio to Ireland in 1643 to stir up rebellion.—Few Protestants realise that Rome is a political church.—Solemn oaths taken to be broken.—Roman Catholic Belief Act in 1829.—Conquest of Canada —The Jesuits fled to Quebec when expelled from Europe.—Statue of Loyola in Quebec.—Rome becomes more liberal. What is she doing *sub rosa*.—Recent meeting of Roman Catholics in Cardiff.—Consequences of allowing the Jesuits liberty in Canada.—The Jesuits' Estates Act.

THERE is a general and very erroneous idea prevalent that the Jesuits are in some way different from other Roman Catholics. Erroneous ideas on serious subjects are always an evil. Although the Roman Catholic Church changes her religious teaching from time to time, as witness the changes which have been made even in the present century, when the whole foundation of that Church was displaced and another foundation substituted, by the change from the infallibility of a united body, the Church, to the infallibility of an individual, the Pope; yet she compels her subjects to move as she moves and to believe as she teaches for the time being.

The Jesuits are also obliged to move with the Church, and to accept her varying changes of religious belief as others do, but there is this difference: the Jesuit can and does interfere with the religious beliefs of the Church, as witness their successful efforts in obtaining the decision of the Pope's infallibility. But all the same, in questions of dogma, the Church and the Jesuits are one—at least publicly. It might, indeed, be said that the Church believes what the Jesuit believes. In Roman Catholic circles so well is the power of the Jesuit recognised, that the General of the Jesuits is called the Black Pope, in contrast to the Pope, who, wearing white always, is called the White Pope. And it is implied that the Black Pope rules the White Pope, even while the former is obliged to make, at least, a show of submission to the latter.

We propose in this chapter to show, not from

hearsay, but from the published works of the Jesuits themselves, what they teach first on the general question of submission to civil authority, and later we shall show what they teach in the confessional to those who come to them for guidance. But, first, though it has been said before it must be said again, so great is the importance of the subject, that the teaching of the Church of Rome is just what it always was on matters of moral theology. It is only the dogmatic theology of that Church which is variable. But just as it is the *rôle* of the Church at present to assure the public that she always teaches the same doctrine, so it is her policy to make every effort to induce a too confiding public to believe that she has changed her moral theology. The world at large is unfortunately so entirely ignorant of what Rome teaches from her own point of view, that it is naturally taken for granted that she should be believed, no matter what proof there may be to the contrary.

The special question to which we desire to call attention here is the much discussed question of loyalty to the state or government under which Roman Catholics live. What can be more dangerous than a traitor in the camp or a citizen with a divided allegiance?

I propose to show first that Roman Catholics are disloyal, not always from inclination, but because they believe loyalty to the Pope in temporal affairs to be their first duty, and secondly to show that they are disloyal on principle. It is just this point of view which is so difficult for Protestants (using the word in its widest sense) to understand. A Romanist protests, and in some cases, at least, protests sincerely, that he is loyal to Queen and country, and honest men find it difficult to question his assertions, and accept his statements. But the Catholic has, so to say, reckoned without his host. There is no Catholic who will or can deny, above all since the definition of the personal infallibility of the Pope, that his first allegiance is due in temporal as well as in spiritual affairs to the head of his Church. The recently published life of Cardinal Manning tells in plain and unmistakable language that there are two classes of Catholics, especially in England. There are Catholics, as he bitterly complains, who would be loyal to the Queen, even if it involved some opposition to the claims of the Pope to infallibility in temporal matters and politics, and there is another class of Catholics who boast of their loyalty to the Pope, and insist on his authority to rule both Church and State.

We can give no higher authority than that of the late Cardinal, and his statements deserve serious consideration. But it should be remembered, that this difference of opinion is really immaterial in the end. Whatever may be the private views of individual Roman Catholics, eventually they must, and do, submit to the commands of the Pope. There have been notable examples of this, even in our own times, so that those who do not recognise the importance of this question as affecting Catholic protestations of loyalty, have only themselves to blame for the consequences. Nor is it necessary to suppose that those Romanists who declare their loyalty to the Queen or State are insincere. The fact is, that the more sincere they are, the more dangerous they are, because it is always safer to meet an open enemy than a doubtful friend. These Catholics know perfectly well, that whatever they may say, in the end, they must submit.

Now Rome is perfectly consistent in her demand for the control of civil government. If her teaching were true, that there is no salvation outside the Church, she is bound to compel all to belong to the Church, even if she has to call in the civil power to help her to enforce submission. This power she has ever invoked and utilised. She aims now, quietly, but none the less effectively, to obtain civil power in this country, her last refuge; and she has already obtained more than she could have dared to hope for a few short years ago.

In the words of the catechism, authorised by Cardinal Gibbons, it is said that the greatest grace bestowed on "us" (Romanists) is that of being called to the "true faith in the *Catholic Church, because without this grace we cannot have the least hope to be saved.*" [The italics are in the original.]

This is the belief of Catholics; and holding such belief they are bound, according to their idea of conscience, to use force and violence to exterminate heresy.

It should be remembered that Rome exercises the most rigid censorship over all publications. Above all the Roman Catholic Church takes the utmost precaution in regard to catechisms, hence the grave authority of any doctrinal or theological teaching which may be found in books intended for the use of children. In the catechism authorised for children by the American bishops, we find the following significant question and answer.

"Q. In what matters is the Pope infallible?

"A. The Pope is infallible in all matters of faith and morals.

"Q. Is the Pope infallible only in matters of revelation?

"A. The Pope is infallible not only in the matter of revealed truths; he is indirectly infallible in all truths which though not revealed, are so intimately connected with revealed truths, that the deposit of faith and morals cannot be guarded, explained and defended without an infallible discernment of such unrevealed truths.

"Q. Explain this truth more clearly.

"A. The Pope could not discharge his office as a teacher of all nations, unless he were able with infallible certainty to prescribe and condemn doctrines, logical, scientific, physical, or political of any kind."

This is plain speaking and it is the language of the Church which may not be gainsaid. For the present, Rome does not find it expedient to use such catechisms in England, but when she has obtained all that she claims in the way of pecuniary endowments, she will speak with no uncertain sound. In the meantime, might it not be well for our statesmen, politicians and voters to ask themselves if this is a doctrine which they desire to have taught to English children, the teaching of which is to be paid for with English money.

How easily the Church of Rome can change her doctrines or her politics, may be seen from the following quotations.

A lecture is reported in the *Catholic Standard* (7th April, 1852), delivered by Dr. Wiseman, wherein he emphatically denied that Papal infallibility was a doctrine of faith in the Roman Church. He said:—

"Clear that from your mind, and let me tell you *authoritatively* as a Catholic bishop, and as one in such intimate connection with the head of the Catholic Church, THAT THERE IS NOT ONE DOCTRINE

OF THE CATHOLIC CHURCH THAT THE POPE IS INFALLIBLE, and that many thousands of Catholics do not hold the doctrine of infallibility. It is a matter of opinion, and not of doctrine."

The italics and capitals are as given in the report of the lecture.

In Father Waterworth's "Faith of Catholics," published in 1846, he says (vol. ii., p. 110):

"It is no article of Catholic faith that the Pope is himself infallible, separated from the Church, even in expounding the faith. By consequence Papal definitions or decrees, in whatever form pronounced, taken exclusively of a General Council or acceptance of the Church, oblige none, under pain of heresy, to nterior assent."

As the question of the Pope's personal infallibility in politics is one which must be felt in this country n the immediate future, we give the authority for accepting the statements of this catechism and some urther extracts from it.

In the authorisation of these catechisms given by Cardinal Gibbons, dated January 3rd, 1888, and printed at the commencement of each volume, he says that they are "strongly marked by soundness of doctrine, simplicity, and plainness of language." The language is indeed very plain as we shall show presently.

The third and most important volume of the

series is called "A Familiar Explanation of Catholic Doctrine for the Family and more Advanced Students in Catholic Colleges, Academies and High Schools; for Persons of Culture, Old as well as Young, with a Popular Refutation of the Principal Modern Errors." It was published in 1888.

The doctrine of the Pope's infallibility in politics is expressly taught in this catechism (see *supra*), and therefore must be accepted by Romanists as "sound doctrine."

At page 117 the very important question is asked:

"How do we know that the Pope as successor to St. Peter possesses the gift of infallibility?" The answer is: "We know it from Christ's own words; for He told St. Peter that by His prayer to His heavenly Father He had obtained this gift of infallibility for him and for all his successors" (Luke xxii. 31).

How is the hapless student to know that Christ never "told" St. Peter anything of the kind?

The next question is (page 117):

"*Q.* 14. Why did Christ pray to His Father that St. Peter and his successors should be endowed with the gift of infallibility?"

"Christ asked of His heavenly Father the gift of infallibility for St. Peter and his successors, because He wished that the never failing faith of St. Peter and his successors should be for ever the foundation stone of his Church, in order that she might be one flock, under *the supreme Pastor, through the preservation of unity of communion as well as of profession of the same faith with the Roman Pontiff.*

"Christ assured us of this truth when He asked the apostles, Whom do you say that I am?"

Further on (page 118) the text, "Thou art Peter, and upon this rock I will build My church," is quoted and the question is asked:

"*Q.* What is the meaning of these words of our Lord?

"*A.* Jesus Christ means to say that, as it is My Father, who has made known to you, Peter, that I am His Son, I also make known to the whole world, that you and your successors will always know and understand who I am and what I have taught, because I have entrusted you with My whole flock, your faith, I most solemnly promise, shall not fail, since no power shall prevail against thee and thy successors, so as to cause you to teach anything else than I Myself have taught."

It is needless to comment on this awful perversion of truth, nor on the terrible guilt of those who put words into the very lips of the Saviour which He never uttered.

Here not only are the words of Christ added to but words are invented, and declared to have been said by Him, which He never uttered. Once more let it be said the Roman Catholic has no means of knowing how he is deceived, because he is placed under the ban of an awful curse if he doubts or questions all this falsehood.

And all this falsehood and misrepresentation of scripture is offered as infallible truth, not merely to the young, but "to people of culture."

The Pope can, then, "*with infallible certainty, proscribe and condemn doctrines, logical, scientific, physical, metaphysical, or political of any kind.*"

[The italics are in the original.

No language could be plainer, or more fully and infallibly authorised by Rome.

In "Essays on Religion and Literature, edited by Archbishop Manning, 1867," we find (pp. 416, 417): "Moreover, the right of deposing kings is inherent in the supreme sovereignty which the popes, as vicegerents of Christ, exercise over all Christian nations. . . . These are not derived or delegated rights, but are of the essence of that royal authority of Christ with which His vicegerents on earth are vested. When, therefore, for the common good, the head of the Church exercises his supreme authority either by excommunicating individuals, by laying nations under an interdict, or by deposing kings, all Christian people are bound to obey his decree."

Again, Cardinal Manning, in his sermon on the

Syllabus, describes the late Pope as saying to those who urged this Pontiff "to be reconciled to Liberalism": "In His (Christ's) right I am sovereign. I acknowledge no civil superior; and I claim more than this. I claim to be the supreme judge on earth, and director of the consciences of men, of the peasant that tills the field, and the prince that sits on the throne; of the household that lives in the shade of privacy, and the legislature that makes laws for kingdoms. I am the last supreme judge on earth of what is right and wrong" ("Sermons on Religious Subjects." Burns, Oates & Co., 1873).

Again, let it be observed, these are not ancient sayings of the dark ages, but they are the utterances of the highest ecclesiastical authority in England in the last half of the 19th century.

Pius IX., in his Encyclical and Syllabus, condemned and anathematised—(cursed)

"Those who maintain *the Liberty of the Press*. Or the liberty of *conscience* and of *worship*. Or *the liberty of speech*."

"Or those who assign to the State the power of defining the *civil* rights (*jura*) and province of the Church."

"Or who hold that the Church may not employ force."

"Or that power, not inherent in the office of the

Episcopate, but granted to it by the *civil authority*, may be withdrawn from it at the discretion of that authority."

"Or that the *civil* immunity of the Church and its ministers depends upon *civil* right."

"Or that marriage, not sacramentally contracted, has a binding force."

"Or that any other religion than the Roman religion may be established by a State."

"Or that in 'countries called Catholic' *the free exercise of other religions may laudably be allowed*."

In this Bull Apostolicæ Sedis, Pius IX. asserted "the immunity of *Ecclesiastics* from *civil* jurisdiction," and "excommunicated all who bring them before civil tribunals. He excommunicated all who enact laws or decrees against the rights or liberties of the Church; all who impede in any way the exercise of the ecclesiastical jurisdiction, or have recourse to the *secular courts* for this purpose; all who impede in any way or have recourse to the *lay* power in order to impede the promulgation or enforcement of the decrees or rescripts of the Church of Rome; all who usurp or retain the properties or revenues of the Church, or of ecclesiastical or of conventual institutions; *all who command Christian burial to be given to heretics*." He further "excommunicated all heretics of *every class*, and all who *favour* them, and all who read heretical or prohibited books, and all who withdraw themselves or secede from obedience to the Roman Pontiff."

When the question of Roman Catholic Emancipation first came before the public, the question at once arose: What do these Catholics believe as to the power of their Church in temporal affairs? Can a Roman Catholic be at the same time a good subject of the king and a good follower of the Pope? Are Roman Catholics free to be loyal subjects of the government under which they live? These were, indeed, important questions, but unfortunately those who asked them in all honest desire for an honest reply, were not always in a position to know whether the replies were sincere or otherwise. It was their misfortune, but unhappily the result has been nearly the undoing of England.

Those who asked these questions naturally supposed that they would receive the most reliable answers from the heads of the Roman Catholic Church. They applied to them, they had special committees in Parliament, but unfortunately they did not know, first, that Rome has approved, and, in fact, requires the exercise of a system of equivocation which renders it impossible to obtain an honest reply from Roman Catholic authority, when it suits Roman Catholic authority to conceal the truth, and secondly, that Rome reserves to herself the right to change her opinions when she pleases on any subject, so that it is never safe to conclude from what she says to-day that she will say the same to-morrow. Take, for example, the questions of the Pope's infallibility. There was no subject on which the heads of the Roman Catholic Church spoke more decidedly. It never was, it never could be a dogma of the Church of Rome, and yet scarce a decade had elapsed ere it was made a dogma which must be believed on peril of eternal damnation.

I have before me now a catechism authorised by the Roman Catholic Church, in which the doctrine of the Pope's personal infallibility is described as "a Protestant invention." When Dr. Murray was examined on his solemn oath before the committee of the House of Commons on March 22nd, 1825, he gave the most solemn assurances that the Pope's infallibility was not and never could be an article of faith. Yet to-day Romanists are as much bound to believe the Pope to be infallible as they are bound to believe in the existence of a God.

Here are the words of the catechism :—

"*Q.* Must not Catholics believe the Pope himself to be infallible?

"*A.* This is a Protestant invention, it is no article of the Catholic faith; no decision of his can bind on pain of heresy, unless it be received and enforced by the teaching body, that is, by the Bishops of the Church."

In all editions printed since the Vatican Council this question and answer is omitted, and without a word of explanation. This catechism had the approbation of the late Archbishop Hughes, of New York, and was in general use. And yet Romanists will tell those whom they can deceive that the teaching of the Roman Catholic Church never changes. Here certainly is a change, and a stupendous one, when what was once condemned as "a Protestant invention" is now the received doctrine of the Church of Rome.

Dr. Murray gave the following quotation from the works of the Jesuit Veron, yet soon after the Jesuits were the great promoters of the dogma of the Pope's infallibility.

"The Pope, in whatever character, or however solemnly he may give his opinion, even in scholastic phraseology *ex cathedrâ*, is not the universal Church, and consequently whatever may be his private opinion, and however declared, such opinion is not, on that account, propounded by the Catholic Church as an article of faith. . . . In fact, it is clear from Bellarmine himself that it has never been defined by the Church that the Pope is infallible when unassisted by a General Council, nor that any doctrine advanced and proposed by him is, in consequence of such a proposal, an article of Catholic faith. All divines consequently are agreed, as Bellarmine allows, that Papal infallibility is no doctrine of the Catholic Church, and this is certain beyond all controversy" ("Rule of Catholic faith," pp. 13, 14).

"It is not of faith that when the Roman Pontiff teaches anything, either assisted by his own private council or by a provincial synod, even though he addressed the Universal Church, or, as it is termed, speaks *ex cathedrâ*, in a word, so long as he is not the supreme judge of controversies, he is not infallible, nor would a decree passed under these circumstances be of faith, unless the opinion of the Church were, from other sources, clearly ascertained to have been pronounced in his favour" (p. 133).

The doctrine of the infallibility of the Pope was first made an article of faith at the Vatican Council, held at Rome in the year 1870. The following are the words in which this stupendous change in the Roman Catholic religion was proclaimed:—

"Wherefore faithfully adhering to the tradition received from the beginning of the Christian Faith, for the glory of God our Saviour, the exaltation of the Catholic religion, and the salvation of the Christian people, We, the Sacred Council, approving, teach and define that it is a dogma divinely revealed; that the Roman Pontiff, when speaking *ex cathedrâ*—that is, when, discharging the office of Pastor and Teacher of all Christians, by virtue of his supreme authority, he defines a doctrine regarding faith or morals to be held by the Universal Church—he, by the divine assistance promised to him in blessed Peter, is possessed of that infallibility with which the Divine Redeemer willed the Church should be endowed in defining doctrine regarding Faith or Morals; and that, therefore, such definitions of the Roman Pontiff are irreformable of themselves, and not from the consent of the Church. But if any one—which may God avert—presume to contradict this, our definition, let him be anathema."

Nothing could have been more sacred, nothing more solemn, than the circumstances under which this Parliamentary inquiry of 1826 was undertaken.

For many years Roman Catholics had been deprived of the privileges which every Englishman enjoyed by right of his citizenship. But this privation had not been enforced without cause. The plots which had all but succeeded and had been attempted by the Jesuits over and over again to deprive Englishmen of their religion and liberties, and to place the country under the control of a foreign power, had excited the apprehensions of statesmen. But at the beginning of the century much had been forgotten which should have been remembered, and it was asked why should not men who appeared to desire to live in amity with their fellow countrymen have the same advantages. The answer should have been that these men considered themselves bound first to obey a foreign power. They were citizens of Rome first, and citizens of England after. Practically a Roman Catholic can never be naturalised, because he can never forego his temporal allegiance to the Pope.

No doubt some of these bishops were sincere when they declared in the most solemn manner, that the Pope never was, and never would be personally infallible. The history of the Vatican Council, which has made every Pope, past, present, or to come infallible, was not then known. But all the same it came.

Protestants were also the victims of what was at that time a very excusable ignorance of Romanism. They met Romanists every day in social or business intercourse, and they asked themselves naturally, What is the difference between these men and ourselves? They love the country of their birth, they assure us that England is their first interest, and that they would obey the King first and the Pope last. They tell us that there is nothing in their religion which forbids them to be loyal to whatever government they live under. What could honest Englishmen do but believe what those whom they supposed to be honest Englishmen said? And no doubt some of these men were honestly in ignorance of the teaching of their Church.

Lord Fingall speaking at the Dublin Convention, as reported in the *Daily Express*, June 24th, 1892, said that "whatever claims individuals may assert, neither my creed [Romanism] nor any other creed represented here to-night contains any tenets or provisions which either directly or by implication can be held to justify 'clerical domination,' or 'religious ascendancy.'" Now an educated gentleman like Lord Fingall must surely know that the Pope distinctly claims the right to excommunicate kings and depose them, and to *interfere in politics* and control them.

But the recently published life of Cardinal Manning proves amongst other important matters, that there always has been and probably that there always will be, a large class of English Roman Catholics who are not ultramontane, who love their native land, and who would fain persuade themselves that they can be loyal to England and loyal to Rome. This same life proves also that even if a man like Newman dares to express himself too openly on this subject, he is denounced in Rome as one whose "spirit must be crushed."*

* It will appear scarcely credible that such an expression should have been used about Cardinal Newman, but the fact is stated in plain terms in the recent life of Cardinal Manning

Of what avail then is the avowed loyalty of these English Roman Catholics? When an emergency arises they will be forced to yield to the dictation of their Church. To rely upon the power of these English Romanists to make good their assurances of loyalty is to ignore history, to deny facts, and to refuse to credit the utterances made by the Romish Church herself.

In the year 1790 an address was published of the "Catholic Committee," protesting against the intolerant attitude then assumed by the Romish Vicars Apostolic, who at that time governed the Roman Catholics in England with Episcopal authority.— This *Catholic Committee* consisted of Delegates, appointed by the Roman Catholics to defend their interests, and to present to the Government their claims for relief from the penal enactments which affected their liberties. Amongst its members were

There is a letter from Mgr. Talbot to Manning, then Archbishop, which contains this remarkable expression, *vol. ii., p. 323.* Rome is indeed famous for crushing the spirit of any one who dares to have a personal opinion on any subject or who expresses even in the most respectful manner any difference, any personal opinion. It suits the plans of Rome, which are simply political, to allow her followers to have apparently a free hand in politics. It looks well when some are found in the ranks of Conservative, some in the ranks of Liberals, some perhaps even Socialists, and this openly, for this impresses Protestants with a false idea as it is intended to do.

included Romish Ecclesiastics of high rank, Roman Catholic Peers, Baronets, and members of the leading Roman Catholic gentry.—(*This address was reprinted in* 1812 *by J. J. Stockdale, No,* 41 *Pall Mall.*)

The address states that "In the eleventh year of Queen Elizabeth, Pius V. fulminated his famous Bull *Regnans in Excelsis*, in which he not only excommunicated that Princess, but declared her fallen from her Sovereignty, and her subjects absolved from their allegiance, and forbade them under pain of anathema to obey her laws;" and it goes on to say; "From this period it has always been asserted that Catholics held principles inconsistent with a Protestant Government, and that they could never reconcile the duties which they owe to the supreme pastor of their Church with the duties which they owe to their temporal Sovereign and fellow subjects;" that "Catholics began to recover from the national odium brought upon them by the unwise and unjustifiable Bull of Pius V.; and under James I., many circumstances entitled them to expect a great degree of relief and toleration. But they were destined to be thrown, by another unwise and unjustifiable Brief, under an accumulated weight of odium"—that "After the infernal horrors of the Gunpowder Treason, James I. caused the Oath of Allegiance to be enacted in Parliament, as a test, by which his loyal Catholics, who were attached to their duties as subjects, might be discriminated from those other Catholics who were under the predominancy of a foreign power:"—that "the Catholics in general were ardent to take the Oath." The address proceeds to relate the events that led to the issue of this Brief, and states:—"*Churchmen* [Roman Catholics] *again interfered, and again blasted their hopes. Three successive Briefs of Paul V. condemned the Oath of Allegiance as containing many things contrary to faith, and hostile to salvation.*"

In the "History of the Decline and Fall of the Roman Catholic Religion in England, by the Rev. Joseph Berrington, Roman Catholic Priest," we find that "the chief clause in the oath objected to by the Roman Court was that which abjured the *deposing* doctrine (claiming a power to the Pope of deposing kings and princes) as *impious* and *heretical*, pronouncing it to be *damnable*."

The address of the "*Catholic Committee*" further recites:—"That in the year 1648, fifty of the most respectable and noble of the English Catholics denied:—

"I. That the Pope, or Church, hath power to absolve any person or persons from their obedience to the civil and political government established, or to be established, in this nation in civil and political affairs.

"II. That by the command or dispensation of the

Pope, or Church, it is lawful to kill, destroy, or do any injury to any person or persons living within the king's dominions, because that such a person or persons are accused, condemned, censured, or excommunicated for error, schism, or heresy.

"III. That it is lawful in itself, or by dispensation from the Pope, to break promise or oath made to any of the aforesaid persons, under pretence that they are heretics."

"Yet," as stated in this address of the *Catholic Committee*, "the authority of the Court of Rome was again brought forward to stop them, and the authority of Paul V. was held out to deter the English Catholics from pledging their integrity as men and citizens."

The address of the "Catholic Committee" then refers to the "Irish Remonstrance" which was subsequently made, and which, as asserted in the address, "was as harmless and free from objection as a profession of allegiance could be. Yet," as the Catholic Committee state, "the remonstrants were excommunicated and several of them perished from want;"* and the Committee add:—"Thus, on the

* The Rev. C. O'Connor, D.D. (a R.C. priest), in his "Historical Address, *ad hiberaos*," states that "those of our gentry and clergy who subscribed the *Irish Remonstrance* in 1662 were excommunicated for so doing, though that declaration implied nothing more, directly or indirectly, than *Tempora*

one hand, the nation refused to relax the severity of the laws against Catholics, till they disavowed the Pope's *temporal* power (in this country) ;—the Court of Rome and her delegates, on the other, forbade them doing it."

Another " Protestation " was published in 1789 by Roman Catholics, which declared :—

(1.) That the doctrine that Princes excommunicated by the Pope might be deposed or murdered by their subjects was execrable and impious, and denied that the Pope had the power to absolve the subjects of this Realm from their allegiance.

(2.) It denied that implicit obedience was due to the decrees of the popes ; and that the Catholics did not hold themselves bound to obey the orders of the Pope, if he should, for the good of the Church, command them to take up arms against the Government, or to suborn the laws and liberties of the country, or to exterminate persons of a different persuasion, and it further declared that they " *acknowledged no infallibility in the Pope,* and that no Prelate, Priest, or Ecclesiastical Power whatever had, or ought to have, any jurisdiction or authority whatever in the Realm."

(3.) The Protestation, moreover, declared that

Allegiance ; and that they were never absolved from that sentence, but on condition of their *submitting to corporal chastisement*, and that, too, of the most ignominious description."

neither the Pope, nor any Priest, nor any Ecclesiastical Power could absolve or dispense with the obligation of an Oath.

The Protestation also rejected and reprobated the doctrine that "no faith was to be kept with heretics" [Protestants].

The *Catholic Committee* state that this "Declaration and Protestation" was signed by "All the Apostolic Vicars and their coadjutors, and with few exceptions by all the clergy (more than 200 in number) out of the four districts." That it was also signed by several "Roman Catholic Peers, and by almost every name respectable among the Catholic Laity in England."

In 1577, Gregory XIII. issued his Bull to all "the Prelates, the entire clergy, nobility, and people of Ireland," urging them to aid James Fitzmaurice in his insurrection against Queen Elizabeth, and giving a plenary indulgence to all who should support Fitzmaurice "by arms or any other means." On the 18th April, 1600, Clement issued a similar Bull urging the Irish to join in the rebellion of Hugh O'Neill. On the 22nd September, 1606, Paul V. issued a Brief condemning the Oath of Allegiance to James I. A similar Bull was published by Urban VIII. in the reign of Charles I.

In 1643, Pope Innocent X. sent to Ireland "a Nuncio, Rinuccini, who summoned an assembly of the clergy at Waterford, and engaged them to declare against that pacification which the Civil Council had concluded with their Sovereign. He even pronounced a sentence of excommunication against all who should adhere to a peace so prejudicial, to the Catholic religion." In the Papal "Instructions" furnished to Rinuccini, by Pope Innocent X., we find that Pope claiming Ireland as "being an ancient possession of the Apostolic See, the sovereignty of which Pope Adrian IV. had conferred upon Henry II., but which sovereignty Henry's successors had forfeited by violation of the conditions attached to the gift." In these "Instructions," Innocent X. referred to the rising of the Roman Catholics in 1641, when, without warning, the cruel and atrocious massacre of the Protestants in Ireland was foully perpetrated. This rising Innocent X. stated "was at first doubtful and tumultuous, *but was gradually organised into a well arranged movement by the Prelates and other clergy*, who willingly gave both advice and assistance." In these "Instructions," given by Innocent X. to Rinuccini, we find amongst the "demands" which that Pope puts forward on the part of the Irish Roman Catholics, the claim, "*that a Parliament should be held in Ireland distinct from that of England.*"

The other demands directed to be urged were "that the Ecclesiastical Hierarchy and the Religious orders should be maintained in their ancient condition; that the Bishops should enjoy the Church property to the exclusion of the heretics; that the Viceroy and other governors and Ministers of the Island should be Catholics; that all the property taken from the Catholics should be restored," etc.

It is not a little remarkable that nearly all the claims made by this pope have been granted gradually by the English government on the specious plea of "Justice to Ireland."

The revenues of the once established and Protestant Church are now enjoyed by the professors and students of Maynooth. The "Hierarchy" are allowed free range to denounce the English people and government, and to set her educational arrangements at open defiance. The religious orders can do as they please, even carrying on lotteries and other schemes for their advancement, which would be treated as illegal if indulged in by others. The principal government offices in Ireland are in the hands of Romanists, and, no doubt, as soon as Trinity College has been confiscated to Italian Cardinals, Ireland will be placed altogether under Papal rule.

How far it will prosper under such circumstances can only be judged by the failure of Rome rule wherever that Church has had a free hand to govern. It might be well, however, for the people of England to remember that Rome, claiming as she does the right of ruling all the world in temporal affairs, will not rest content with Ireland.

At the present day the question seems to be not will this or that measure proposed for Ireland be of benefit to that country and to the Empire at large, but will it please the Pope.

The fact is that very few Protestants have realised how entirely Rome is a political church, and that she always makes her political advancement her first object; nor do they realise that is not only permitted but approved, that solemn oaths should be taken which are never intended to be kept.

In 1826 the Irish Roman Catholic bishops swore solemnly that there was no enactment or bull of the Roman Catholic Church which would interfere in any way with their loyalty to the English crown and constitution. Unfortunately they were believed, and in 1829 the Roman Catholic Relief Act was granted by Parliament—yet they knew, none better, that the bull which makes disloyalty compulsory was in full force.

Further, in 1869, Pius IX. promulgated the Bull *Apostolicæ Sedis*. Even Cardinal Newman, though he was so bitterly accused by Cardinal Manning of disloyalty to Rome, said in his letter to the Duke of Norfolk:—

"That the British Ministers ought to have applied

to Rome (p. 14) to learn the civil duties of British subjects;" and that "*no pledge from Catholics was of any value to which Rome was not a party.*" Mr. Gladstone, in commenting on these words, urged too by such a man as Cardinal Newman, writes: "Statesmen of the future, recollect these words, and recollect from whom they came. . . . . The lesson received is this. Although pledges were given, although their validity was firmly and even passionately asserted, although the subject matter was one of civil allegiance, 'no pledge from Catholics was of any value to which Rome was not a party.'"

We now turn to the action of the Jesuits in America.

On the 13th September, in the year 1759, an event took place which will for ever stand pre-eminent in the annals of Canadian history. At sunrise on that memorable day Wolfe and his gallant army, having climbed the rocky steeps of Quebec, stood upon the Plains of Abraham prepared to strike the blow that was to result in the fall of that imperial power, which for more than one hundred and fifty years had ruled the destinies of New France. The story is so familiar that it needs no repetition. How bravely the French fought under the chivalrous Montcalm, and how utterly their lines were broken and repulsed by the

English veterans, is well known to every schoolboy. As Wolfe lay dying on the plain, he caught the cry, "They run, they run!" "Who run?" eagerly inquired the expiring hero. "The enemy, sir; they give way everywhere," was the reply; and so the battle of the Plains was won. This was the last act in the long struggle between England and France for colonial supremacy. Five days after, on the 18th of September, Canada ceased to be a French possession, and was added, by right of conquest, to the domain of the British Crown.

Unfortunately the "British crown" did not realise the consequences which always result from giving unlimited liberty to Rome. Protestant liberty is restrained, exactly in the proportion in which liberty is given to Roman Catholics. If an example is needed, surely we need go no further than Ireland. There Roman Catholic ecclesiastics reign supreme, and openly defy the government which fosters and caresses them. But when has the all powerful voice of the Church ever been raised to put down insurrection, or even to denounce outrages not only against persons but against helpless animals?

But to return to Canada.

When the Jesuits were expelled from Europe they fled to Quebec, and in 1886 became an incorporated body through the state craft of one of their most brilliant students, and soon afterwards received an endowment of $400,000. Since that time the Order has become more aggressive, and the attitude of the people more exclusive, until in the autumn of 1892, the Jesuits obtained a foothold in a diocese not covered by the Act of Incorporation, and have secured by underhanded means, the use of a splendid property in the wealthiest and most fashionable portion of the city of Quebec. The "Bennett Estate" has become "The Jesuit Retreat." The abode of these fathers stands upon the great battle ground, whose soil is drenched with the blood of our fathers, and out of its garden plots there may, even now, be unearthed the missiles of war used in 1759-60. In front of the main entrance of the retreat, and in full view of a fashionable promenade, there has lately been erected a colossal statue of Ignatius Loyola, the founder of the Order, of which we have given an illustration from a photograph taken on the spot. It will be seen that Loyola has a man under his feet, that the man is clinging to the Bible or some other *bad* book, and that he is in the throes of death, his tongue protruding from his mouth—Rome's victory over independent thought, or Protestantism in the throes of death!*

This symbol stands there a menace to civil and

* The ignorant Roman Catholic population are told that the figure whom Loyola is trampling on represents Luther, and the book, the Protestant Bible.

STATUE OF IGNATIUS LOYOLA ERECTED IN CANADA.

religious liberty in the Province of Quebec, and an insult to the Protestant minority which, after all, is the financial backbone of the country.

Government in Quebec is according to Canon law. It is not what is the will of Queen Victoria, but what is the will of Leo XIII. Here, in the midst of a simple-minded, peace-loving, religious, but in no sense wealthy population, are Sulpicians, Redemtorists, Oblats, Jesuits, Dominicans, Franciscans, Benedictines and Trappists, who have come to settle in this poor province, to feed upon the poverty of the people, and to reproduce here the worst conditions of life in old Europe. The attitude of the religions in this Province is not "live and let live." On the contrary the clergy encourage the growth of the most extreme intolerance and exclusiveness. Quebec, according to their teaching, must be French, French only, and ultra montane. In this way they are goading the people on to a kind of religio-racial madness. Educated, liberal-minded Roman Catholics, who understand English thought and know the Protestant position and the fairness of its spirit, deplore the extremism of the people as fostered by these foreign orders— orders which have been hived in Quebec and provided for out of the public chest.

Rome is asking every day for more concessions, more liberty, more money, all in the name of religion. She is assuring us in public that she has become more liberal, but it might be well to ask what is she doing and teaching in private. After all she does not find it necessary to make much concealment of her intentions and plans. She knows her public, and she uses her knowledge to her very great advantage. An Englishman's great characteristic is his love of liberty; Rome knows this, and trades on her knowledge. But should not Englishmen ask—What will Rome do with all this money and all this liberty? In the matter of education, Rome has so far made all her demands for separate endowments on the plea of religion—she has a right, so she says, to teach her own people the form of religion which she believes. But if matters were reversed, would Rome give us the same liberty? Rome herself has declared that she would not, again and again. We do not consider it a sacred duty to persecute the Roman Catholic Church: Rome considers it a sacred duty, and indeed it is one which she cheerfully undertakes, to persecute us, when she has the power.

Why then should we put this power in her hands? But Rome wants liberty to teach some other things besides her religion, and to this point special attention should be given. The heads of the Church know well, none better, that to appeal to an Englishman on the ground of liberty of conscience is the surest way to win. But are the English people willing that Rome should teach history, and science, and in fact every branch of education, according to Rome, and not according to fact. Yet this is what Rome demands now, what she has intended all the time. The reader will have already seen how history is spiritually peptonised in French Jesuit colleges ; are English children to have the same process undertaken for them ? Certainly they will, if Rome is allowed her own way. And what will be the result. It is self-evident that English children will know history simply in a distorted fashion, and will be deprived of real education. What an appalling injustice to the coming generation.

A public meeting of Roman Catholics was held recently at Cardiff, at which the Roman Catholic bishop of Newport gave an address on the school question. On such questions, what one bishop says, all say. The following extract from his speech as given in the Roman Catholic papers, shows what Romanists require. He said : " The board schools not only prevented Catholic training, but in many cases were the instruments of positive perversion. Sometimes non-Catholics would ask with amazement, what objection Catholics could have to a board school where no religion was forced upon them. In board schools history and geography were taught by teachers trained in Protestant views, and general information was imparted by men and women who were saturated with anti-Catholic prejudice. Catholicism touched history and general knowledge at a thousand points."

The usual talk followed about the rights of parents to have children brought up in their own religion. It sounds well in English ears, but when has Rome ever acknowledged or sanctioned that right when it was opposed to her? If the bishop had spoken truly he would simply have said, "We insist that all children shall be brought up in our religion, at present we cannot compel Protestants to learn history or religion as we think right to teach it, but we are content with one step at a time, the rest must follow."

We now proceed to give some information as to the consequences of allowing the Jesuits liberty to do as they please in Canada, and endowing them with enormous sums of money. We may add, that the information has been given to us by a friend in Canada, and that it has been the subject of much newspaper comment, as indeed it should be. It is well also that English Protestants should know how the English government is upholding Rome in that country.

In July, 1888, the Quebec legislature passed an Act, called the Jesuits' Estates Act, granting $400,000 and the Laprairie Common to the Pope to satisfy an alleged "moral" claim to the Jesuits' Estates. As the grant has been endorsed by the Dominion Parliament, and yet very generally condemmed throughout the country, and has led to widespread discussion, a short historical statement concerning the Jesuits Estates is given. These Estates, when Canada was very young, were given to the Jesuits by the Kings of France, the Duke of Ventadour, the commercial Company of Canada, and by private donors; some, it was said, were purchased. Some of these Estates were granted on condition that the Jesuits would employ themselves in instructing the Indians and young Canadians.

In the year 1760 judgment was given in the Consular Court of Paris for thirty thousand livres against Father Lavalette, as agent of the order, in certain transactions connected with the purchase of estates in the Windward Islands, and the court declared that the whole Jesuit body was liable for his acts as principal. In the following year the Superior-General of the order, and in his person the body and Association of the Jesuits in France, were condemned to pay one million, five hundred and two thousand, two hundred and sixty-six livres, two sols, and two farthings, the amount of certain bills of exchange which the body had not paid in connection with the purchase of these Windward Island estates, and also fifty thousand livres damages and all costs and expenses. During the trial the counsel for both the plaintiffs and defendants referred to the constitution of the order, and the Parliament of Paris, on April 17th, ordered that it be produced in court, specifying a printed copy of "the edition made at Prague in 1757," which had been cited in the court. A copy of these important volumes was produced in the Parliament and given to a commission, on whose report, on account of the teachings of the society as contained in the constitution, the Society of Jesuits was stripped of all its property, put out of existence as a society (it had no legal existence even at that time,) and the portion of its estates that had been devoted to education was continued for that purpose with some notable exceptions, but under the directions of others than the Jesuits, though ex-Jesuit teachers were allowed to remain in France and teach on certain conditions. The following year Louis XV. addressed a letter to the General of the order at Rome, Ricci, and also to Pope Clement XIII., asking that the statutes of the society be amended.

Ricci answered: "Let them continue as they are, or cease to exist." The Parliament of Paris decided they then must cease to exist in France and they were expelled by law, although they were given the option of remaining on condition that they retired from the order, severing their connection in truth and forever from the General in Rome. Only five or six out of some five thousand accepted these conditions.

This decree of expulsion extended to Canada as

well; and was made in 1762—one year before the Treaty of Paris in which the King of France ceded all his rights to "His Britannic Majesty." In 1765 the right of the Jesuits to these Estates came before Parliament, and Sir James Marriott, King's Advocate, in a letter to the Attorney General and Solicitor General in answer to certain questions, reported that the Estates were undoubtedly the property of the Crown, and gave reasons for his contentions. In 1770, the Estates were granted by the Crown to Lord Amherst in recognition of his services. The grant, however, was never carried out, principally because of the difficulties in securing the necessary information to draft the legal documents. In the year 1773 Pope Clement XIV., issued a bull "abolishing," "suppressing," and "dissolving," the Society of Jesus "forever." This bull was dated July 21st, and promulgated at half-past one o'clock in the night of August 16th, when the Jesuits were asleep, and were securely penned up in their houses.

In the following year instructions were sent from the King of England to the Governor of Canada, that the Society of Jesus be suppressed and dissolved, and that all their rights, privileges, and property should be invested in the Crown for such purposes as the Crown might hereafter think fit to direct and appoint, "and the Royal intention was further declared to be that the present members of the society, as established at Quebec, should be allowed sufficient stipends during their lives." As the Jesuits had had no corporate existence since 1762 in Canada, and as the Imperial Government shortly after the conquest prohibited any more Jesuits from coming to Canada, the society gradually died out, and in 1689 there were only four Jesuits living in the province of Quebec. Father de Glapeau, one of these, wrote to Monsieur Louis German, merchant of Quebec, stating that these Estates had been given them in full property for purposes of education, but "they had been reduced in number to four, all of an advanced age, consequently they were not in a condition to acquit themselves of the stated obligations, and therefore they renounced purely, simply, voluntarily, and *bona fide* all property and provisions thereof to the Canadian citizens in whose favour they were made."

In the year 1786 a commission in Canada was appointed by Lord Dorchester, the Governor of the colony, for the purpose of describing the Jesuits' Estates that they might be transferred to Lord Amherst. In the course of their work, they had a dispute as to whether the Jesuits' Estates could be taken even by the Crown for any purpose except those of education and the advantages of the young Canadians. Lord Dorchester referred this legal question to Alexander Gray, Attorney-General of

Quebec, and J. Williams, Solicitor-General. The next year, 1790, the Attorney-General and the Solicitor-General, submitted their report, which held that the proceedings of the Parliament of Paris in 1762 applied to Canada. The nature of their institution prevented them individually from taking anything under the capitulation of all Canada; nothing could be conveyed to the head of the order, and the order itself was finally dissolved and suppressed in 1774, so "the existence of the few members of the order in the province can in no shape be considered as forming a body politic or corporate, çapable of any of the powers inherent in and enjoyed by communities." The report further said these persons were living on the charity of the Crown and should be very grateful.

In 1792 a petition was presented to the king by the newly constituted Legislature of Quebec, asking that the revenue of the Jesuits' Estates be set apart for educational purposes. In the year 1800 Father Cazot, the last of the Jesuits in Quebec, died, and the Sheriff of Quebec was directed to take all these Estates into possession, which he formally did. And thus these properties for lack of any heir, real or apparent, escheated to the Crown. Let it be noted that since 1762 there was no corporate society of Jesuits in the province—at which date the society lost all legal status, i.e., one year before the Treaty of Paris—that since 1773 they had been dissolved and abolished by the Bull of the Pope—that the individual members of the society in Canada became extinct in 1800—that one of the four survivors in 1689 renounced all claims upon the property, on account of inability of the members to fulfil the trust conferred upon them—that from 1800 to about 1850 there were no Jesuits in Canada to receive the trust and to discharge it—and it will, I think, be tolerably evident to every one that a new society organised about 1850 could not have a very strong claim to property given in trust to a former society which had ceased to exist nearly a century before. The claim of the first society lapsed through the cessation of the order and consequent failure to fulfil its trust, even if it were not forfeited by the conduct of the order. The claims of the new society of Jesuits seems to be of that vague, shadowy kind that ordinary people cannot discover, and politicians can only see when it is backed up with good strong political support.

In 1814 the general society which had been "forever," abolished by one pope was revived by another. From 1824 to 1828 a lively agitation went on in Quebec, to have these Estates formally set aside for educational purposes. And accordingly in 1831 a dispatch was received from Lord Goderich, handing these Estates over to the Legislature for the purpose of advancing religion and "sound learning." From 1800 to 1831, about one fourth of the revenue of these Estates had been granted to educational purposes. In 1831 the Legislature passed an Act requiring that all the revenues of these Estates be kept in a separate chest, and applied to "educational purposes exclusively," as that or other Acts might direct. About 1841 Bishop Bourget went to Rome and invited the Jesuits to come and set up a college under the shadow of the episcopal palace in Montreal. The invitation was accepted, and the charter granted eleven years later.

About 1846 the agitation began to place the revenues from these Estates under control of the Roman Catholic Church.

The British troops had occupied the Jesuit Barracks, the old college, until the departure from that city conquered by Wolfe. In 1873 the property had been made over like the other property to the Provincial Government. The Jesuits thought this a good time to put in a claim, and M. F. David in their behalf, asked the Government whether it was its intention to indemnify the ancient proprietors, as though they had not all been dead and buried three-quarters of a century ago. The Government replied, in writing in substance that under the law all the property which had belonged to the ancient order of Jesuits, and all money received from the sale of any part thereof, formed a fund for the support ot education ; that the building which had served them for a college formed part of this educational fund, and was held to contribute to the support of superior education. "Any indemnity," the reply goes on to state, "or sum of money diverted from the direction which the law assigns, would necessarily cause a reduction in the grants in favour of superior education, and would be prejudicial thereto. The appropriation of these lands and this property is conformable to their destination, and consequently the Government is not required to indemnify any corporation whatsoever." This reply was made on the 10th of December, 1873, and rejects the claims of the Jesuits for compensation entirely. This grant of public money is therefore based on a claim that cannot be made good in law or equity, a claim rejected entirely by the Imperial Parliament a century ago, a claim not only ignored but positively denied by the R. C. Legislature of Quebec fifteen years before the same Legislature made the grant, a claim that exalts the Canon law of the Roman Catholic Church above the laws of the British realm, a claim combatted by seven out of the ten of the R. C. bishops of Quebec, a claim that would have been laughed out of the Legislature and Parliament, but for the solid electoral following that the Jesuits have now at their back. Many other objections to the Act have been urged, among which we may mention its unconstitutionality, the charges implied in it of robbery, spoliation against the British Crown and Government, and its infringements of the sovereignty of our Sovereign Lady the Queen, by investing His Holiness the Pope with civil authority in Canada. There can be no doubt whatsoever that the Pope's permission was sought, and is recognised as necessary to the sale of the Estates, that the Act requires the Pope's sanction to make it law, and that the funds arising from the sale of the Estates is to be kept as "a special deposit to be disposed of with the sanction of the Holy See."

CHAPTER IX.

The Disloyal Teaching in Jesuit Colleges.

Disloyal Teaching in Jesuit Colleges.—Case of Prince Boris.—"Are Heretics to be tolerated?"—Jesuit encouraged Popish plots against English sovereigns.—Extracts from the *Month*, a Jesuit magazine.—The Jesuits in the United States.—Jesuit scheme for the Romanising of England.—Father Parsons.—General of the Jesuits has the power of life and death.—Jesuits hung by Jesuits.—The General can sentence to death without trial.—Jarridge's case.—Teaching on Murder.—The Secret.—Immense Printing concern of the Jesuit fathers.

THE object of the last chapter has been to show, from authority which cannot be disputed, the disloyal character of Roman Catholic teaching. Nothing can excuse it, and nothing can explain it away. But the Jesuits are necessarily, and naturally the great exponents of this teaching, hence we now turn to their authorised books of theology. It was shown, exclusively on Roman Catholic authority, in the preceding chapter, that Roman Catholics are *obliged* to be disloyal. The government of the country in which they live may, or may not, hold the same opinions as to what is best for the prosperity and peace of their native land, as the pope. But whatever may be the opinions of those who rule or decide public affairs, the opinion of the pope must be considered first, and must be obeyed first.

Many instances might be given here of the interference of the popes in politics, but one must suffice. It is chosen merely because it shows in what details this ecclesiastical pressure makes itself felt.

In the *Morning Post*, August 15th, 1893, we read that the Marquis de Breteuil resigned his seat in the Chamber, and in a letter of explanation addressed to his constituency at Argelès, refers to the profound perturbation caused in the Conservative ranks by the recent action of the Vatican in regard to the Republic, and expresses his conviction and that of his constituents, that a republican form of government is synonymous with the persecution and destruction of faith.

Now the French Conservative party have always been the most devoted Catholics, yet at one word the Pope compels them to abandon the policy they have pursued for years, and they are obliged to abandon it.

The case of Prince Boris is contemporary history. This case of interference with parental rights is noteworthy, because we hear so much from Romanists in England of these rights as a solemn duty not to be interfered with, no doubt to impress the people of England by whom they are specially respected. But what of parental rights in Bulgaria? What, indeed, it may be asked, of national rights? But what makes this case especially oppressive and high-handed, is the fact that while Rome might denounce such a proceeding, if the transfer of faith were made to what she would term an heretical church, Rome actually acknowledges the rights of the Greek Church to a valid priesthood and lawful sacraments. However, whenever Rome dilates on parental rights, she always means her own rights, for she recognises no others.

The teaching of the Jesuit must, as we have said elsewhere, be always the same as the teaching of the Church. The Jesuit therefore is obliged, whether he will or not, to teach this disloyalty. But the great evil is, that the Jesuit always practises disloyalty, and has opportunities which other priests and teachers have not, of enforcing his dangerous doctrines.

The Jesuit teaches them in his schools, he teaches them in his colleges, he teaches them to his penitents, not the least important part of his work. Further, he publishes books in this country which teach this disloyalty, and then he comes before a too confiding public and declares that he is a devoted Englishman, and would almost lay down his life in the service of his Queen and country. He plots treason for the greater honour and glory of God, and he proclaims himself honest, while he is practising deceit of the worst kind. And all this is done in the sacred name of religion.

The Jesuits have their own printing press, their own compositors, their own workmen. They can print what they please, and do what they please, because this is a free country. But surely it is carrying liberty rather far to allow such license for such a purpose.

One of the works recently published by the Jesuits is called "Aquinas Ethicus," and consists of extracts from the "Summa Theologica" of St. Thomas Aquinas. The translator is the Rev. Joseph Rickaby, S.J.; we give the following quotation from this work from vol. i., pp. 332, 333:—

"*Are Heretics to be tolerated?* R. With regard to heretics, two elements are to be considered, one element on their side, and the other on the part of the Church. On their side is the sin whereby *they have deserved*, not only to be separated from the Church by excommunication, but also *to be banished from the world by Death.* For it is a much heavier offence to corrupt the faith, whereby the life of the soul is sustained, than to tamper with the coinage, which is an aid to temporal life. Hence if coiners or other malefactors are at once handed over by secular princes to a just death, *much more may heretics*, immediately they are convicted of heresy, be not only excommunicated, *but also justly done (sic) to* DIE. But on the part of the Church is mercy in view of the conversion of them that err; and therefore she does not condemn at once, but 'after the first and second admonition,' as the Apostle teaches (Titus iii. 10). After that, however, if the man is still found pertinacious, the Church having no hope of his conversion, provides for the safety of others, cutting him off from the Church by sentence of excommunication; and further, she leaves him to the secular power TO BE EXTERMINATED FROM THE WORLD BY DEATH."

He states that as things are, it is a question whether "it would *be prudent* in her (the Church) nowadays to visit heresy with *all* the ancient penalties," even if "she had might on her side;" yet he impresses on his readers the fact that the Church of Rome "still *insists* on her *right* to punish by corporal inflictions."

Certainly it cannot now be said that English Jesuits have deceived the English people. If our immediate descendants are "done to die," either by civil war, stirred up by the Jesuits to win England for Rome, or in the horrors of the Inquisition, presided over by priests as it always has been, they can justly say, "We told you this, why did you add to our power every day socially and politically, until we were able to crush you."

This is also the doctrine taught and approved by the present Pope, who is credited with being a Liberal.

When it is remembered that every one of the Popish plots for the deposition of English sovereigns were of Jesuit origin, it is time to ask if such men should be encouraged and supported in this country. When popes, cardinals, and bishops have feared their power, and tried often and vainly to control them, there is surely a justification for fear of the secret work, which even now they may be plotting in England.

Indeed Romanists seem to take a pride in declaring their contempt for the laws of the country, which has helped and sheltered them when they have been restrained and banished from countries once exclusively Roman Catholic. The following extracts from Roman Catholic papers, supported and authorised by the Church, will show that the above statement is not mere assertion :—

" Upon the passing of the 14th and 15th Vic. cap. 60, A.D. 1851, forbidding the assumption of R. C. Ecclesiastical Territorial Titles within the United Kingdom—an assumption forbidden, also, by the 24th Section of 10 Geo. IV. c. 7—the R. C. leading Paper, the *Tablet*, of July 26th 1851, p. 478, said :—

"' Neither in England nor in Ireland will the

Catholics obey the law of Parliament. They have before them two things called law, which contradict each other. Both cannot be obeyed—one of them is the Law of God, the other is not law at all. It pretends to be an Act of Parliament, but in the direction of legislation it has no more value than a solemn enactment that the moon is made of green cheese. The law of God, that is the Pope's command.'"—"If carried into effect the Parliamentary lie" will be "treated as all honest men treat a lie, that is rigorously disobeyed—will be spit upon and trampled under foot."

The utter contempt shown by Engish *Romanists* of the laws of their country is further aptly illustrated by the *Weekly Register*, another R. C. Paper, of June 21st, 1868. This Paper wrote:—

"It [*the Ecclesiastical Titles Act then in force*] is broken every day in the year. It has been broken without hesitation or intermission ever since it received the Royal assent, and it will be broken without hesitation every time that its infraction becomes necessary, so long as it defiles the Statute book."

The *Weekly Register* makes no secret of the intentions of those it represents, and says plainly:—"If we like the laws, we obey them; if not, we defy them."*

* In the United States the Jesuits are still more active, and all public organisations are at their mercy. Mgr. Satolli, the

Amongst other works published openly by the Jesuits, there is a magazine called the *Month*. The name was chosen, we believe, so that Protestants might not suspect that the serial was Roman Catholic. The venture at first promised failure, but when it was taken in hand by the Jesuits it proved a brilliant success. A remarkable article was published in this magazine in October, 1889. It is headed "A Jesuit Scheme for the Reformation of England." The word Reformation is, we suspect, purposely misleading, it should be "A Jesuit Scheme for the Romanising of England," when it is added that this scheme originated with, and was arranged by Parsons, the value of the title will be better understood. We may do the Jesuits the justice to say that they never put their personal safety in competition with the success of their work. When therefore the Jesuit who writes on this subject declares that the scheme was not published for some time after it was written, because it was not "safe" to do so, we know that he refers to the necessity for concealing the conspiracy, not to the security of the conspirators.

Probably it is thought quite safe to publish the

Apostolic Delegate in the United States, has promulgated an edict of the Pope, placing under the ban of the Church, as secret societies, the Oddfellows, the Knights of Pythias, and the Sons of Temperance. December 21st, 1894.

"scheme" now the people of England have been hypnotised into acquiescence with whatever Rome pleases to do. Parsons was a pervert, and had been a fellow of Baliol College, Oxford. Archbishop Abbot says he was expelled for bad conduct and peculation, the Jesuits say that he abandoned his fellowship because he desired to become a Romanist. Perhaps one statement is not irreconcilable with the other. His treatise was published in London with a biographical notice by the Rev. Edward Gee, the rector of a Protestant church in London in 1690. Mr. Gee had a bad opinion of Parsons, and had special opportunities for forming it. Parsons' book is at all events another proof that the Jesuits were the active partners in every effort to overthrow the Protestant government in England. His Protestant biographer says that he was "fierce, turbulent, and bold."

Parsons' Roman Catholic editor says, that he had to account for the rapid return of the people of England to the Protestant religion after the death of Mary, and gives his reasons. He says:—

"Many priests that had fallen and married in King Edward's days were admitted presently to the altar without other satisfaction than only to send their wives out of men's sight; and of some it is thought they did not so much as confess themselves before they said Mass again. Others that had preached against

Catholics were admitted presently to preach for them, and others that had been visitors and commissioners against us were made commissioners against the Protestants, and in this Queen's time were commissioners again of the other side against ours; so as the matter went as a stage play, where men do change their persons and parts without changing their minds or affection."

But Romanists in general, and the Jesuits in particular, have always a sharp eye on temporal affairs, and the weakness or indifference of Protestants too often affords them ample ground for concluding that, if they ask with sufficient importunity they will be sure to receive.

It grieved the heart of the Jesuit, that even Roman Catholics should possess the lands which the Church had sagaciously grasped in preceding reigns, and he blames the Church for allowing these lands to return to their original Catholic owners even by the Papal permission.

There can be no doubt that Rome has full details of all the estates which she claims to be the property of her Church in the United Kingdom, and when she has secured the spoils of Ireland, she will turn her attention to England and Scotland, beginning, no doubt with the plea of requiring funds for "educational purposes." Parsons' says:—"Now, in Queen Mary's reign, all possessors of Church lands had, with a few exceptions, retained them. Some had applied to Rome for a Bull of toleration, others had never taken the trouble to do so." Many of the applicants, he tells us, had sent false information as the ground of their petition, and yet thought themselves safe in conscience. "Yea, he was taken for a great Catholic who would so much as ask for a Bull." This accounts, in his opinion, for the transitory character of the change, and "for the fact of the second scourge of heresy having proved so sharp and heavy."

From all this it is evident that the greatest crimes in the eyes of the Jesuits were the honest marriage of a priest, and the holding of money or land which the Church claimed as her own.

The Jesuit writer in the *Month* make several remarks which are noteworthy. He expresses his "no small astonishment" that so many of Father Parsons' plans and recommendations have been already carried out in England. Whether his "surprise" is real or assumed, the fact can be easily accounted for. For some years the Jesuits have had their well trained pupils in every department of state, in the army, in the navy, in Parliament, on the judicial bench, and it can scarcely be a matter of surprise that they have carried out the teaching of their masters.

The foundation-stone was to be the placing of a

"Catholic" monarch on the throne. This the Jesuit writer appears to consider quite possible at the present day. He says:—"Father Parsons' object in his book, however, is not to criticise the past, but to provide such plans for the future that Catholics may avail themselves of them if the occasion offers of restoring the [Roman Catholic] Church in England."

No doubt the "occasion" will be made, and probably it is already in the process of making:—"Father Parsons is constructive throughout, and his constructive scheme is not only that of a good and prudent man, but of one who knows by experience the nature of the evils to be met and the best remedies for them. He is very practical, and sometimes enters into details into which we shall not attempt to follow him. But the main features of his proposal are of permanent interest, not merely as an historical study, but as affording some valuable suggestions for the guidance of Catholics, even in circumstances very different from those which the headstrong House of Stuart turned to such ill account."

Having had access to the original, we note two special points which the Jesuit writer in the *Month* has thought it prudent to pass by, at least for the present. Father Parsons insists on securing a Roman Catholic king, and still more on securing a Roman Catholic Parliament and a Roman Catholic succession. As far as Ireland is concerned his plans for a Roman Catholic Parliament are already carried out, as the bishops either nominate, or approve, the candidates for the greater part of Ireland, and "no others need apply." Parsons say: "that the king can in no wise be better able to satisfy his duty to God, and to assure his own possession and estate, than by making account that the security of himself, his crown, and successor dependeth principally on the assurance and good establishment of the Catholic religion within his kingdom." For this purpose he must not only give "singular care for restoring perfectly the Catholic religion in the realm," but must "uphold and maintain the same, and provide for the perpetuation thereof," and to insure this, he must "first of all assure the succession of the crown by good provision of laws, and in such manner link the state of Catholic religion and succession together, as the one may depend and be the assurance of the other."

Upon the important question of the constitution of Parliament, Father Parsons gives the most explicit instructions in his "memorial." The higher house is to be strengthened by the admission thereto of "the principal men of the religious orders," a device, no doubt, for placing that august body under the control of the Jesuits.

He then proposes that "for chcosing knights of the shire and burgesses, a more perfect and exact order should be set down, and less subject to partiality and corruption, and that information should be taken of their names and religion." In the election of their representatives, Father Parsons recommends that, for a time at least, power should be given to the bishop of the diocese, "to judge of their virtue and forwardness in religion and to confirm their election, or to have a negative voice, when cause should be offered." This is not all, for this Jesuit adds, that these representatives shall be required "to make public profession of their faith before their election could be admitted."

He makes provision for instituting an inquiry as to all the rights and privileges taken from Parliament since the entrance of heresy, which are to be restored by the Crown; and then he directs that "every man be sworn to defend the Catholic Roman faith; and, moreover, that it be made treason for ever for any man to propose anything for change thereof or for the introduction of heresy." When Rome acts thus in her own interests it is all right, but if Protestants protect themselves in a similar manner it is bigotry and illiberality.

Father Parsons then furnishes instructions *for the making of laws* by the "Catholic Parliament," which he would establish, and first he proposes:—"To abrogate and revoke all laws, whatsoever have been made at any time, or by any prince or Parliament, directly or indirectly, in prejudice of the Catholic Roman religion; and to restore and put in full authority again all old laws that ever were in use in England, in favour of the same, and against heresies and heretics."

Here is Father Parsons' idea of toleration:—"To be provided that this toleration be only with such as live quietly, and are desirous to be informed of the truth, and do not teach, and preach, or seek to infect others."

"For wilful apostates, or malicious persecutors, or obstinate perverters of others, how they may be dealt withal," this distinguished Jesuit states, "it belongeth not to a man of my vocation to suggest, but rather to commend their state to Almighty God, and their treaty to the wisdom of such as shall be in authority in the commonwealth at that day; admonishing them only, that as God doth not govern the whole monarchy but by rewards and chastisements, and that as He hath had a sweet hand to cherish the well affected, so hath He a strong arm to bind the boisterous, stubborn and rebellious, even so the very like and same must be the proceeding of a perfect Catholic prince and commonwealth; and the nearer it goes to the imitation of God's government in this and all other points the better, and more exact, and more durable it is, and will be ever." The astute Jesuit suggests a military order for suppressing heretics. Are the "Ransomers" the outcome of this suggestion?

The "Council of the Reformation" was also to consider how some new Order of Knights, similar to the "Order of the Knights of St. John of Malta," might be erected in the realm, for the exercise of the young gentlemen and nobility, whose rule should be "to fight against Heretics in whatever country they should be employed;" and Father Parsons adds, that "whereas their ancestors, to fight against infidels, *less dangerous and odious to God than these Heretics,* undertook long and perilous journeys into Asia and other countries," so the members of this new order "should show their valour against Heretics and enemies of God and His church, of these our days, as well at home among us, as also in divers kingdoms round about us."

Care was also to be taken for the expurgation of all Heretical books. "Public and private libraries are to be searched and examined for books; also all book-binders, stationers, and booksellers' shops, and all *Heretical books and pamphlets were utterly to be removed, burnt, suppressed,* and severe order and *punishment* appointed for such as shall conceal these kind of writings."

Successive Protestant Governments in this country have been wearied with applications, and have used their best endeavours to relieve Roman Catholics from every possible religious or legal *disability;* but we learn from this "memorial" of Father Parsons, that when the Roman Catholic power is restored, it is to be considered "whether it shall be fit to disable some great and able heretics and their posterity—especially if they have been principal authors in the overthrowing of the Catholic religion—not only from priesthood and ecclesiastical dignities, but also from other honours and preferments temporal of the commonwealth, for warning and deterring of others."

Father Parsons also suggested in this memorial that in order to put the Commonwealth in joint again, it would be desirable to appoint a Council of Reformation.

This "Council of the Reformation" was to consist of "certain prudent and zealous men put in authority by the prince and Parliament and the Pope's Holiness, and, for that the name of Inquisition may be somewhat odious and offensive at the beginning," Father Parsons proposes that the name given to these men should be, "the Council of the Reformation."

But it is advised "that before this 'Council' make an end of their office, when they shall have settled and secured the state of Catholic religion, it would be very much necessary that they should leave some good and sound manner of Inquisition established for the conservation of that which they have planted;

that perhaps it would be best to spare the name of Inquisition, at the first beginning, which, in so new and green a state of religion as ours must needs be, after so many years of heresy, may chance offend and exasperate more than do good. But afterwards it will be necessary to bring it in, either by that or some other name, as shall be thought most convenient at the time: for that, without this care, all will slide down and fall again."

The memorial proceeds to the consideration of "the form and manner of Inquisition," which it will be desirable to bring into this kingdom. The merits of the respective Inquisitions set up in Spain, Italy, and Rome are severally discussed, and it is suggested that possibly "a mixture of all will not be amiss for England when the day shall come." Nevertheless special commendation is given to the "diligent and exact manner of proceeding" that then prevailed in Spain, as being "so necessary as without this, no matter of moment can be expected." It is also stated that "some high council of delegates from his holiness must reside in the court, as in Spain is used; or else all will languish." "The prisons of the Inquisition are also to be separated from the concourse of the people," and "some sharp execution of justice is to be made upon the obstinate and remediless."

We are hearing a great deal at the present day of

the "liberality" which we ought to extend to our "Catholic brethren." It would be well if we knew a little more of the kind of "liberality" which they propose to extend to us as soon as they have power. Every concession to Catholics, whether that concession be small or great, is hastening the day when they can carry out the plan of which the Jesuits at the present day have so boldly and openly approved. Let us hear no more then of the Jesuits as the benefactors of mankind, as amiable gentlemen who merit our consideration. Let it be noted that we make no doubtful or calumnious charge against them. What we have advanced are stern facts, and facts which should sink deep into the heart of every reader. Nor can the matter be referred to the past. Romanists are very anxious to persuade us that the age of persecution and intolerance has passed.

It has not passed, and those who say this know that well. Here is the proof that Rome is as intolerant, as narrow, as cruel, and as determined to exterminate Englishmen, we do not even use the word Protestants, as ever she was in the darkest ages of her dark career, if they do not accept her creed.

The Jesuits must know that they have hope of success or they would never have made their plans public. It was a daring act, but they are daring men.

I use no harsh or bitter language about them. I have known Jesuits in my Roman Catholic days to whom I was indebted for many a kindness, men who I believe would have shrunk from the cruelties which are proposed in this vile plot on English liberties, religious, social, and political. The danger is that those who may have known such men should suppose that they are real representatives of the order, or that they would dare to be anything else but cruel if they were commanded to be cruel. These men, if ordered by the church or by their ecclesiastical superiors, would not hesitate for one moment to torture their nearest and dearest relatives, or bring them to the stake, such is the power of religious fanaticism. Once more let it be said, the fact is there, and there is no evading it. So lately as the year 1889, the Jesuit Editors of the Jesuit representative magazine, published such parts of Parsons' scheme as they dare, and approved what they were too prudent to publish in these words: "his scheme is not only that of a good and prudent man, but of one who knows by experience the nature of the evils to be met, and the best remedies for them. The main features of his proposal are of permanent interest, not merely as a historical study, but as affording some valuable suggestions for the guidance of Catholics, even in circumstances very different from those which the headstrong house of Stuart turned to such ill account." This is plain speaking, and the Jesuits mean what they say.

We now proceed to show from historical evidence that the Jesuits claimed for themselves the power of life and death.

MURDER OF JESUITS.

We give the following extracts from Griesinger's "History of the Jesuits":—

Page 649. "In the underground vault in the Munich Jesuit College, eleven human skeletons, hung in chains, were found, which were all dressed in Jesuit clothing, and had apparently fallen victims to the extreme justice of the Order.

"The commissary had to be satisfied with the declaration of the rector, that these were eleven brethren who had lost their reason."

This was on the suppression of the Order in 1773, in the time of Joseph II. of Austria.

At the college of Ingolstadt were found things "which strongly compromised the Order of Jesus, as, for example, a crucifix, which, when it was kissed, the person kissing it was killed by a dagger springing out. Also, an executioner's sword, with the remarkable inscription, *Hoc ferrum centum et decem reis (regibus) capita demessait.*"

JARRIDGE'S CASE—GRIESINGER.

Page 498. "In 1648, Jarridge, a professed Jesuit of the four vows, escaped from La Rochelle to Leyden in Holland.

"At Leyden he published a book called 'The

Jesuits on the Scaffold,' owing to the high crimes perpetuated by them in the province of Guyenne."

Page 501. "Ponthélier, a Jesuit, well disguised, was sent to Leyden, where Jarridge was; they were known to have met, but he suddenly disappeared, and so did Panthélier, and no researches, officially instituted, ever cleared the matter.

"In 1651 the Order published Jarridge's so called Recantation, but his exposure of the Order and the recantation are not in the same style or by the same hand, which is quite evident, and the Recantation is a palpable forgery."

I have examined both books in the British Museum.

Page 502. "There was an exposure of the Order in 1645, evidently written by a member, called 'The Monarchy of Solipsen, by L. C. Europœus. The Jesuits never discovered the author, it was first published in Venice."

TEACHING ON MURDER—GRIESINGER.

Page 488. "Escobar, 1655, in his Moral Theology teaches, 'That it is absolutely allowable to kill a man whenever the general welfare or proper security demands it.'"

"To defend his life or his honour, a son may murder his father, a monk his abbot, and a subject his prince."—HERMAN BUSENBAUM.

Father Francis Laing, (Disp. 36, Num. 148.) "It

is an established truth, that ecclesiastics must save their honour and consideration at any price, even at that of the life of the person insulting them. This is especially the case when the loss of their honour would tend to the disgrace of the whole order.

Father Henriques Summa Theologiæ Moralis (Venic. 1600). "If an ecclesiastic murder the husband of a woman with whom he is caught in adultery, he is quite justified in doing so."

Benedict Slattle, vol. 1, p. 337, of his "Moral Philosophy." "A real injury, bringing disgrace, may be retaliated by the murder of the insulter.

THE SECRET—GRIESINGER.

Page 474. "Bishop Palifox wrote to Innocent X. in 1649.

"'But the Jesuits alone, shroud themselves intentionally in a darkness, which the laity are completely forbidden to penetrate, and the veil is not even uplifted to many of the members. There are among them a large number who have taken merely three vows, but not the fourth, and who are in consequence, not at all, or at any rate, not properly, instructed regarding the true principles, institutions and liberties of the order; this secret, on the other hand, is entrusted, as is known to His Holiness, to only a small number, and whatever is especially important is known only to the Superior and the General.'

"The Duke de St. Simon in his memoirs, one hundred and fifty years later, says the same thing.

But there is another class book which needs careful attention. This work is a translation from the German of Dr. Joseph Hergenrother. In this work, one of no small Roman Catholic importance, the doctrine of the lawfulness, or rather the duty of killing heretics, and deposing heretical sovereigns is fully defended and carefully taught. And this is done openly in the 19th century. Much capital is made in this book of certain expressions and acts of Protestants at the time of the Reformation, who declared it lawful for their brethren to fight for their religion, and to depose in open war those kings or princes who were persecuting Protestants. But surely this is something very different from the blessing of secret assassins by the head of the Romish Church, and the fulmination of spiritual cursings on the head of a lawful sovereign, merely because that sovereign was a Protestant.

It would occupy more space than can be given to this matter here to go fully into the teaching of this book. But in it the doctrine of the Romish Church, that it is a duty to exterminate heretics is fully taught and earnestly defended. The Pope's plans for the assassination of Queen Elizabeth are justified; indeed, his Bull of excommunication of that sovereign placed her at the mercy of any one who pleased to kill her, and who could plead the Pope's authority for so doing. Many other cases are brought forward for justification, in which the Popes at various times exercised what they are pleased to call their spiritual rights to incite to the murder of princes and people, who would not submit to their rule. Some of these Popes were men of infamous character, but they were infallible all the same.

And this doctrine is fully approved at the present day by the present Pope, for in his Encyclical on Scholastic Philosophy, Leo XIII. ordered his ecclesiastics throughout the world as follows :—" Let the teachers whom you shall discreetly choose make it their aim to instil the doctrine of Thomas Aquinas into the minds of their scholars, and to set in a clear light *his solidity and excellence above all other teachers*."

In the " Relations of the Church to Society," by the late Father O'Reilly, S.J., with preface by Matthew Russell, S.J., the author teaches that " A Protestant clergyman or a Protestant layman as effectually introduces the child whom he validly baptises into the Catholic Church as the Pope could, and into no other ;" and " to conclude what has been said concerning persons *subject to the Church's laws*, I may add, though the statement seems rather superfluous, that *no temporal dignity, however exalted, exempts from the obligation of obedience to them. A King, as such,* has no prerogative of spiritual independence, any more than he has of spiritual authority."

The object of this statement may not be immediately apparent to those who are not familiar with Roman Catholic teaching. It is none the less important. Rome claims every lawfully baptised person as her own, no matter how strongly the person may object to this appropriation : thus, on her theory of church government she claims the right to dispose of that person's body and soul at her pleasure. She claims the right to put him to death in this world and to damn him eternally in the next, as she so pleases, no matter whether he has ever given his consent to her usurpation of his immortal soul or not. Further, the delicately conveyed hint about royalty being on the same level with others is not without its intention also. It simply means that Leo XIII. has the same right to depose or sanction the assassination of Queen Victoria, as his infallible predecessor Pius V. had to ex-communicate and, as far as his power could go, to depose Queen Elizabeth.

One fact is worth a thousand assertions, and the fact that the Jesuits and indeed all Roman Catholic professors are teaching to-day in England this horrible doctrine as being the very truth of God, ought not to be overlooked by those who care even for the material prosperity of their country.*

* We have been informed that a very large sum of money was given to the Jesuit fathers to purchase all that was necessary for an immense printing concern. They are by no means content with leaflets or pamplets, but are issuing large volumes, and having them placed in public libraries. May we not hope that some Protestants will have the same zeal for the circulation of books which may counteract this danger ?

CHAPTER X.

The Spanish Armada and the Jesuits.

The Spanish Armada and the Jesuits.—The Pope's one idea to re-enslave England.—England's unique position.—Cardinal Manning commends the Gunpowder Plot conspirators.—Englishmen must clearly understand Roman Catholic principles and motives.—The Pope's claim to temporal power. — The *Civilta Cattolica.* — Jesuit plots in England.—The Jesuit the "Wandering Jew" of the Romish Church. — Queen Elizabeth wished to exercise toleration towards her Roman Catholic subjects.—The Jesuits tried to assassinate Elizabeth.—Roman Catholics had liberty to practise their religion privately under Elizabeth.—Elizabeth inclined to clemency.—Mary Queen of Scots.—Philip of Spain.—The Armada, a Jesuit plot.—Execution of Mary Queen of Scots.—The Jesuits persecute the Pope and the King of Spain for men and money.—Both are unwilling to act.—The Pope angry and hysterical; throws his plates and dishes about.—Refuses to give money till the expedition has started.—Everything planned by the Jesuits who were sure of success. — Cardinal Allen's proclamation. — The Pope can make or unmake sin.—Elizabeth would have been his "dearest daughter" if she had placed herself and her kingdom at his feet.—The Armada defeated in spite of relics and prayers to the Virgin.

TO obtain control of England has been the one absorbing idea of the Papal court since the Reformation freed us from its yoke. Indeed, Rome has always had a quarrel on hand with this country, for history records the determined resistances which the people of England, even when Roman Catholic, made again and again, to the encroachments of Rome, and at a time when Rome held her own all over the Christian world.

There are many reasons why Rome greatly desires to govern us. England has a position unique in the history of nations. France is complimented on occasion as the eldest daughter of the Church, but from time to time the daughter has proved unfilial and refractory and has more than once thrown off the Papal yoke. France cannot be depended upon as an appanage to the Holy See, and the Holy See knows it.

Germany may support Rome politically for a moment, but Germany is not Catholic or likely to become so. Italy has spoken for herself, or rather, has been tried too long by Papal government to submit to it again, unless under military compulsion, which the Pope would use if he could find fitting tools for his purpose. Might not England, if once under the control of Rome, be made to play the part of compulsory dictator? It would be the duty of England, if Catholic. England is rich, she holds under her hand nations and principalities which are mines of wealth, and whole vast populations might be compelled to bend to the Papal power, if once her army was placed at the disposal of Roman cardinals. England has a prestige all her own.

The people of England are reliable and not given to sudden change, but it may be said that such a change as that which is here suggested would not be possible at the present day. Events move quickly in this 19th century. Already a noble lord openly and without reproach has made statements as to the property of the Church of England which would have cost him his lordly head in Tudor times. He has declared that the property of the Established Church is really the property of the Church of Rome.

It matters little whether this statement was made as an unworthy attempt to obtain popularity and continuance in office, through the voters of the persuasion which he seems so anxious to accommodate with the money of the nation, or whether the statement is the result of his own convictions. We are only concerned with the fact that such a statement could be made publicly at the present day. To say the least, it is ominous of coming changes. Canada, through her too complaisant politicians, has already handed over large sums of money to the Jesuits, which they claimed as "restitution of church property," but this is not all.

Another noble lord has publicly declared in his corporate capacity, and with the express approval of many clergymen of the Church of England that he desires to have England placed once more under the spiritual guidance of the Pope, and it is no secret that all this encouragement has impressed the present head of the Roman Catholic Church, and has led him to hope that what was not accomplished by violence in the reign of Elizabeth, may be accomplished by diplomacy in the reign of Victoria.

Hence it is of importance that the manner and the methods which have been employed in the past for the subjugation of England to the Papacy should be fully understood, even if the subject was not so intimately connected with the history of the Jesuits.

It may be said that the methods of the times of the Gunpowder Plot and of the Spanish Armada would not be practised now. Roman Catholic authorities do not think so, and they are surely the best authorities as to the plans and belief of their Church. The late Cardinal Manning, who was a Catholic first and an Englishman after, as indeed every good English Catholic is bound to be, has spoken very plainly on this subject. And if in the near future Englishmen find themselves under Papal control or driven to deadly warfare to free themselves from it, they cannot reproach Rome with having deceived them as to her intentions. No words can be plainer than the words which Rome uses at the present day. No authority can be higher than the authority which has made the statements which we quote. There is no uncertainty when Rome declares her opinions officially. The Cardinal has frankly given the special reason why Rome desires to conquer England and subdue it. He says:

"If ever there was a land in which work was to be done, and perhaps much to suffer, it is here (England); were it (heresy) conquered in England, it would be conquered throughout the world. All its lines meet here; and, therefore, in England, the Church of God must be gathered in all its strength."

This is plain language, because it proves how fully Rome realises the importance of converting England to her interests and of placing England once more under Papal rule. Nor can it be said that Rome has hoped without cause. We have but glanced at two sources of encouragement on the part of leading Englishmen, who would appear to emulate their Roman brethren in looking to the advancement of the Church of Rome first, and to the good of their native land a long way after. It is noteworthy also that these men too often agree with Rome in her appreciation of those of her members who suffered for disloyalty to their country but whom Rome would fain reckon as martyrs to her faith.

Cardinal Manning commends the rebellious Becket and the arrogant Anselm as model Englishmen, because they were loyal to a foreign power. He commends the men who suffered justly for the Gunpowder Plot as true heroes, and holds them up to the admiration of the rising generation.

It is noteworthy that the service for the commemoration of our deliverance from the same plot has of late years been disused, principally, if not exclusively, through the influence of those who have expressed their preference for Roman customs and Roman doctrines so openly, as to give rise to grave suspicions as to whether they are not themselves not only of the opinion of the lapsed Cardinal, but also secret members of his faith.

It is extremely difficult for an honest Englishman to understand a divided allegiance, and Rome has greatly profited by this difficulty. To an Englishman who fights openly for the cause which he espouses, and always says so, it is almost incomprehensible that others should act differently. But it is all the more desirable that Englishmen should very clearly understand the principles and motives of Roman Catholics. It is no reproach to a Roman Catholic to say that he is true to his own principles, but it is very important that we should very clearly understand what these principles are.

The sooner and the more clearly it is understood that the canon law of the Church of Rome only tolerates civil law when it is practised in complete subjection to canon law, the better for all concerned. This is after all but carrying out the teaching of the Church of Rome to its inevitable and logical end. If Rome's contention is admitted, that the canon law is God's law, and exercised by Divine right, it is self-evident that all other law holds its authority by mere delegation.

Hence the claims of the popes, not only in the past, but at the present day, to depose kings, and to permit, and by permitting to encourage, the assassination of rulers who disobey her mandates. Every Roman Catholic subject of the Queen, or of any other power, is first a subject of the Pope, that is to say, if there should be any conflict of obedience between the two powers, obedience to the Pope comes first, and not only does it come first, but such obedience is a solemn religious duty.

The Pope bases his claim to temporal sovereignty on the ground of his spiritual sovereignty. The conclusion, as we have said, is perfectly logical, but what of those who from indifference or prejudice deny the temporal power, while they admit or encourage Papal claims to spiritual power, though they would scarcely care to submit to the Pope's temporal sovereignty. It is true that some English Catholics, as, for example, at the time of the Spanish Armada, may have given their loyalty to their country first. But no English Catholic dare act in this manner at the present day. Circumstances alter cases. The realisation that the Pope is personally infallible by Divine right, and that this infallibility is an article of faith as much binding on the faithful Catholic as a belief in the existence of God, adds enormously to the importance of Papal pronouncements. Indeed, the Pope's personal and political infallibility is taught in Roman Catholic catechisms approved by the Holy See in the United States. Hence, for example, if the United States went to war with England, American Roman Catholics would be obliged to fight on and help whichever side the Pope chose. There is no personal liberty of any kind allowed in the Church of Rome.

The English Roman Catholic who took the side of England against Spain had not the full opportunity of knowing the Papal desires which he would certainly have at the present day. Communication with Rome was slow and difficult, Roman Catholics in England were comparatively isolated. They may have doubted, certainly they took the benefit of whatever doubt there might have been. At the present day such doubt would be impossible. Again, at that time English public opinion was against Rome. To-day public opinion is to a large extent greatly impressed by Rome. The pressure of excommunication, which Rome has never been slow to use, either in the past or the present, would soon be brought to bear with terrific force on any English Roman Catholic who took the side of his country, when his country took a side against Rome, or even against what Rome decided.

DESTRUCTION OF THE SPANISH ARMADA.

It is also difficult for an Englishman to understand that what he calls "toleration," or considers a favour, where Roman claims are concerned, is not accepted as a favour by that Church and is never accepted as a toleration. 'Any larger liberty granted to Roman Catholics, whether political or social, is considered by them simply as a right. No thanks are due, and none need be expected, unless, indeed, policy may suggest some appearance of gratitude, which is not and cannot be felt. On the contrary, if all the revenues of the Church of England were handed over to-day to Roman cardinals, those sanguine individuals who suggest such a course would find to their surprise that far from receiving thanks, they would be informed that they only deserved punishment for having kept Rome out of her rights so long.

The Pope's claim to temporal power being an admitted doctrine of the Roman Catholic Church, Catholics must give their first temporal allegiance to Rome, no matter what may be their nationality. *Roma locuta est causa est finita* is an axiom as much in force to-day as when it was first propounded. But while the Church can always bind in temporals as well as in spirituals, she can never be bound. It is part of the Divine right under which she claims to govern the world that she can be "subject to none" while all must be subject to her. She is also logically the sole arbitrator of the manner in which her rights shall be enforced. To-day she may secure what she claims to be her Divine power by fair means, by persuasion or influence, to-morrow she may put to the sword all who dare to disobey her. And still she is answerable to none. If people but realised to the full the power which Rome claims, and the right she claims as to its exercise, they would be slow indeed before they strengthened her hands, or gave her the power to bind them in fetters from which they may never obtain release.

We do not enter into the proofs of the statements which are made above, as it will probably be more satisfactory to the reader to place them in the appendix. It will be seen there how abundant and undeniable is the evidence. Also it will be seen that the Jesuits are the special defenders of the Papal claims to personal and universal sovereignty. The Jesuits have writers everywhere to uphold this doctrine, and the *Civilta Cattolica* is the special and Papal organ for the exponent of Papal claims.

It would be impossible to enter here into the political state of England when the Jesuits planned and carried out the plot for the subjugation of England to the Pope through the hoped for success of the Spanish Armada. The discovery of state papers and the perfect freedom granted in England for their publication has enabled the present generation to form opinions from facts. It is a curious and remarkable fact that the Jesuits were not allowed in England during the reign of the Roman Catholic Mary. Cardinal Pole, who knew them well, had a deep distrust of them, and like others of his religion and profession, thought that one cardinal could govern with more advantage to the Church than a dozen Jesuits, who would act as spies on his conduct if they observed their rule faithfully.

Ireland has always been used by the Papal court as a stepping stone to effecting a landing in England, and accordingly in 1550 Davis Wolfe, a Jesuit, was sent to that hapless country. A bishop and two other Jesuits followed three years later. But a far more important step was taken when Father Chinuage was sent to England on the plea that his health required a return to his native air; who, it was asked, could be so unjust or ungenerous as to refuse a temporary shelter to one who only asked to recruit a shattered constitution. In 1551 a certain Father Sandon was sent to Scotland to encourage Mary Queen of Scots, and to obtain reliable information as to her position and prospects. But the Jesuit father was discovered and obliged to leave the country, not, however, without having seen Mary three times and obtaining all the information for which he had been sent.

But the great danger to England was from the

seminary priests, who were under the complete control and guidance of the Jesuits; of these seminary priests, William Allen was the chief. He was an Englishman. A man's foes are often those of his own household. It is a mistake to suppose that those who differ from us are all actuated either by mercenary or irreligious motives. Religious fanaticism is responsible for the greatest evils which the world has ever seen, and fanatics, with a very few exceptions, are men who believe in their religion, whatever it may be, and will suffer for it to the death. Allen believed in his religion, he believed in the Order to which he had joined himself. The great idea of the Jesuit has always been a universal spiritual monarchy, in which, *bien entendu*, the Jesuit should reign supreme. England has always been the place desired for the base of the operations necessary for this end. Hence the blood, the tears shed, and the schemes undertaken in this country by the Jesuit. He has by no means ended his efforts for the subjugation of the world to Rome through England. On this subject, so important for us, more shall be said later.

In the reign of Elizabeth, the attempt was made through the plots to murder her (of course for the good of the Church), and anything which might help, however remotely, to this end was eagerly availed of. The English Roman Catholics did not like these schemes. The English Catholics did not like the Jesuits. But the Jesuits were a united body, they had the ear of the Pope at Rome. They had power, they had prestige, they were always in evidence, above all they had, and have, enormous wealth at their command. The parish priest was confined to his parish, he could not run over to Rome, or to Douay, or to Paris as he pleased. The other religious orders were located in certain places, and could not leave their monasteries without difficulty or special permission. But it was not so with the Jesuit. He was the free lance of the Church. While it was the business of the parish priest to look after the interests of his particular flock, and of the monk to work in his particular monastery, the Jesuit had the world for his parish and any house where he could obtain an entrance for his monastery.

It is true that he could only move on the chess board of his Society, at the express will of a superior, but it was the express will of his superiors, that he should be in the front of every movement which promised to increase the power of the Church and of the Order. He had a large field of labour, and he occupied it. When the Jesuit is expelled from one place he is not slow to find another. France may reject him, not without cause, but England opens her arms to him. Catholic Italy may deprive him of the glories of his once famous home in the *Gesu*, but America opens her doors to him. He is the wandering Jew of the Romish Church; he is followed by the execrations of those by whom he was once beloved, until they discovered his iniquities.

It is an historical fact that Queen Elizabeth was most desirous to exercise the utmost toleration towards her Roman Catholic subjects. It was only when they were required, by their Roman Catholic superiors, to become rebels against her lawful authority, that she exercised her right as a sovereign, to protect her person, her throne, and her subjects from their disloyal plots.

The Jesuits were naturally the great movers in the rebellion against their Queen. Their motive was twofold. Pope Pius V. had excommunicated Queen Elizabeth by a Bull issued on the 5th of February, 1570, and the Jesuits were bound to carry out their vow of obedience to the Pope to the bitter end, and to see that this excommunication bore fruit. It was not possible, as it would have been in earlier times, to bring the excommunicated Queen to the scaffold, but it was possible to attempt to assassinate her privately, and the Jesuits set all their most skilled men to work to accomplish this object.

A great deal has been said, and a great deal has been written on this subject: the facts are not denied because they are too evident. But on the Catholic side the men who died for their treasonable practices are called martyrs, and applauded to the highest heavens by English Roman Catholics even at the present day. By honest men they are simply reprobated as traitors, who met the doom which they courted and deserved.

This difference of opinion is worth consideration. History repeats itself. Evidences are not wanting that efforts are being made at the present moment to set aside the Protestant succession to the throne.

It is true that the attempts to announce and honour a new line of kings of England are apparently insignificant in the extreme. But things are not always what they seem, it is significant that such an attempt should be possible. It is significant that such public efforts are being made to overthrow the Established Church at the same time. We point to this simply as a sign of the times, without any reference to the rights or wrongs of these efforts against the Church of England. It may be said that any attempt to change the dynasty of England at the present day is too impossible to be worthy of notice. A straw is insignificant, but it serves on occasion to show which way the wind blows. There are a good many straws blowing about just now, if people would only see them. Besides, small beginnings often have great endings. If Rome cannot bend a dynasty to her will, she will leave no means unused to break the dynasty. Elizabeth was cursed by the Pope with all the powers which he possessed to curse. The Jesuit, as the special servant of the Pope, was bound to leave nothing undone to make the curse a success. It was his duty; it would seem that his duty was a pleasure.

The Pope could only curse, he could not command the civil power, as he had done in past ages, to execute his vengeance on the object of his displeasure. The Jesuits, his military organisation, undertook that task. If they failed, it was not for want of loyal efforts to succeed.

There were two ways in which the Pope's curse could be made effective. One way was by the assassination of Elizabeth. The Jesuits, as we shall show later, tried to do this. The other way was by attacking her throne through a foreign foe. The Jesuits tried this also.

It was a dicta of the famous O'Connell that there was no fool so dangerous as a pious fool! We may, perhaps, be allowed to say there is no fanatic so dangerous as a sincere fanatic. Fanatics, with few exceptions, are sincere. And here we find a key which explains Roman Catholic disloyalty. Roman Catholics have maintained that the executions of their co-religionists, which took place in the reign of Queen Elizabeth, were executions for their religion, and reproach Protestants with cruelty and religious persecution. If ever there was a case in which men were executed, and executed justly, for treason against their lawful sovereign and country, the case is that of those Roman Catholics who paid the penalty of their crimes of disloyalty in the reign of Elizabeth. These Jesuits came to England with the deliberate purpose of carrying out the effects of the excommunication which had been pronounced by the Pope.

Elizabeth had been cursed by the Pope, and the Jesuits were the chosen instruments of carrying out the effects of this curse. She was no longer a queen, but a woman, whom it was their duty to murder, as soon as she could be murdered.

She was no longer the lawful ruler of the fair realm of England, she was an outcast, against whom every man was bound to raise his hand, who believed in the power of the Pope to make or unmake kings at his pleasure. This is a question about which there can be no dispute. It is a question of to-day, as well as a question of yesterday. More so. The past is past. But the Pope of to-day claims the same power, the Mannings, and the Howards, and the Arundels, and the Vaughans, are as much bound to do their duty to the Pope first, as were the Jesuits who compassed the destruction of Elizabeth by assassination and by war. They must be loyal to the Pope first, and if loyalty to the Pope conflicts for a moment with loyalty to the queen they have no choice as to which they shall obey.

There is ample evidence that Elizabeth gave large and free liberty to Roman Catholics to practise their religion, at least privately; but they wanted liberty to deprive her of her crown, in order to rule England through a Roman Catholic dynasty, whether England desired it or not. Elizabeth punished disloyalty to her throne and punished it justly. If the punishments were barbarous, it can only be said that the age was barbarous and she simply allowed the law to take the usual course. Further, Roman Catholics when in power inflicted even more barbarous punishments on Protestants. But there is evidence that Elizabeth was inclined to the side of mercy, until the discovery of Babington's plot to murder Elizabeth and place Mary on the throne of England. Tichbourne, one of his accomplices, did not pretend that he was innocent, but said he expected to be forgiven, so notorious was the clemency of the Tudor Queen. In September, 1586, when the plotters were executed, the usual barbarities were carried out to the letter, and the men were cut down alive and disembowelled, but Elizabeth gave orders that the men who were reserved for execution on the following day were to be hung till they were dead. Indeed, Babington actually wrote to Elizabeth the day before his execution imploring her clemency.

But neither executions or intimidations could restrain the impetuous Jesuit. If the plans for the assassination of the excommunicated Elizabeth failed, all the more reason why they should stir up a war in which they were sure that the saints and the Virgin were on their side. They held the strings of three puppets in their skilful hands—Philip of Spain, who was dazzled by the hope of securing the English crown, if not by an alliance with Elizabeth, then by conquest ; Pope Sextus V., who was bound at least to appear anxious to secure England for Rome; lastly Mary Queen of Scots, who was beating her somewhat soiled plumage against the bars of her cage. But there were difficulties. Mary was too impetuous and received humiliations from her Jesuit advisers which must have been very galling to her. She was told by Father Martellito, "to take care what she was doing," she must not offend the Catholic powers. She forgot the risks which others run in serving her, she must beware, or she will ruin herself fatally, she thinks only of her own misfortunes ; nay, it is even hinted very broadly that she is not as good a Catholic as she should be, and that there are those who will not be sorry if she gives them an excuse to complain of her. She had not trained her son as she should have done, and he was therefore doubtful and unreliable as a Roman Catholic, and lastly the King of Spain cannot be made a laughing stock by failure, if he sends an imperfectly provided army to England and the enemies of God go to war with him. The view taken by the Jesuit as to the enemies of God is amusing. No doubt he believed, as a good Catholic, and still more as a good Jesuit, that every Englishman was bound to join the Spanish invasion the moment it appeared on the shores of old England, but did he really suppose that the "enemies of God" would sit down quietly and let any foreigners capture their native land? We shall give at least a considerable part of the Pope's Bull of excommunication, which made this Spanish invasion justifiable, and even a duty in the eyes of Romanists. We may add that our authority for the above letter, and the extracts which follow, are the state papers which are given in Froude's "History of England," all these he verified personally.

Philip was not very much inclined to push matters on for the conquest of England; one reason was that he needed money, another reason was that he had just received the present of an old (or shall we say new?) relic which absorbed his thoughts and his devotions. Cardinal de Medici had presented him with a fragment of the broken shoulder bone of St. Lawrence, the corresponding fragment had been long the most precious of the Spanish objects of religious worship. This saint was the particular saint of the king, but it does not seem to have occurred to him that he might have supplied him with the money he so greatly needed for his expedition to crush the English heretics, and compel them to adopt his religious views. The Pope was the great resource relied on by the Jesuits, and they made him do all that a pope could do for the ruin of their native land, for most of these Jesuits were Englishmen. The Pope was quite willing to utter spiritual fulminations, and to place Elizabeth at the mercy of every scoundrel who for any reason, or for none, wished to kill her; but to give money, that was quite another affair. The Jesuits wanted to keep the business quiet, with their usual regard for secrecy, and their usual skill in diplomacy; the blow should be struck, but if they could have concealed the hands which were preparing to strike it, if they could have made the Spanish fleet invisible until it arrived on English shores, they would have been content. The Pope was their great difficulty. They had implored him to be silent. And they had implored him to advance the necessary funds. But the Pope was not to know everything, he was not to know that the Jesuits had arranged to give the crown of England to Philip of Spain. A letter from Allen, the Jesuit, and the promoter of the expedition, to Philip reveals all this.

"We are of opinion," he writes, "that it will be well to say nothing for the present either to the Pope, or anyone, about your Majesty's succession;

it cannot do good, it may do harm, through the sinister interpretations of enemies, and even friends." Prudent Jesuit! Even at the present day popes prove troublesome to their followers, and the late Cardinal Manning complains that Pius IX., whom he helped to make infallible, "could not be trusted with a secret," and had become "garrulous" in his old age. France had also her eye on England. France was never, even in later ages, the very ready tool of Rome. France has not greatly affectioned the Jesuits.

France had already put in her word against the Jesuit scheme, and had advised the Pope against it. The Jesuit Morgan had reported to the Queen of Scots, that the French King had been "at hand with the Pope, to provide that nothing be attempted against England." *

France was afraid lest England, after all, might be strong enough to defeat the Jesuits, and the Pope, and the King of Spain; that in the rebound the Catholic faith might suffer, and that France might suffer through her Protestant and cruelly persecuted subjects. Further, if the expedition succeeded there would be the danger that Spain, if aroused by conquest, might annex French provinces.

The Jesuits implored the Pope to be silent, but he

* State papers quoted by Froude. "History of England," vol. xii., p. 224.

would not. He talked to every one of the plot, perhaps from pure love of talking, perhaps to relieve his troubled feelings. The only comfort the Jesuits had was that "he" the Pope, "was such a notorious liar that nobody believed a word he said." They wrote this to the Spanish King and the original manuscript remains underlined by Philip, in a manner which shows that he appreciated the communication. There was also another matter about which the Pope was so irritated, that he even became hysterical, "and cursed and swore at his attendants, and flung his dinner plates about." Altogether the Jesuits had a hard time. Philip, we may presume, consoled himself with his relic of the shoulder bone, and he was never very much in earnest in the scheme. Possibly he understood the English better than either the Pope or his advisers.

In the meantime Allen never lost heart or ceased from pursuit of his object. He had already been made an archbishop, he looked to have a cardinal's hat, and obtained it eventually, but the Pope never liked him, though he may have been too much afraid of the all powerful Jesuits to show his dislike openly. All that could be got from the Pope was the promise of 700,000 crowns, but even this moderate sum would not be given until Philip had actually landed in England. The Pope had at least profited by experience in dealing with sovereigns, even of his own faith.

And then came the news of the execution of the hapless Queen of Scots. This scarcely changed matters. Mary was never of much account in Papal plans, as an individual, and we have seen that her piety and devotion to the Church was not quite as much credited in her life time as it has since her death. A pope of the 19th century may canonise her, but the pope of the 16th century was not very anxious to afford her the rites of the Church in Rome after her death. But the Jesuits triumphed, and the Spanish Armada became an accomplished fact, but only to end in a most disastrous failure. Two things, however, are certain. The Spanish Armada was the exclusive work of the Jesuits; neither the Pope nor the Spanish King would have taken the initiative, if they had not been driven to it by the perseverant efforts of these disloyal Englishmen. English Catholics who suffered death or other penalties, either before or after this event, suffered solely for treason. If Rome to-day declares they suffered for their religion, she must admit that to commit treason is a religious duty when commanded by the Pope or other ecclesiastical superiors.

Many of these so-called martyrs were men who were acting as spies in the pay and interests of a foreign power, and would have been promptly hung or shot if they had carried out similar practices in ordinary warfare. Their actions were none the less treasonable towards their lawful Queen, because they were acts of loyalty to Rome. Their religion taught them treason as a religious duty, and they only seek to throw dust in the eyes of the world when they cover over evil with a pretence of suffering for good. Yet, while Roman Catholics at the present day call loudly for sympathy with their martyrs, they show a very clear discernment of their views as to the fate which should be reserved for those who are what they considered disloyal to their head, and rebel ever so mildly against his authority.

If there was no other evidence of the character of the men who suffered at this time for their attempts against the throne and peace of England, we may find full confirmation in Father Allen's correspondence with Philip of Spain. As the matter is important, we give a few extracts from his letter here. He writes: "As soon as God shall have given your Majesty victory, you can then allege your descent from the house of Lancaster."

Philip was ambitious of the English crown, if it could be had without trouble, and this is the bait held up to him by the Jesuits; for, notwithstanding his love of relics, Philip was less zealous to fight for the Church than for his own interests. "The Archbishop of Canterbury (Cardinal Allen was to be appointed to that office by the Pope), who gives his vote first, and whom all the Catholic peers will follow, can easily bring to pass what you desire. The Pope will then acquiesce and all will go as you desire. With the sword of the Lord and of Gideon you will chastise the English heretics."

But a public manifesto was necessary also. Allen prepared an important document, which cuts the ground from under the feet of those who fancy they can make men of common sense believe the invaders of England did not want to make rebels of Englishmen, or to change the dynasty. This document was printed in Flanders, and was intended to be issued as a pastoral letter to the people of England, by their new and self-appointed spiritual ruler, Cardinal Allen. Copies of this document were smuggled across the channel, and distributed amongst the Catholic party.

The burden of the whole was the wickedness of Elizabeth. Her father had been excommunicated, she, therefore, for that and a hundred other reasons, had no right to the throne. His Holiness confirms and renews the sentence of his predecessors against Elizabeth. Allen addresses the people of England thus:—"Being of your own flesh and blood, His Holiness has chosen me for his legate, for the restoring of religion and the future ordering of the realm," a large office for one individual. "He discharges you of your oath of allegiance, and requires you no longer to acknowledge her as your sovereign." "The angel of the Lord," he declares, "will scatter the heretics," which, as the event proved, was precisely what the angel of the Lord did not do. He assures them that if they will but forsake their Queen, and hand their country over to his control that their property will be spared. A weighty bribe for those who might have no settled religious convictions, but who might have a very settled desire to keep their possessions. If they took the side of their country and their Queen and died in battle, they would certainly go to hell, temporal bribes and spiritual punishments were well interspersed in the carefully prepared document. The heretics, he said, were few (surely he knew better), but was not the lie written for good ends? The angel of the Lord will scatter them. This so important and self-confident document is dated, "From my lodging in the Palace of St. Peter at Rome, this 28th of April, 1588. The Cardinal."

But the Lord fought on the other side, and we do not hear what view the Roman Catholic authorities took of the failure of their promises and prophecies.

We shall show later how much the English Catholics, and the English Catholic priests, dreaded and resented Jesuit plots and interference. The Jesuits had a plan, all their own, for reconciling the conscience of honest Catholics, and there were then, as there are now, many such disloyal devices.

The Bull, deposing and excommunicating Elizabeth, was the great difficulty, according to the law of the Roman Catholic Church, then as now, any Roman Catholic who obeyed the Queen, disobeyed the Pope.

To enter fully into the Jesuit system of morals would require a volume. It may be summed up in a sentence. The Jesuits offer the world at large a system of theology by which every law, Divine and human, may be broken with impunity, and by which the very bulls of popes may be defied. It is a ghastly religion, it is a religion to be abhorred of all honest and honourable men.

But it may be said the Jesuits of to-day do not teach these doctrines, and do not practise this theology. Would to God that this was the case. We have already shown how recently they have brought forward, with full approval, and an earnest recommendation, the plan outlined by the Jesuit Parson for the overthrow of the Protestant succession in England, and for "removing" Protestants from all offices of State, and introducing the Inquisition. This does not look like repentance for past crimes. We have quoted from the works published by the Jesuits at the present day, and the works of the Jesuit authors quoted in this present work are the class books of their schools and colleges. What then can be expected in the near future but civil war, religious anarchy, and the privation of an

Englishman's dearly bought right of liberty of conscience.

Lord Robert Montagu, who left the church of Rome some few years since, has indicated not a few of the preliminary steps which have been taken to further the plans of Rome for the subjugation of England. He says, "By the Ballot Act, the influence of the landlord was destroyed, while the power of the priests which is exercised in the confessional by the threat to refuse absolution was not touched."

It was far, indeed, from being touched, it was simply secured. English statesmen have signed away their birthright of liberty for a mess of political pottage. A recent Jesuit writer, Father Amherst, has declared that "The admission of Catholics into the Legislature, by the Emancipation Act of 1829, was the first great blow which Protestant ascendency received. England has, indeed, been since called an essentially Protestant country, and no doubt there are many who would still so call it. But when Catholics were admitted to an equality in the making of laws, the principle of a purely Protestant State was surrendered."

We can now only briefly indicate the Jesuit teaching as to our duty to our neighbour, and the duties which we owe to each other. But let it be remembered that what the Jesuits teach the Church teaches and that the class books of moral theology, written by the Jesuits, are also the class books of all Roman Catholic colleges, and that in all schools under Roman Catholic control the same teaching is given.

Before blaming the Irish people for crime and discontent, it would be only justice to them to remember that Maynooth has been endowed, and is largely supported by Protestant money, and that the priests who rule Ireland are taught there that it is no crime to " remove " a tyrant, and no sin to refuse the payment of debts which man considers he need not pay.

EQUIVOCATION.

Both Liguori and Gury teach "that it is lawful to use equivocation—that is, language in which words or phrases of a double meaning are employed—for a just cause, and to confirm the equivocation with an oath ;" and he defines a just cause to be "anything designed to maintain things good for the spirit or useful for the body."

" A man may swear that he never did such a thing (though he actually did it), meaning within himself that he did not do so on a certain day, or before he was born, or understanding any other such circumstance, while the words which he employs have no such sense as would discover his meaning. And this is very convenient in many cases, and quite innocent, when necessary or conducive to one's health, honour, or advantage."

The same author suggests a surer method of avoiding falsehood, which is, after saying aloud, I swear that I have not done that, to add in a low voice, "to-day," or, after saying aloud I swear, to interpose in a whisper, "that I say."

"A confessor, if asked by a tyrant whether Titus has confessed a murder, can and ought to reply, I know not, because a confessor knows it not so as to communicate it. Moreover, if the tyrant should persist and say, Is it the case that you know not this by sacramental knowledge? he can still reply, I know not. The reason is, because the tyrant well knows that he has not the right to ask this, neither does the confessor, as a man, know that he knows it, but as the Vicar of God, and with an incommunicable knowledge."

Theft.

Thus Gury, in his chapter "On the causes excusing theft," says:—"A man may in extreme necessity use of another man's goods as much as is sufficient to free himself from such necessity. The reason is that the division of goods, in whatever way it may have been made, cannot derogate from the natural right, which belongs to everyone, of providing for himself when he is labouring under extreme necessity. Whence, in such a case, all things become common, and therefore anyone taking anything belonging to another, for his own relief, takes a thing truly common, which he makes his own, as happened before the division of goods. Therefore he does not commit robbery."

The Rev. Daniel O'Hanlon Walsh is reported in the *Wexford People*, October 7th, 1885, as saying:—"If you are going to pay the rent, you must first of all consider your liability to pay the honest shop-keeper, and make provision for yourself and family. I am not going to tell you that you are bound to pay the surplus. I am merely telling you if you resolve on what to do; but if you think it prudent to put it in your pockets, you will have my blessing and support."

"A man may steal the property of another, not only in order to relieve his own necessity, but also that of another. The reason of this is that he, as it were, acts for the needy person, and shows that he loves his neighbour as himself."

Surely this is making the commandments of God of no account.

How Nuns Should Act in Hospitals.

A nun, attached to an hospital in which not only Catholic but also heretic patients are admitted, is requested by a Protestant, grievously ill, to bring to him a minister of his own sect, from whom he may receive the aids of his own religion. But the nun does not know whether she can comply with his request. The question is asked, Can the nun bring in a Protestant minister? Answer, No. The reason is evident; for it would be communication and co-operation, properly so called, with heretics, in a matter pertaining to religion. This also follows from the following reply of the Holy Congregation, 15th March, 1848:—Most blessed Father! D. N—— lays humbly before your Holiness, that in the city of M—— there is an hospital, of which he is rector and chaplain, and in which nuns nurse the patients. But since, from time to time, the followers of an uncatholic religion are admitted, who continually ask for a heretic minister from whom they may receive religious help and comfort, it is asked whether it is lawful for the aforesaid nuns to call in a minister of a false religion. It is also asked whether the same solution is to be given in the case where a sick heretic is living in the private house of a Catholic: whether then a Catholic can lawfully call in a heretic minister." The reply given to this by the Inquisitors was, "That, according to what is laid before us, it is not lawful;" and they added, "let them remain passive."

No doubt some isolated case may be found in which nuns will have complied with a request for a Protestant minister, because the Church always considers expediency. But the rule is as given above. The same rule holds good in regard to Protestant children who are sent to Roman Catholic schools.

It is the duty of the nuns to teach them as much as possible of the Roman Catholic religion, and this is always done, no matter what promises are made to the parents, unless in cases where the risk of discovery would be too great, and pecuniary loss might result to the nuns.

CHASTITY.

We do not propose to enter here into this subject. It is sufficient to say, that the Jesuits condone sins under this head quite as freely as they condone theft and murder. One example must suffice, and it is selected because the whole case was brought before the public tribunals and admits of no dispute.

In 1817, Niembauer, a Bavarian priest, was found guilty of the murder of his mistress.

In his confession of his guilt, he related at length how this woman, whom he had seduced, having threatened to denounce him to his ecclesiastical superiors unless he received her into his lodgings, and provided for his child, he deliberately cut her throat while she was sitting with him in his room, and gave her absolution as she expired. In explanation and justification of his conduct he said, in his confession of his crime:—"My honour, my position, my powers of being useful,—all that I valued in the world was at stake. I often reflected on the principle laid down by my old tutor, Father Sætler, in his 'Ethica Christiana,' a principle which he often explained to his young clerical pupils, that it is lawful to deprive another of life if that be the only means of preserving one's own honour and reputation. For honour is more valuable than life; and if it be lawful to protect one's life by destroying an assailant, it must obviously be lawful to use similar means to protect one's honour. My case appeared to me to fall precisely within this principle. I thought, if this wicked woman should pursue me to Lauterbach, and do what she threatens, my honour is lost . . . Father Sætler's principle became, therefore, my *dictamen practicum* . . . . Her death has always been a source of grief to me, though the motives which led me to effect it were praiseworthy. These motives, my only motives, were to save the credit of my honourable profession, and to prevent the many evils and crimes which a scandalous exposure must have occasioned . . . . As these calamities could be prevented only by the getting rid of Anna Eichstädter, I was forced to get rid of her. The end was good—her death was the only means. Therefore I cannot believe that it was a crime."

The most painful feature in all this Jesuit teaching is the entire absence of any thought of God or of His law. All turns on the opinion of a few men and on their view of good or evil. And this system is being endowed with the wealth of a Protestant, or shall we not rather say, of a Christian nation.

Surely God will judge the supporters of such infamies, as well as those who perpetrate them.

It might, indeed, be said with perfect truth that if St. Peter had gone to a Jesuit confessor he would have found excuses for his denial of Christ, if not a complete justification, and that even the awful crime of Judas would have become excused if not extenuated.

THE FLOGGING MANIA OF THE MIDDLE AGES.

Religious manias break out from time to time which are sometimes more dangerous in their results than civil war. The dancing mania was one of these scourges which went nigh to overset the mental balance of thousands. The flogging mania was a still more dangerous epidemic, and in this the Jesuits bore a considerable and guilty share. Devotees are always cruel, and Catherine de Medici took up the lash and used it with effect on her hapless maids of honour. It need scarcely be said that she took care that no such suffering should be inflicted on herself.

She indoctrinated her son, Henry III., with this passion also, and induced him to give added prestige to these abominations by assisting at them. Under Henry IV. a more sensible *régime* was commenced, and all these processions and exhibitions of religious immodesty were strictly forbidden.

A public scandal occurred at the commencement

of the 18th century which gave a considerable blow to the Jesuits as a body. That some members of every association may, and do prove unworthy is no argument against the rest, but if the evil-doer is supported and his crime extenuated by his brethren, then indeed one must believe that they are partakers of his sin. Such was the case in the famous trial of the Jesuit father, John Baptist Girard, whose illicit amours, under the cloak of religion, with a very beautiful young woman named Catherine Cadiere ended in a public trial and exposure. At first the poor girl came to the father with an earnest desire for spiritual advice, after her fall, probably from a feeling of remorse, which even the priest's assurances failed to remove. Then she became, as she supposed, possessed by the devil, and no doubt she was the victim of a terrible hysteria. No one could console her but this one particular father, and consequently he passed long hours with her alone, during which he was supposed to be occupied in exorcising the demon.

Though long since forgotten, the scandal rang through the whole of Europe, and the result was a blow to the Jesuits, from which they did not soon recover. At the public trial the unhappy woman was acquitted, for in order to shield her priestly paramour the blame was thrown on her. It is said that great efforts were made to have her punished in some way, but the judges were resolute. They declared that they had acquitted the real culprit, and that they certainly would not pass even the slightest censure on his victim.

The extent to which the practice of public scourging was carried during this century under the direction of the Jesuit fathers is a pitiful record of human weakness. The idea that the creatures of a good God could please Him by self-mutilation or torture is sufficiently degrading, but when such humiliations involved acts of the grossest immodesty, the source of the inspiration from which they proceeded is self-evident.

A disguised, but none the less certain, sensuality was concealed under all this mortification. We had almost said that the animal in man predominated, but animals are not guilty of such refinements of evil.

Certainly the administration of the Spanish discipline by the priest to the penitent became at last a source of terrible danger, not only to the Order, but to the Church which permitted it, and in permitting it sanctioned it. We must never forget that what Rome permits she sanctions, because Rome has but to say the word, and at the moment her commands are obeyed.

There were two kinds of discipline, the discipline *sursum* and the discipline *deorsum*, or the *secundum supra* and the *secundum sub.* The discipline was applied in the one case over or on the shoulders, and in the other case on the lower part of the body. This method of administering flagellation was called the Spanish discipline, because it was introduced by the Spanish Jesuits. It is not to be supposed that the penitents of these fathers submitted all at once to the shameful exposure which was considered necessary, the fathers were indeed far too wise to proceed otherwise than cautiously. The shoulders, but slightly bared, were at first considered sufficient for the infliction, but as soon as the penitent had become accustomed to this mode of administering penance more was required.

In 1552 a community of women was formed in Louvain, where the Jesuit fathers had considerable influence, as, indeed, where had they not at this time? This community, which was composed of some of the ladies from the first families of Louvain, submitted to the Spanish discipline, and processions were organised and constantly carried out, in which these penitents walked through the streets scarcely clad and flogging themselves or allowing themselves to be flogged until they bled.

The matter was at last taken up by the professors of the university and by some of the secular clergy, and these processions, with the public administration of the discipline, were forbidden by law. At last the scandal became so great, for the use of the Spanish discipline had become a mania, and as infectious as such manias must always be, that the Archbishop of Toledo commanded that the "Book of Spiritual Exercises," as used by the Jesuits, should be revised; and in 1570 the Inquisition interfered and positively forbad these disgusting exhibitions. The Jesuits, however, were not to be silenced so easily. They at once increased their processions instead of causing them to be discontinued, and they found ready supporters amongst a number of ladies, who walked the streets of Marcia, Toledo, Seville, Saragossa, and other towns, in a state in which it might have been supposed that no self-respecting woman would have allowed herself to be seen. And this was called the religion of Jesus!

But though the Jesuits were obliged eventually to abandon these public processions and flagellations, they were still continued in secret, and with worse consequences.

CHAPTER XI.

THE GUNPOWDER PLOT AND THE MASSACRE OF ST. BARTHOLOMEW.

The Jesuits the sole originators of the Gunpowder Plot.—Futile efforts to deny this.—How Rome teaches history.—Pope Paul IV. tries to bribe Queen Elizabeth.—Offers to condone her supposed illegitimacy.—Excommunicates her when she refuses submission.—The secular clergy praise Elizabeth for her clemency, and bitterly accuse the Jesuits of making disturbances. — Letter of the Pope complaining of the immorality of his own priests.—The Pope obliges English Romanists to commit treason.—The present Pope canonises them for it.— James I. succeeds Elizabeth ; banishes the Jesuits.—They then declare him illegitimate.—They approve and help the Gunpowder Plot.—A plot lately revealed of a similar character to be carried out at the present day.—Assassination approved in the confessional. — Contrast between the fair and open trial given to the Jesuit Garnet, and the secret practices of the Inquisition.—Falsehoods written by a dying man to shield Garnet.—The massacre of St. Bartholomew.—How planned and how executed.

THERE is no event in English history which should be more carefully remembered than this of the Gunpowder Plot. Yet it has become the fashion to ignore it, or speak of it as if it had been an event of long past ages. Romanists, who not so long since were thoroughly ashamed of it, speak of it now in an airy fashion, as something with which they really had no concern. Even the Jesuit fathers, whose Society was the sole origin of this, and so many other plots, to deprive Englishmen of their religious and political liberty, give lectures on the subject, and declare that it is all a mistake to credit them with the plot; it was a "put-up job" to throw them into discredit. Fools may believe them, but the historical evidence against them is far too strong to allow of honest denial. Facts are "stubborn" things, and the facts and the history are all against the Jesuit.

However, it may be said, because it can be proved that neither history nor Scripture are of much account with these men, and either can be re-modelled to suit their peculiar views. We have already given evidence of this. Besides, when the Church of Rome has power, she will at once destroy all historical evidence which tells against her. It is useless to say that she will not do this, for she has already announced her intention to do it, to a generation which will not listen to a voice of warning. In the Jesuit scheme for the "reformation" of England, re-published by the Jesuits in 1889, with the highest commendation, this one particular point is insisted on. "Public and private libraries are to be searched and examined for books, also all bookbinders and stationers," and all books which the Church pronounces heretical are to be at

THE CONSPIRATORS FROM A CONTEMPORARY PRINT.

once destroyed. What havoc will be made one day of the British Museum when it becomes the Pope's library. What has been done in England may be done again. In the reign of that Queen who has been justly called Bloody Mary, a law was passed that any one who had heretical books, if they did not burn them at once, without showing them to any one, should be hung. How terribly afraid Rome is of knowledge.

Romanists naturally make light of the persecutions of Mary, but when did Elizabeth ever issue such a tyrannical enactment. But for Romanists, history must be believed and written according to Rome. We have already shown how this is done in colleges under Jesuit control; it is remarkable that Romanists are now declaring openly that they require not only that they shall have schools where they may teach their own religion, but that they must also have schools where they may teach their own history.*

* A speech was made by the Roman Catholic Bishop of Newport at Cardiff, in which it is plainly stated that Romanists will insist on teaching their own history, and even their own geography, as well as their own religion. He said: Sometimes non-Catholics would ask with amazement what objection Catholics could have to a Board school, where no religion was forced upon them. In Board schools history and geography were taught by teachers trained in Protestant views, and

As a specimen of how history is expurgated for the use of Romanists, we may say here that in the Clifton Tracts, a Roman Catholic publication, it is stated that the persecutions under Mary and the cruelties practised by the Inquisition are all "nursery fables."

The Gunpowder Plot was simply a last despairing effort of the Jesuits to secure a Roman Catholic succession for England, and to place her under the heel of Rome. Plot after plot had been discovered and frustrated ere this fiendish scheme was planned. And here it should be noted that Romanists are constantly bringing forward those who suffered in the reign of Queen Elizabeth as martyrs for their faith, and thereby securing the sympathy of a certain class of Englishmen. But the facts are very different. In the reign of Mary, men, women, and even those who might also be called children, were burned alive and tortured, simply because they would not submit to the Roman Catholic Church. In the reign of Elizabeth those who were executed had an open, public, and fair trial, and they were executed simply and solely for treason. But here, again, the duplicity of Rome comes in to falsify history.

general information was imparted by men and women who were saturated with anti-Catholic prejudice Catholicism touched history and general knowledge at a thousand points.—*Tablet*, January 18th, 1896.

These men knew well that they were simply hung for plotting and doing their evil best against the Queen and throne of England; but they did not call this treason, for they openly avowed and openly taught that they owed no allegiance to Elizabeth, that their sole allegiance was to the Pope, and that as he had excommunicated Elizabeth, it was their duty to assassinate her, and an act of loyalty to the Pope. A consideration of the subject from this point of view is important, because there is so much historical misrepresentation at the present day. For all the facts here stated there is ample historical proof. How sad it will be if English children are not allowed to read for themselves the true history of their native land.

Now the facts of the case are very simple, and there is abundant indisputable evidence to prove them. When Sir Edward Carne, the English ambassador at Rome, notified Paul IV. of the accession of Elizabeth to the throne, "he told Carne that England was a fief of the Holy See, and that it was great temerity in Elizabeth to have assumed, without his participation, the title of Queen." Pope Paul IV., finding that Elizabeth was firm and determined to hold her own, offered to let things remain as they were, provided she would acknowledge his primacy and a Reformation from him. Pius IV., his successor, proffered the same conditions to the Queen by letter, written May 5th, 1560, wherein he offered to comply with all her requests to the utmost of his power, provided she would allow of his primacy; and Pius V. (the same Pope who afterwards issued the Bull of excommunication against Elizabeth), thirty-three years after Elizabeth's birth, and in the seventh year of her reign, offered to reverse the Papal sentence which declared her illegitimate, if she would submit to his rule. The Spanish ambassador in England, De Silva, assured Queen Elizabeth that she had only to express a desire to that effect, and the Pope would immediately remove the difficulty.

Camden, in his "Annals of Elizabeth," gives the text of a letter addressed by Pope Pius IV. to Elizabeth, under date May 15th, 1560, wherein he addressed her as "our most dear daughter in Christ, Elizabeth, Queen of England," expressing his "great desire . . . to take care of her salvation, and to provide as well for her honour as the establishment of her kingdom!"

It is one of the special prerogatives of a pope to be able to make or unmake sin at his pleasure. The Roman Catholic Church teaches that it is a sin of incest for a nephew and niece to marry. But the Pope can unmake the sin and allow it to be committed, provided a sufficiently large sum of money is paid into the Papal treasury.

So in the case of Queen Elizabeth. If she had

submitted herself and her kingdom to the Pope, and allowed his Italian Cardinal to rule her country, we should have heard nothing of her illegitimacy.

One scarcely knows which to admire most, the courage of Queen Elizabeth or her moderation under circumstances which were of the most exasperating character, especially to a woman of her temperament, and these noble traits are fully admitted by so many Roman Catholic priests that we can only make a selection from their writings on this subject.

Bitterly, indeed, did the secular priests complain, and not without ample cause, of the ruin brought not only on England, but on the Church of Rome itself, by the plots and intrigues of the Jesuits.

In the year 1601 "sundry secular priests" published, during the reign of Elizabeth, a statement of their case, with an epistolary introduction written by priest Watson. It is entitled "Important Considerations which ought to move all true and sound Catholics, who are not wholly Jesuitised, to acknowledge, without all equivocations, ambiguities or shiftings, that the proceedings of her Majesty [Elizabeth] and of the State with them since the beginning of Her Highness's reign, have both been mild and merciful." "It cannot be denied," say the secular priests, the writers of this document, "but that for the first ten years of Her Majesty's reign, the state of England was tolerable, and, after a sort, in some good quietness."

These secular priests tried even to induce the Jesuits to cease from their disloyal and felonious attempts to murder Elizabeth and overthrow her government. They said, " In the beginning of her kingdom, she did deal somewhat more gently with Catholics; none were then urged by her or pressed, either to her sect, or to the denial of their faith. All things, indeed, did seem to proceed in a far milder course—no great complaints were heard of." And these secular priests for themselves state:—" For whilst Her Majesty and the State dealt with the Catholics as you have heard (which was full eleven years, no one Catholic being called in question of his life for his conscience all that time), consider with us how some of our profession proceeded with them." And they then describe the plottings of the Jesuits in this country, which brought upon them the retribution they richly deserved. They conclude by admitting that " these foreign Jesuitical practices had been the cause of all their troubles;" and that " they might have continued in peace, and none making them afraid, were it not for the treasons and rebellions stirred up by the Jesuits and their party against the Queen and the lawful government of the country."

It should be observed here, however, that these

priests make no objection to the teaching of the Jesuits, they themselves would teach the same moral code. They do not object to the Jesuits because their teaching is unscriptural, but because they are busy bodies, plotters and incessant disturbers of the public peace, and because they wanted to control everyone.

Before it is said or believed that Rome has changed, it would be well to know what Rome is doing to-day. At the urgent solicitation of the late Cardinal Manning and of the Jesuit and Oratory Fathers, and of his own infallible will, the present Pope has canonised the men who defied the authority of their Queen, and one of whom, John Felton, posted a copy of the Bull of Pius V., excommunicating Queen Elizabeth, his lawful sovereign, on the doors of the Bishop of London's palace.

Elizabeth was no longer the Pope's "most dear daughter in Christ." The Bull of "damnation and excommunication of Elizabeth, Queen of England, and her adherents," bore date "5th of the Kalends of March, 1570." The Bull anathematised and excommunicated Elizabeth as a slave of impiety, a heretic and a favourer of heretics. The Pope deposed her, and deprived her of her alleged pretended right to the crown of England, as illegitimate. He absolved all her subjects from their allegiance, and all others from their oaths, and that for ever. He positively enjoined disobedience under penalty of the same anathema and excommunication as were denounced against the Queen, and placed the whole land under his curse and interdict. This was an open declaration of war against England, and the Pope was the aggressor. John Felton, who published the Bull as stated above, was canonised recently for the act, and it is worthy of note that when Pius V., who issued this bull was canonised, one of the "great deeds" for which he was given this honour, was the issue of this bull deposing the lawful Queen of England, and for urging her secret assassination. Romanists declare that these men whom they have so recently canonised were martyrs for their religion, thereby making it the duty of the good Catholic to murder and rebel against their rulers, since the doing of it procures for the doers the highest honours which their Church can pay them.

So many are the inconsistencies of Rome that one is not surprised to find the same canonised Pope at one moment denouncing Queen Elizabeth for allowing married priests, and in the next declaring in no measured language, that his Church was reeking with the impurities of his unmarried priests. In an apostolic letter, addressed to the Archbishop of Saltsburg, Pius wrote "that he had been informed by the best authority on the spot, that the greater part of the beneficed and dignified clergy in Germany, who ought to set the best example without fear of God or man, kept concubines openly, and introduced them into churches and public places like lawful wives, giving them titles of their own dignities and offices; that from the contempt thus brought upon the clergy by themselves, they had lost all authority, and hence the increase of heresy which can never be repressed till the abominable vice of concubinage is extirpated."

It would be impossible to relate here the many plots which the popes and the Jesuits made to assassinate Elizabeth, and to ruin England. That the same treason would be practised to-day were it at all possible, and that it may be made possible and practised ere long, there can be no manner of doubt, since to-day the men who perpetrated these crimes have received the highest honours which the Church can pay them. Before the Church of Rome canonises anyone she makes the most exact and rigorous inquiries as to their life, and the books, if any, which they have written, are all most fully approved down to the most minute particular. In the case of those who "shed their blood for the faith" no such minute inquiry is considered necessary, but it is clear that when the Roman Catholic Church canonises men solely because they were hung for treason, she thereby sets the seal of her highest approval on treason, indeed, she could scarcely do otherwise since Rome claims universal and temporal sovereignty.

It should also be said that treason and assassination were especially taught as a religious duty in Roman Catholic colleges, as, indeed, they are at the present day.

Camden informs us that out of these seminaries (the Jesuit colleges in France and Rome), first a few young men, and then more as they grew up, entering over hastily into holy orders, and being instructed in such principles of doctrine as these, were sent forth into divers parts of England and Ireland to administer (as they pretended) the sacraments of the Romish religion, and to preach. But the Queen and her Council found that they were sent underhand to withdraw the subjects from their allegiance and obedience due to their prince, to bind them by reconciliation to perform the Pope's commandments, to raise intestine rebellions under the seal of confession, and flatly to execute the sentence of Pius Quintus against the Queen.

Evidence of the seditious instruction given to the missioners sent forth from these colleges is furnished by the letter of Cardinal d'Ossat to Henry IV. of France, November 26th, 1601, in which the Cardinal writes that "the chief thing attended to in these colleges is to instil into the youths the belief that the

King of Spain is the rightful heir to the crown of England."

THE GUNPOWDER PLOT—THE REIGN OF JAMES I.

But as all the attempts made during the reign of Elizabeth proved abortive, and as the Jesuits were enraged to madness by the failure of their plots, they saw now that assassination of kings and princes was not so easily accomplished, so they devised a new and horrible scheme for the attainment of their ends. As usual, their plans were laid with consummate cunning. The Provincial of their Order, Henry Garnet, came to England attended by Jesuits chosen with the greatest care for the work. These men disguised themselves in every way possible, so as to escape notice, and to reach and converse with Roman Catholics without detection.

Again they used the confessional for their fell purpose. Though Catholics had then perfect liberty for the exercise of their religion, it was often a matter of some difficulty for them to get confession, as priests were comparatively scarce, and locomotion was then very slow and difficult. Besides, the prestige of the Jesuits made them especially acceptable as confessors, and they did not fail to uphold their own cause, or to extol the special privileges which they had forced or cajoled from the Holy See from time to time. This, then, was their opportunity, and they knew how to use it. Words said in the confessional are viewed by Romanists as veritably and actually said by God himself. How easy then was it to arouse the feelings and inspire the hopes of the kneeling penitent! The one word was, Claim England for Rome. No sin could be committed which would not be pardoned, if the penitent placed himself, and above all his fortune, in the hands of his Jesuit confessor for this purpose. It needs to know something personally of the tremendous power of the Church of Rome to realise the way in which it controls and possesses the bodies and souls of men. No doubt many of these men were very unwilling to embroil their country again in a religious war, above all when there was no question of being deprived of the free exercise of their religion. But what matter; the word of the priest, above all the word of the Jesuit, must prevail, and the consent was given to any measure that might be proposed.

Garnet was attended by other Jesuits, all disguised, and all bent on the same fell design. But there was need for great diplomacy. It was necessary to throw odium on King James, and it is so easy for infallible popes to make and unmake legitimacy, or to make and unmake sin, that it needed only a whisper from the confessor that after all James had no right to the throne, for he was "probably" illegitimate. Not a word, be sure, would have been said on this subject if James had played into the hands of the Jesuits. A candidate was also provided. The Jesuits do not do their work by halves. The king once got rid of, no matter how, it was absolutely necessary to have a substitute ready on the spot, and the substitute was found. The Jesuits, who could make and unmake kings and nobles at their own sweet will, discovered that after all the "rightful" heir to the throne of England, was not James I., but a Lady Arabella Stuart, the daughter of the Earl of Lennox. She was prepared to accept the crown from the Jesuits, and it only needed to assure the Romanists, who wavered, that it really was their duty to see that the right heir "had her own." And then there was the name of Stuart to conjure with, fatal as it has been to its possessors.

It is amazing, and if the subject were not so serious it would be amusing, to see with what consummate skill the Jesuits have hoodwinked the public. How they must rejoice at their success, and what a fund of amusement their dupes must afford them. They ask the deepest sympathy, and too often get it, for men who were hung for treason, who would have been hung or shot for the same crime in any country, but whom they represent as having been martyrs to their religion, because that tells so well, and so effectively with the English public. In modern times the position of our by no means remote ancestors is scarcely understood, subject as they were to continual plots against their liberties and treasons against their Government and Queen.

After a time the "Manchester martyrs" will be proposed for canonisation, and they will be quite as worthy of it. The spies whom the Jesuits sent all through the length and breadth of England, are also represented as suffering for "their faith" when they were discovered and justly punished. These men would simply have been shot on sight if they had attempted such exploits elsewhere. They came to spy out the land for a foreign prince, and to excite, by every means in their power, those who were most inflammable against their lawful rulers. Short work should be made of all this nonsense, and the common sense of the people of this country should be aroused to see its true character. If any English king or queen had acted in a similar manner in regard to the popes who made war on them, how very differently the matter would be represented by Romanists!

And, in the meantime, while all these beguilements are being used to blind honest people, Rome is teaching openly the doctrine of rebellion against lawful kings, and the duty of freeing subjects from their allegiance whenever she pleases to depose a sovereign.

In his "Essays on Religion," Cardinal Manning says: "If, therefore, an heretical prince is elected or succeeds to the throne, the Church [of Rome] has a right to say, 'I annul the election, or I forbid the succession;'" and, again, that "The Pope can inflict temporal punishments on sovereigns for heresy, and deprive them of their kingdoms, and free their subjects from obedience."

There is ample historical evidence that Romanists had almost absolute liberty for the exercise of their religion during the first twelve years of the reign of Queen Elizabeth. Nor were they ungrateful, as they frequently declared. It was not until the restless and evil spirit which possessed the Jesuits had its sway that a renewal of severities was commenced. During the closing years of the life of Elizabeth severe laws were enacted and enforced against the Catholics. But this was an absolute necessity. If the kingdom was to be preserved from a deluge of blood, if Englishmen were to rule their own country and possess their liberties, something needed to be done for their protection from a foreign foe. There is one remarkable difference between the manner in which Protestant and Christian England acted when obliged to prosecute her enemies and the enemies of God, and the way in which Papal and half-pagan Rome acted when she desired to possess herself of these fair realms. We do not find that Englishmen made plots for the assassination of the Pope, or carried on secret war in his country, as he did in England. And such has ever been the marked difference between the action of the children of light and the children of darkness.

Unhappy Ireland! taught and practically governed by papal Rome, has her secret crimes and midnight assassinations, her cruel outrages on dumb animals, her thefts of property. England, too, alas! has her crimes; but they are the crimes of a fallen humanity, and not the crimes of demons.

The death of the brave Elizabeth gave new hopes to the plotters of treason. James I. was believed to be a Catholic at heart. The Jesuits, at least, hoped that he would repay them for all they had done, or tried to do, for his hapless mother, Mary Queen of Scots. But they soon found their mistake. Probably he had seen quite enough of their restless plotting to have learned a lesson which stood him in good stead. He at once issued a decree, by which the Jesuits must still remain abroad, in fact, he placed them in the same position as that in which they had found themselves during the latter part of the reign of Elizabeth. Probably his indolent and easygoing nature made him averse to political broils or secret plottings, and so he took prompt precautions to free himself and his kingdom from those who were sure to embroil it. But he gave a large measure of toleration to English Romanists, who, if they pleased, could have lived as peaceful Englishmen in amity with their fellow countrymen.

There is ample evidence that English Catholics would have been contented and peaceful subjects if they had been left in peace by the ever-restless and ever-plotting Jesuit. But this was not to be. The Jesuits determined on a wholesale massacre of heretics, and acting on the principle so lately and so highly approved by their fathers, they determined to secure a Roman Catholic succession by murdering all the Protestant royal family at one fell blow.

The history of the Gunpowder Plot is so well known that it needs only to be related here in outline. Garnet had made the acquaintance, on the continent, of Robert Catesby, an English Catholic of good family. Catesby was ambitious and ready for revolt. Garnet applied to him on his arrival in England, and induced him to join in the plot. It was necessary to be most circumspect in the selection of his fellow conspirators, so that the number was not complete till the close of the year 1604. Their names were Thomas Percy, a young profligate and spendthrift, but bold even to rashness, from the celebrated family of the Earls of Northumberland; Thomas and Robert Winter, two brothers, who had suffered under the government of Elizabeth; Guido Fawkes, a soldier and formerly an officer in the Spanish service, Francis Tresham and Ambrose Rookwood, both of noble blood, and intimate friends of Catesby; Everard Digby, a man of considerable means and great talents:

Robert Keyes, Christopher Wright, John Grant, and lastly, Tom Bates, a servant of Catesby, just the man for such a purpose, as he had been initiated into his master's secret from the beginning. Still, Catesby considered it well, before the formal commencement of the conspiracy, that this latter, on account of his vacillating scruples of conscience, should be especially schooled by Father Oswald Tesmond.

But the Jesuit leader of the conspiracy found an unexpected difficulty amongst his followers. More humane and more just than he was, when they had realised the enormity of the plan and the fearful loss of life which it must cause, they asked what was to become of so many of their own faith who most certainly would be present at the opening of Parliament, and who must also perish. But the Jesuit would have his end, even if it needed to wade in the blood of his own people to attain it. He assured the unhappy men who hung on his word as on the word of God, that this would be merely the usual fate of battle, that they might be obliged to attack a walled-in city and that many Catholics might suffer as well as the heretics whom they must destroy; and they were satisfied. The word of the priest was all that was needed to make crime a virtue.

But, after all, these men were human. They had, some of them at least, the best instincts of humanity, and these instincts triumphed over their false religion. We shall show later that Garnet was fully cognisant of the plot, and that the only scruples which these unhappy men had were removed by him. They asked if it was right to kill so many of their own faith who would inevitably suffer in the general massacre. But Garnet promptly silenced all their difficulties. Let us give a meed of pity to these victims of a cruel and Christless religion. The conspirators should indeed be condemned and condemned justly for their crime, but our just and most earnest reprobation should be reserved for the Church which urged them to commit it, and which has not only never repented of her evil deed, but rather has at the present day, placed the seal of her highest approval on her dupes by canonising them.

The people of England are indebted to the humanity of one of the conspirators, for deliverance from one of the most horrible plots and outrages which has ever been attempted in the world's history. And yet there are those at the present day who listen with attention to Jesuit fathers who declare that this plot was none of their doing, and then laugh at the folly of the dupes who believe them. The conspirator Tresham was the revealer of the plot. His sister was married to Lord Mounteagle, and Lord Mounteagle would certainly be present at the opening of Parliament, perhaps also Lady Mounteagle might be there. There is ample corroborative evidence to show that the mysterious letter addressed to this nobleman was written by his brother-in-law. This, and this alone, saved England. God alone knows what misery, what bloodshed, what fiendish atrocities would have resulted if the Gunpowder Plot had succeeded.

Everything had been planned to follow up the blow. For the moment Protestant courage might have been crushed when the mangled corpses of the king, the princes, and hundreds of the leading men of the country had been seen lying in their gore in Westminster precincts. But it is quite certain that the shock would have been only temporary, and the reprisals would have been terrible and sure. Who could have blamed the Protestants if, after such a destruction, they had risen up in their strength and enacted a massacre which would have included every Catholic in the land? Yet such a massacre would have been justified if any enemy had adopted such tactics in ordinary warfare.

England was saved, but how near England was to this most awful peril at the hands of Rome should never be forgotten.

The acumen or the fears of the king saved England. The Stuarts were generally fools when their own interests were in question, but they were not without wit in other matters. The result is well known. It

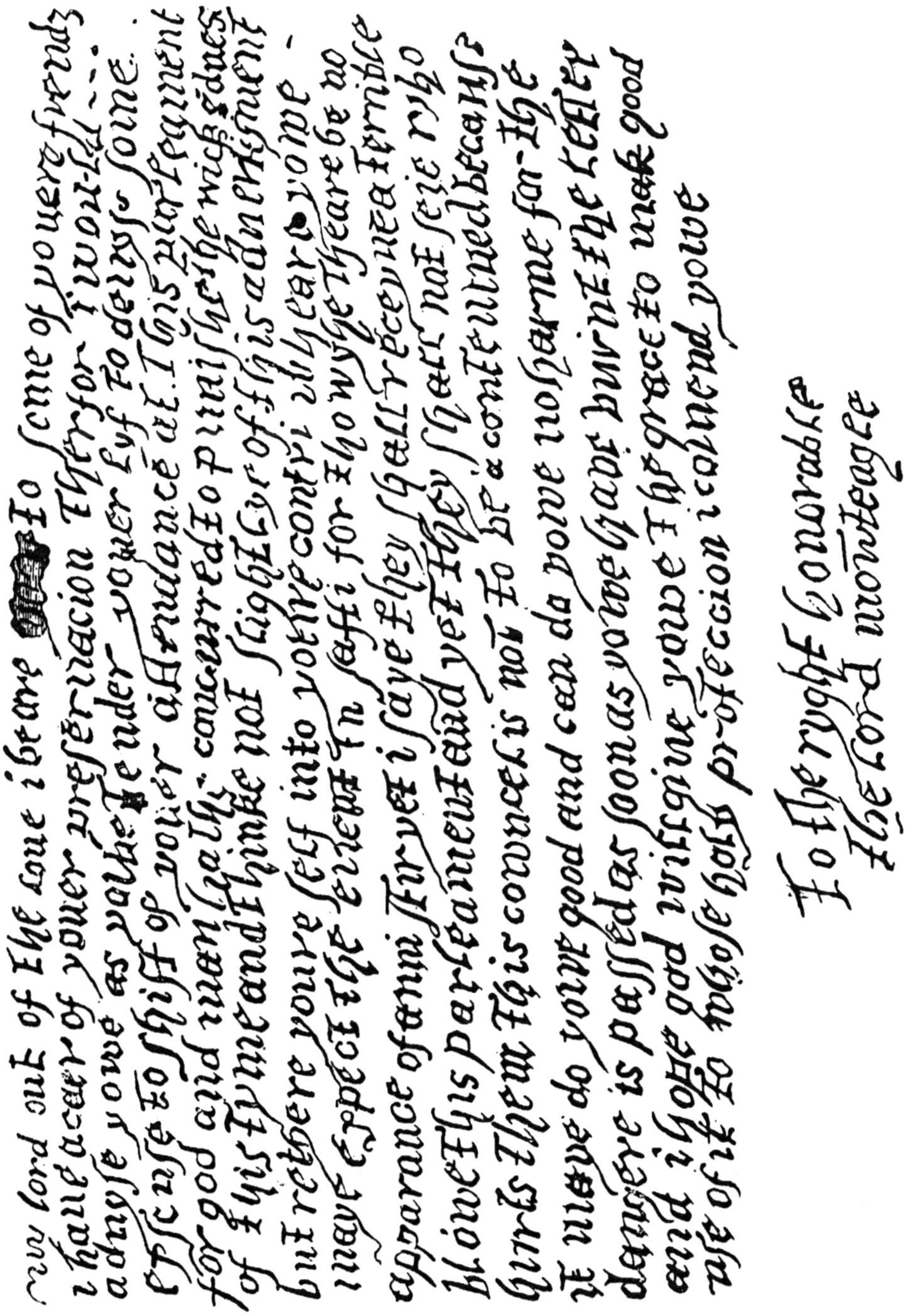
my lord out of the love i beare to some of youere frends
i have a caer of youer preseruacion therfor i would
advyse yowe as yowe tender youer lyf to devyse some
exscuse to shift of youer attendance at this parleament
for god and man hath concurred to punishe the wickednes
of this tyme and thinke not slightlye of this advertisment
but retyere youre self into youre contri wheare yowe
maye expect the event in safti for thowghe theare be no
apparance of anni stir yet i saye they shall receyve a terrible
blowe this parleament and yet they shall not seie who
hurts them this cowncel is not to be contemned because
it maye do yowe good and can do yowe no harme for the
dangere is passed as soon as yowe have burnt the letter
and i hope god will give yowe the grace to mak good
use of it to whose holy proteccion i commend yowe

To the ryght honorable
the lord mowteagle

is a matter of history. It is history which is well known, but which should never be forgotten, though Rome makes useless efforts to conceal her share in this and kindred subjects.

On the night of the 4th of November the vaults were searched, the conspiracy was discovered, and England was saved from the most diabolical plot which the mind of man has ever conceived.

But we shall be told by confiding Protestants and even by worldly minded Christians, that such terrors are impossible at the present day. Can we be sure of this? Has Rome changed? She declares herself solemnly that she cannot change. I admit, however, that one proved fact is worth a thousand assertions. In a serial now publishing, which I do not wish to advertise by giving the name, a plot to murder every Protestant, *i.e.*, every member of Parliament who is not avowedly Roman Catholic, a plot quite as clever and, if possible, more diabolical than the Gunpowder Plot, is openly revealed.

The plotters are named because they have died recently, but they were Irish Roman Catholics. Irish Roman Catholics do not commit deadly crime without the knowledge and full approbation of their "spiritual" guides. God help them, and may God forgive the Christian people who support and encourage this cruel religion.

The Jesuit conspirators did not all escape. The

principal men engaged in the plot were taken alive, but Catesby and several others were killed by the soldiers who were sent to effect their capture, but not until they had suffered themselves from an explosion of gunpowder which took place by accident when they were drying powder. Even these hardened men, when the suffering came to themselves, realised in some slight degree the crime which they had committed. But it was too late to repent even if they had any desire to do so.

The details of the various trials of the conspirators are simply a sickening history of equivocation and subterfuge. Each was anxious to know what had been revealed by the other, and each made admissions however trifling, which, when compared, helped to the utter condemnation of all.

But here we must observe the wide difference between these trials and the practices of the Inquisition. The prisoners were all allowed to speak in their own defence. The Jesuit Garnet especially took considerable advantage of this permission. It is true that torture was used in some cases in the Tower, but this was the evil custom of the age, which had been introduced by the Roman Catholic Church and persistently practised by the Inquisition. It is remarkable how easily Protestants are led astray on this subject. Rome demands the utmost sympathy from them for those who were tortured in this and other cases, but Rome smiles grimly when she does so, knowing that she first introduced these cruelties, and that she practised them as no other church ever did. Where or when has she ever expressed her sympathies with her victims?

A word must be said about Tresham, the betrayer of the plot. In order if possible to save himself he blamed and accused the conspirators one after another, and especially included the Jesuit Garnet. But as he lay dying, such is the power of Rome and the terrible fear which it impresses on its followers, he dictated a letter which he gave to his wife to deliver to the Earl of Salisbury after his death, in which he retracted what he had said of Garnet, and swore "on his salvation" that Garnet knew nothing of the plot and moreover that he had not seen him for "sixteen years before." He swore too much, for there was already undeniable proof that he had frequent intercourse with Garnet, and that he had stayed at Tresham's house in Northamptonshire, a few days before the discovery of the plot.

"This is the fruit of equivocation," writes Sir Edward Coke to Lord Salisbury, "to affirm manifold falsehoods upon his salvation when he was in *articulo mortis*." When Tresham was apprehended, a book, which he had apparently well studied, was found in his desk entitled, "A Treatise of Equivocation," an alteration on the title page in Garnet's handwriting was found, which ran thus: "A Treatise against Lying and Fraudulent Dissimulation." This book was published at the close of the reign of Queen Elizabeth. No doubt Garnet's equivocal title was well adapted to induce honest people to read this dishonest book, and perhaps to lead them to appreciate practically the advice which it gave.

Even from a worldly point of view honesty is the best policy, for the Jesuits have failed again and again in their most important undertakings, and have not even gained the ends which they sought in such an evil fashion.

Digby, Winter, Grant and Bates, were executed at the same time and place. Digby said he had committed no offence against his religion, which was true: but what a religion it is which justifies and indeed requires such crimes. Winter never asked mercy of "God or the King." According to his religion he had committed no offence against God and none against the king. Grant excused himself also on the ground of "conscience" and religion. Bates asked forgiveness of God and the king, and said what was probably true, that he had been led into the plot from love to his master.

The next day, Winter the "younger," Rookwood, Keyes, and Guido Fawkes, were executed, and no doubt all these men will be canonised later by the Church which they served so well. Winter expressed some regret for his crime, but declared his faith in the religion which had practically obliged him to commit it. Rookwood spoke in much the same manner. Keyes did not attempt any excuse, and was followed by Guido Fawkes, who seemed somewhat sorry for his crime; and so ended life in this world for the tools of the Jesuits.

One and all were inspired by the same idea, that they were meriting heaven by attempting the murder of a whole nation in their representatives. Their descendants have at least the consolation of knowing that the Church, in whose interest they suffered so cruelly, has shown, even at the present day, her high appreciation of their efforts, by placing the seal of her highest approval on their conduct. Surely they have the best encouragement which their Church can give for any attempt, however diabolical, which may be made at the present day to alter the succession to the throne of England.

The one great object of these unhappy men seems to have been to screen the men who taught them to murder from the consequences of their crime But one and all admitted that both the Jesuit Garnet and the Jesuit Greenway knew all the plans of the conspirators "under the seal of confession." Now a great deal has been made of the sacredness of the seal of confession, and even Protestants have been taken in by the idea that it is a question of honour.

They say, naturally, as honourable English gentlemen, these priests are to be respected because they will not betray such a sacred confidence. This is all very fair they say, if we are to have confession we must have secrecy. But there is another and a very grave side to this question which is quite overlooked; one word of disapproval from the priest would at once put an end to such plots. Let us take an example. When Guido Fawkes, or Digby, or any of the conspirators went to confession to their Jesuit guides, one word of disapproval from the priest would have at once put an end to the whole matter. When any of the Irish "invincibles" went to confession, as all such men admit they have done before committing crimes, one word from the priest would prevent the murder. But the priest never says the word, and the priest gives absolution, and the men know that the work which they have taken in hand has the blessing, and even the highest encouragement of the Church, and hence they believe of God.

Hence the excuse of the priest that he cannot reveal plots which have been told to him in the secrecy of confession is a mere pretence. He knows them, he could prevent them with a word. He is therefore not only guilty in an ordinary sense, but he is guilty in the highest sense, for he places the seal of the Divine approval as far as it is in his power to do so on the most deadly crime. He may blind a confiding public with the supposed high sense of honour, but he cannot deceive the Almighty.

A man who will not prevent deadly crime when he could do so with a word, is far more guilty than the hapless wretches who have committed it.

Garnet was tried at the Guildhall, London, on March 28th, 1606. Never had criminal a fairer trial. A special commission was appointed, amongst whom were the following noblemen and gentlemen: The Lord Mayor of London, the Earls of Nottingham, Suffolk, Worcester, Northampton, and Salisbury, the Lord Chief Justice of England, and several judges and aldermen. The king and many of the nobility were present secretly. The charge was high treason. Garnet having objected to one of the jurors, he was at once removed. How very differently would a Protestant have been treated in the Inquisition! How very differently would Garnet himself have been treated if he had offended his own society! In that case there would have been no trial, and no defence, for life and death then hung without trial or inquiry, on the word of the General.

Garnet's defence, if such it can be called, was one continued tissue of equivocation, and of excuses for equivocation. The matter was after all very simple, though he was obliged to cloud it with as much verbage as possible to deceive the public. He had committed the crime of treason according to law and justice; but as this crime was an act of the highest virtue, according to the teaching, then and now, of the church to which he belonged, he considered himself justified not only in committing it, but also in denying it. The full details of his trial were published at the time. We had purposed to have given large extracts from it, but space will not admit, and they would not be of interest to the general reader. Some valuable documents concerning it have "disappeared" from public offices, the only wonder is that so many have remained.

Garnet was executed on May 3rd, 1606, not for his religion, except in so far as in the exercise of it he committed treason, and gave his sanction and encouragement to a vile and cruel crime. Sir Dudley Charleton said in a letter still preserved, that he doubted not that Garnet "would equivocate on the gallows, but that he would be hanged without equivocation."

It should be noticed here that Garnet was accused of having had improper intercourse with a Mrs. Anne Vaux, and that he denied this on the scaffold, but of what avail were his denials. Whether he was falsely accused or not, it is at least certain that she followed him everywhere, and that they had a very close correspondence and friendship. It was also remarked by those who were near him on the scaffold that he appeared very much frightened, and that his prayers were uttered with little apparent devotion, and were chiefly addressed to the Virgin Mary. There was no earnest expression of hope in the love or mercy of God, nor of love for Christ or desire to go to Him.

By the king's command he was left hanging from the gallows until he was dead; a merciful deed, considering how Garnet had prepared so cruel a death for his lawful sovereign.

The usual story of miraculous events was got up after his death. A youth, named Wilkenson, declared that he visited the place of Garnet's execution for the purpose of finding a relic, and naturally did find one. This was a bit of straw, on which the appearance of a man's face was rudely pictured, and which was reputed to have been done miraculously. Probably this relic was neither more nor less genuine than the "straws" which were venerated in Belgium for some time, which the poor people were assured had been taken from the bed on which the Pope was obliged to be when put in prison by Victor Emmanuel, his cruel persecutor.

THE MASSACRE OF ST. BARTHOLOMEW.

The story of the Massacre of St. Bartholomew must be briefly told. In the whole history of Christendom never was such an outrage perpetrated. It is idle to say that it had not the approval of the Pope. There is too much evidence to the contrary.

The teaching of the Church of Rome is so plain and clear on the subject of equivocation that no Roman Catholic can be believed on his most solemn oath on any subject whatsoever, and denials are of little avail when facts are opposed to them. No wonder that Rome has special men trained to write for the Press of this country, and to supply the leading magazines with essays and articles teaching insidiously her own views on all subjects, especially on history. No wonder that she depreciates the late professor of history in Oxford. Mr. Froude was far too honest, and made too many revelations which disclosed facts that Rome would fain have hid, to obtain even her toleration. Ere long she will have the Protestant universities of England in the hands of her own professors, since the thin end of the wedge has been put in, and when those who have been accepted by Protestants as "liberal Roman Catholics" shall have served her turn, she will replace them by others who will teach all she desires.

The Massacre of St. Bartholomew was carefully and deliberately planned. The object was simply the extermination of the Protestants of France, men who had fought for their country and loved it. The bloody plot was arranged by Catherine de Medici and the Duke of Alva. These worthies met at Bayonne, in the south of France, in the year 1565;

and while they amused the public with games, they spent their own time planning the murder of their defenceless subjects, whose only crime was that they loved God better than the Pope, and that they worshipped Christ and looked to Him alone for salvation, instead of to the Church and the Virgin. The Pope wrote to Catherine, "It is only by the entire extermination of Protestants that the Roman Catholic religion can be restored completely." Henry of Bearn, subsequently Henry IV., and then a little child, who it was supposed was too young to understand what was said, overheard and remembered a sentence in the conversation of the plotters. "The head of one salmon is worth that of ten thousand frogs;" this he repeated to his governor, who at once suspected danger, and warned the Protestant party without delay, the result being that the massacre had to be deferred. But it was only deferred. A wedding took place in the cathedral of Notre Dame, in Paris, on the 18th August, 1572. This was part of the plot. Protestants were invited, who came, suspecting no evil, when Margaret of France and Henry of Bearn were united in holy wedlock Jeanne d'Albret, mother of the bridegroom, was a noted Protestant, but in a week's time she died with every appearance of having been poisoned.

The massacre commenced at daybreak on Sunday,

August 24th, 1572. The unfortunate King, Charles IX., hesitated long before he would consent to the crime, but his mother and the priests were too strong for him. Lest he might relent at the last moment, and forbid the savage act, the queen-mother had the signal given an hour earlier than the time which had been decided on. The brave and noble Admiral Coligny was the first victim, and then the fiendish butchers waded in the blood of the best, the noblest, the purest men and women of France. So well had the plot been arranged, and so far in advance, that even the Protestant troops had been removed from Paris on a specious pretence.

Nor was the massacre confined to Paris. The same bloody deed was enacted all over France, so that it was estimated that some 70,000 persons perished. Charles, it is said, became maddened by the sight of the rivers of blood which flowed before his eyes at the very gates of his palace, and then himself shot down his faithful and loyal subjects who fled to him hoping they might find mercy at his feet.

But God's retribution was to come. In less than two years after the massacre Charles was stricken down by an illness, which the most indifferent admitted to be a just judgment. He died in agonies of remorse, crying out perpetually, "Blood, blood." And blood poured from all the pores of his body until at the last it gushed from his mouth, and so he died.

Not all the consolations of the Church, for which he had committed one of the blackest crimes in history, could save him from despair. There is deep in the heart of every man a conscience which tells him what is good and what is evil, and that conscience will speak. The unhappy king was but in the twenty-fifth year of his age when he came to this miserable end. Nor did his inhuman mother fare better. She died at Blois some years after her son, universally execrated and hated.

In Rome great rejoicings took place at the success of this diabolical massacre. The messenger who took the dispatch received a reward of 1000 gold crowns. Cannon was fired from St. Angelo, bonfires lighted, and, Pius V. being then dead, Pope Gregory XIII. went in great state to the church of St. Mark to return thanks to God for so great a blessing to the Roman Catholic Church. Over the portico of the church a cloth was hung on which the Papal share in the guilt of Charles IX. was directly acknowledged in letters of gold, stating that the massacre had occurred after "counsels had been given." Thrice the Pope went in state with all the Cardinals and foreign Ambassadors then in Rome to return thanks to God for the massacre. He caused medals to be struck in commemoration, and the Vatican to be decorated with paintings representing the murder of Coligny and his friends.

Now with regard to this medal a word must be said. Romanists, however much they may glory in the massacre, know well that it is something which tells against them in the minds of all honest men, hence they wish to clear the Pope of all complicity in the matter as far as possible. To this end, they have strenuously denied that the Pope ordered this medal to be struck, and as many copies of it as possible have been destroyed. But facts are the best argument. One copy remains at present in the British Museum. I have seen that medal, and compared it with a fac-simile which I possess. The initials of the name of the maker of the medal are on it, he was a well known artist of the time and age. If it be said that the Pope did not order the casting of the medal, and it should be remembered that the Pope was then both spiritual and temporal king of Rome and the Italian States, is there anyone who will dare to say that such a medal could have been struck without his full permission ? The doer of such a deed would have soon found himself in the Inquisition.

But there is yet another, and if possible a stronger proof that the "Church" approved the crime. We find in the lately published life of Cardinal Manning the following statement:—

"It is, therefore, undeniable that the Pontiffs were morally within their right in the Crusades, the Armada, and in the condemnation of boycotting and the Plan of Campaign."—"Life of Manning," vol. II., p. 625.

Why then should they not have been "within their rights" in approving this wholesale massacre of Protestants?

THE REVOCATION OF THE EDICT OF NANTES.

On this subject we do not propose to enter here, except so far as to show that it was directly the act of the Jesuits. The letter in the appendix will prove this past dispute. The Jesuit in the confessional, and the Jesuit as director, has never failed in doing what he believes to be his duty. Who is there who will not give a meed of pity to the hapless princes who believed in them, and submitted to their dictation like whipped hounds? The pity of it is that to-day these men are invited to England and encouraged there, and their pupils are given the first places of trust and importance in this country.

CHAPTER XII.

THE SUPPRESSION OF THE JESUITS BY CLEMENT XIV.

The Jesuits suppressed.—Cardinal Ganganelli's ambition to be made Pope.—The Spanish king promises to support his claim if he will suppress the Jesuits.—Sevrious complaints against them from kings, nobles, and the general public.—They are denounced severely by the secular clergy.—Called "a public plague."—What Clement XIV. said of them.—He was slow in fulfilling his election pledges.—The Spanish king offers to send troops to protect him.—Nothing can protect him from poison.—Cardinal Bellarmine's threat.—The Pope prepares the bull of condemnation with great care.—He signs it.—He cries in agony that he has signed his death warrant.—Evidence that he was done to death by slow poison.—How the Jesuits exulted in his death.

THERE are few more remarkable events in the history of the Church of Rome, than that of the suppression of the Jesuits. Popes may be infallible in the eyes of their subjects, but infallibility has its difficulties, however infallibilists may gloss them over for the benefit of the unbeliever. That one infallible pope should have established the Jesuits, that another should have denounced them as utterly unworthy to exist, and that a third should have reinstated them in all their ancient privileges, is, shall we say a political, or a theological puzzle, which we are not able to solve. They all differed on a most important subject, they all made *ex cathedrà* declarations, which flatly contradicted each other, but they were all right, and all equally infallible.

At present, we have only to inquire into the facts connected with the suppression of the Jesuits.

Although Spain was the cradle of the Order, and the native place of its founder, and of some of its most famous men, Spain has not been over anxious for its continuance. The Order has always shown itself far too much concerned with politics, and its own temporal advancement, to meet with the approval of statesmen. When Cardinal Ganganelli was, shall we say negotiating for, or praying for, the triple tiara, it was very important for him to secure the vote and interest of the Spanish Cardinals. The Spanish king was very anxious to get the Jesuits out of his dominions, if not to abolish them altogether. There were indeed complaints of them on all sides. It would seem that there could not be peace where the Jesuit had power.

This is no mere "Protestant" calumny. We give Roman Catholic evidence for the above statement :—

At the close of the 16th century the parish priests of Paris preferred a formal indictment against the

Jesuits, with a prayer for their removal, because they put the Pope above the General Councils, and proclaiming there was no bound to his power; put themselves above bishops; supplanted the parish clergy; trampled under foot Gallican liberties; claimed for the Pope the right to excommunicate kings, interfere in state affairs, and call the temporal power to his aid; and above all, because they corrupted by their doctrines, and taught their pupils the lawfulness of regicide.

In the year 1700 an assembly of the Roman Catholic clergy of France passed unanimously a sentence of the severest censure upon the lax morality of the Jesuits, and especially on the pernicious character of their doctrine of probabilism.

Pope Clement XI., in spite of his known sympathy with the Society, censured the Jesuits for having sanctioned the use by their converts in China, of a combination of the superstitions of Confucius with the ordinances of Christianity.

The theological faculty of the Sorbonne censured the conduct of the Society as "false, rash, scandalous, contrary to the Word of God, and subversive of the Christian faith and religion," which sentence was ratified by the Pope.

Lavalette, the head of the Order in France, being brought into Court for irregularities in regard to his financial operations in 1762, the Society in the trial were obliged to produce their "Constitutions." When these, which had been heretofore hidden from all eyes except their own, became known, intense indignation against the Society was aroused. Louis XV. sent a letter to Ricci, the General of the Order at Rome, and also to the popes, asking that the Statutes be amended.

But the condemnation of the Order by Pietro Sarpi, the Roman Catholic historian of the Council of Trent, is as important and reliable as that of the many popes who have denounced their teaching and practices. He says: "They are a public plague, and the plague of the world," and that "the education of the Jesuits consists in releasing the pupil of every obligation to his father, to his country, and to his natural prince. From the Jesuit colleges there never is sent a pupil obedient to his father, devoted to his country, loyal to his prince."

Pope Clement XIV. in his famous Bull of July 21st, 1773, suppressing the Jesuits, whilst giving the grounds of his condemnation of the Society, witnesses to the following facts:—

1. "That thousands of complaints against that religious community were laid before our predecessors, upheld by the authority of some princes."

2. "That the very bosom of the Society of Jesus was torn to pieces by internal and external dissensions."

The Spanish Cardinals were politicians, as Cardinals will be. They had not much faith in verbal promises, and wanted things in writing, and took care to get what they wanted. Cardinal Ganganelli had already secured French interest; he now secured that of the Spaniards. He wrote a letter in which he declared that the "Sovereign Pontiff might abolish the Jesuits without violating the canonical regulations." In fact, as we have said elsewhere, it is difficult to know what the Pope cannot do infallibly, or undo, infallibly. Happy popes! And yet, and yet, "uneasy lies the head which wears a crown," and the Pope after all wears three.

Cardinal Ganganelli was made pope by the votes of the Spanish and French Cardinals. No one seemed greatly concerned as to what share the Holy Spirit of God had in the election, though professionally and ceremoniously His influence was invoked.

Ganganelli took the title of Clement XIV., but, like many another politician, he was slow in fulfilling his election pledges. Constituents may be put off or trifled with, but kings, especially when they are very much in earnest, have unpleasant methods of enforcing their demands. The Spanish king expected his protégé to keep his word, pope and all as he was. The pope, pope and all as he was, did not like to keep his word. Poor pope; but, pope and all as he was, he was none the less afraid of the Jesuits. They have unpleasant ways of revenging themselves on those who interfere with their affairs. But Charles would not be gainsaid.

The Spanish king was firm; he was something in the position of an Irish landlord. If his agent was shot for enforcing his commands it would be a pity; but then he could get another, and he must have his rents. If the Pope was removed another pope could always be got, but the Jesuits were very much in the way and could not be "removed" individually, so they must be got rid of altogether.

The Pope had made a promise, and in writing, too (alas! poor pope), and the pope was expected to keep his election pledges. Charles offered to land troops at Civita Vecchia for his protection. Of what use? All the troops in Spain, or, for that part of the matter, in Europe, could not save him from poison, and poison was then so easily and freely administered. At length the Pope had to yield; but, to his credit it must be said, he did not do so without long and careful deliberation.

After all, Pope Clement decided that, if he must die for his deed of daring, he would die like an honest man, and he deserves the respect of posterity. The celebrated historian Griesinger, says: "The Pope who ventured to censure the Order of

Jesus undertook an act of far greater daring than a warrior who placed his cannon against them in a field of battle; while, too, every representative of Christ on earth who had contemplated anything of the kind before—I call to remembrance among the Popes, Sixtus V., Clement VIII., and Innocent XIII.—had been quickly removed from the face of the earth." There are certainly some remarkable coincidences as regards the premature decease of popes who had interfered with, or attempted to control, the "Society."

Sixtus V. had died, as Cretineau Joli says, "quite *à propos* for the Company," just as he was planning material changes in its rules and in its designation. In the Brief Clement XIV. makes significant allusion to "the salutary project" of Sixtus V., in regard to the Order failing of effect owing "to his premature death." Clement VIII. died when ready to pronounce sentence against the Jesuit Molina, whose cause had been warmly advocated by the General Acquaviva. Fuligati relates in his "Life of Cardinal Bellarmine," that Cardinal Francis del Monte having spoken to Bellarmine of the Pope's resolution to condemn the doctrine of Molina, the latter replied, "I know he wishes it, and I acknowledge he can do it; but I say he will never do it, and if he attempts it, he will die first." The Jesuit Cellot, who also reports this fact, extols this prediction of Bellarmine as a true prophecy, inspired by the Holy Spirit, and he carefully attests its accomplishment in 1605, when Clement VIII. was about to publish his censure of Molina's Book. [Vita Bellarmin. Leodii, 1626, Lib. vi., Cap. vii.]. Innocent XIII. died suddenly when planning the suppression of the Order. Innocent XIII., on the 13th September, 1723, solemnly declared the Jesuit Missionaries in China guilty of idolatry, of rebellion against the Holy See, and of profanation of the name of God. This act was the occasion of the General Tamburini's addressing a *Memoire* to the Pope, which was, without contradiction, the most hypocritical that can be imagined. On receiving this document, it is said that Innocent XIII. determined to abolish the Jesuits, but he died two months after, in 1724. Benedict XIV., after signing a Brief for its reformation on the 1st April, 1758, died on the May 2nd following.

No document could have been worded more plainly, no document could have been issued with more deliberation than this papal Bull which suppressed the Jesuits "for ever." If ever Peter spoke from the chair of Peter, he spoke by the mouth of Pope Clement XIV., when he denounced in scathing language the iniquities which had made this act of papal censure imperative on the head of the Papal church. It was no wonder that the Pope was deliberate: it was no wonder that the Pope was afraid.

Though bearing the date July 21st, 1773, it was not at that time made public. The Pope, first of all, wished that its contents might be proved to be correct, and on that account nominated a Commission or Congregation, consisting of Cardinals Corsini, Marefoschi, Caraffa, Zelada, and Casoli, of the Prelates Macedonio and Albani, and, lastly, of two celebrated theologians, Brother Mamachi, a Dominican, and Brother Christopher de Monferrate, a Franciscan. They assembled daily with the Pope, and went over the contents of the brief word by word; each of them, however, was solemnly pledged not to divulge a single syllable as to their transactions. On the 16th of August the Pope signed the Bull, which, from the words with which it began, received the title *Dominus ac Redemptor noster*.

Some one has said, "Oh, liberty, how many crimes have been committed in thy name?" Have Christians even realised how many evils have been committed or sanctioned in the name of Christ.

It seems scarcely needful to quote from this famous Bull. Its validity has never been disputed and if papal infallibility means anything it is still in force. If popes can contradict each other on points of doctrine, morals, and politics, when does infallibility speak?

The Bull concludes thus:—"We forbid that this Bull shall be censured, impugned, invalidated, retracted, brought to law or controversy, or taken to the courts of law; and we forbid that there shall be obtained against it any act restoring matters to their original position, any re-trial, any bringing of the case into the courts of law, or any other remedy of law, of fact, of favour, or of justice; and if any such remedy should by any means whatever be conceded or obtained, we forbid anyone to use it, or to avail himself of it, either in a court of justice or out of it; but we ordain that this present Bull shall always and perpetually be, and continue to be, valid, firm, and effective, and shall have and obtain its full and complete results, and shall be inviolably observed by all and every one whom it affects or will in any way affect in future."

If ever any deed was done with calm, earnest, and may we not say Christian deliberation, surely this act of Pope Clement XIV. was thus accomplished. What makes the matter so important, is, that he refers to all the decisions of previous popes who had in vain tried to reform the Society, and to the complaints of so many kings and princes who had declared that they could have no peace in their dominions while the Jesuits existed. Lust of gain, and the insatiable greed of power were but too obviously the one end of the Jesuit. It is, as we have said before, no Protestant voice which has condemned them, it is the voice of the Universal Church of which they even proclaimed themselves the special defenders. Yet, strange to say, with all their profession of deference to popes and prelates, they seem to have taken special pleasure in acting in open defiance of their commands. Even Bellarmine, the admired of many Protestants, used language which can only be described as threatening when submission to the decisions of a pope was in question.

We can well believe with what a terrible sense of responsibility the Pope signed this document. He did not indeed know that he was personally infallible, but he did know the awful power with which his Church has invested her pontiffs. Even the wording of this document shows his deep sense of responsibility and his conscientiousness.

And he had but too good reasons for personal fear. He had done and dared what none of his predecessors would have attempted; he knew the penalty and paid for it.

When he had placed his signature to the fateful document he cried out in the agony of his soul, *Sotto scriviamo la nostra morte,* "I have signed my death warrant." The signature was made on July 23rd, 1773. On September 27th, 1774, he died. There is strong contemporary evidence that he died of slow poison. From the day on which he signed the Bull he faded away. His sufferings were terrible, and almost intolerable. His life was one long agony of physical torture. One thing is certain, he could at any moment have recalled the condemnation of the Jesuits, but he did not recall it. 'Perhaps it was a nobler courage which enabled him to persevere to the end in an act of duty under such pressure, than to have signed it.

Strange to say, a Protestant historian has discredited the belief that Clement was poisoned. That it was contradicted at the time, would of course be expected. The question is simply what contemporary evidence is there for the assertion? And this evidence is abundant and reliable.

Report is not always reliable, but the fact that such reports were current while the Pope lay dying, and were credited by ambassadors and statesmen, is an indirect evidence. In such a case, probably, there never could be actual proof, but there is such a thing as circumstantial evidence, and in this case the circumstantial evidence is strong. Cardinal de Bernis, the French ambassador to Rome, wrote to his government that the Pope had been poisoned, and that the Pope had declared openly that he was assured that he had been given poison. Don Monino, the Spanish ambassador, wrote to his government to the same effect. It is surprising, considering the secret fear which was felt everywhere for the Jesuit, that anyone should have dared to speak openly on this subject. The physicians of the Pope declared that they could not find any symptoms of poisoning. They may have been right, but at the time secret poisoning was a fine art, and the desired end could be attained without any possibility of discovering the means by which it had been effected. Besides, the physicians may have been in the secret. One thing is certain, the Pope suffered the most terrible agony from the date of the promulgation of the Bull until the hour of his release by death.

Prophecies of that event were very freely made by women of reputed sanctity. The mystic letters P.S.S.V. appeared suddenly on walls and in every public place. They were explained to mean *Presto sede sara vacante*, The Papal chair will soon be vacant.

But the strongest evidence of Jesuit complicity may be found in the conduct of the Jesuits themselves. And here again we avail ourselves exclusively of Roman Catholic authority. The Abbé Guettèe (Hist. des Jesuits, iii. 303), says : "They displayed the most lively joy at his illness and death, and spread abroad rumours about his last moments as horrible as they were absurd. They would have it believed that God had punished him by a horrible malady for the measure he had taken against the Company. The affection with which they spoke of this malady gave more consistency to the report which imputed to them the poisoning of the Pope. They have been too habituated to acts of this nature for these suspicions to be rejected as ill-founded, even though the accusation has not been juridically proved."

The Jesuits were restored to some of their ancient privileges by Pope Pius VIII. by the *Bull Solicitudo Omnium Ecclesiœum*, but they were far from being satisfied. It is observable that Pius VIII. does not in any way deny the accusations against those whom his predecessor so solemnly condemned.

On July 13th, 1886, the Brief *Dolemus inter alia* Pope Leo XIII. reinstated them in the canonical status which they had held previous to the suppression in 1773, restoring all the privileges withheld by Pius VII., when he re-established the Order in 1814. The Jesuits are by this Brief exempted completely from all jurisdiction, supervision, and control of bishops, archhishops, and ordinaries; they may occupy any pulpit; teach and found professional chairs; hear confessions, read mass, and administer the sacraments everywhere, without the consent of the local clergy or of the bishop; they have full power given them to act as they wish, uncontrolled by either the secular or ecclesiastical power; their estates and possessions are free from any tithes, taxes, or dues whatever; and ecclesiastical and secular powers are warned, under the penalty of excommunication, not to hinder or disturb them in the exercise of the privileges conferred on them. They have, in fact, full power given to them to act as they please, unrestrained by either ecclesiastical or secular authority.

The Roman correspondent of the *Times* (August 23rd, 1886), stated that it was reported that Leo XIII. was driven to this by poison, that he endured three days of severe illness, and then did what was required of him.

CHAPTER XIII.

THE JESUIT IN THE CONFESSIONAL—THE FLOGGING MANIA OF THE MIDDLE AGES.

THE JESUIT IN THE CONFESSIONAL—THE FLOGGING MANIA OF THE MIDDLE AGES.—The Confessional.—The Romanist is followed by the confessor from the cradle to the grave.—Every subject is discussed and decided there.—All the affairs of life controlled.—Children terrified.—*Hell opened to Christians.*—Books to terrify children.—A man-made religion.—How Rome influences Protestants.—It is a system of organised and deliberate deceit.—Why the Jesuits make confession easy.—Cardinal Manning afraid of the Jesuits.—The Jesuits denounced for their immoral teaching by the French Roman Catholic clergy again and again.—Denounced for practising idolatry by Romanist bishops.—Caught in their own trap.—Denounced for interfering in politics.—The flogging mania of the middle ages. How the Jesuits were concerned in it.—Catherine de Medici practised it on her court ladies.—Cruelties and immoralities the result.

THERE is no subject of such importance as that of which we are about to treat. In the Roman Catholic Church every one, from the trembling child to the aged and feeble man and woman, is obliged to confess if he hopes for eternal salvation. What a terrible bondage, what an awful crime. And all this must be done and suffered at the dictates of a church which, after all, has confessed herself very doubtful if her priests really possess the "orders," without which they cannot absolve. Enough has been said on that subject, but it is of such grave importance that we would ask the reader again to glance at the pages in which the question is discussed. If all this pain, if all this shame, if all this agony has to be endured for nothing, what shall be said of those who inflict it? and they know, as few of their penitents know, that the probabilities are against them.

It is no wonder that Rome discourages investigation, and silences thought as a deadly crime. No wonder that she falsifies history, that she dreads honest biography, that she dares not be true. Truth would be her death-blow. But for us, shall we submit to her commands, and bow before her dicta? Shall we do all that in us lies, as so many are doing at the present day, to support such a system, or shall we do all that in us lies to defeat it?

The moral, or rather the immoral teaching, of the confessional has been a subject of much discussion, and perhaps has had more exposure than any other subject connected with the Church of Rome. This system is necessary for Rome, and it is one of the notes against her that it should be so.

Perhaps only those who have had a large experience of the system can understand all its evils. It is obviously true that there must be a serious moral contamination to both the priest and the penitent, but this is by no means the only evil. One important point has been somewhat overlooked by those who have treated of it, that point is the question of direction. This touches every affair of life, and is the real source of the power of the Church of Rome. We commence, however, with the question of confession as far as it is merely the confession of sin.

And first, in order to understand the power of Rome, in this and all else, we must try to realise the fact that Roman Catholics believe in the power of the priest to forgive sin, as truly and absolutely as we believe in the power of Christ. We must remember that from the very dawn of reason the Roman Catholic child is taught to look on the priest practically as a god, whose word is absolute, whose power is Divine. The confessional is repulsive to every Catholic, not because it is always a source of evil of a certain kind, but because human nature shrinks from exposing its faults and foibles to any human creature. Hence it has been necessary to make the confessional a source of absolute obligation under the most terrible penalties. Better, cries the priest, to be ashamed here than to be ashamed for all eternity. Hence it is that the priest insists on the child going to confession at the very earliest age possible. No child, they say, is too young to be damned (and horrible stories are told to children to frighten them on this subject), so no child is too young to go to confession. The chain is wound round the soul at such an early age that its power is not realised, and, in some cases, at least, the chain is never broken.

A book called " Hell Opened to Christians," was published in Ireland some years ago, but was withdrawn from circulation for a time at least, in consequence of the exposure of its horrible teaching by Protestants. The tortures which even children of seven years of age endured in hell because they would not go to confession, were described with all the realism of a Dante.

In the " Examination of Conscience, etc." by Liguori, we read : " Tell me, my sister, if in punishment of not confessing a certain sin, you were to be burnt alive in a cauldron of boiling pitch ; and if, after that, your sin was to be revealed to all your relatives and neighbours, would you conceal it ? You certainly would not conceal it, if you knew that by confessing it your sin should remain secret, and that you should escape being burnt alive. Now, it is more than certain that, unless you confess that sin, you shall have to burn in hell for all eternity ; and that on the day of judgment it shall be made known to the whole human race."

How far all this man-made religion is from the pure Gospel of Christ we need not say, the Eternal God cannot be unjust, and it would be a ghastly injustice when the penalty of sin has been once for all paid in blood to exact it again. This is one of the many things which makes the system of Rome so derogatory to the Majesty of Heaven.

But the power which the confessional places in the hands of the Church is almost inconceivable. Rome claims the right to decide on every question of family relationship, on every event in life, on every change of state, on every political and social matter. Rome rules with a vengeance terrible to its subjects, and beyond compare dangerous to every human being who can be reached by her influence. She forbids all intercourse with heretics where and when she dare, she regulates all intercourse with heretics where she cannot forbid it. Which is the more dangerous to the public peace it would be difficult to say. Intercourse, even at the present day, and in this free country, is absolutely and sternly forbidden with those who have left the Church. A word of explanation might be said, a question might be asked, that would arouse a doubt, hence there must be no possibility of such a danger. How weak the Church of Rome is with all her boasted strength. The weakest saint can face all the world with Christ, but Rome is afraid of the poorest child, if that child has been taught a pure religion, and can read the Bible.

So far-reaching is the influence and power of Rome

to-day even in England, that we have known Protestants who have declined any social intercourse with those who have left the Church of Rome, because it might offend their Roman Catholic friends. Thus Rome obtains added strength from those who, if they were asked solemnly, do they desire to see the fires of Smithfield re-lit, would declare they could not imagine such an event possible. Yet Rome has declared openly and plainly that she does desire such a consummation.

There is one of many points to be noted about the confessional, and that is that it is a system of deliberate deceit. Apart from the consideration of a certain class of moral evil, on which we do not propose to touch here more than briefly, there is the question of deliberate deceit, and in this matter the Jesuits are the chief offenders.

The object of the Jesuits has been to attract to the confessional by making confession easy, and this has been done in two ways. First, confession has been made easy by giving the lightest possible penances for even grievous sins, and by having a "moral" code which make the most grievous sin appear as a mere bagatelle. The Jesuit books published with authority for the use of confessors, prove this beyond question, and it is indeed lamentable that English gentlemen, who once prided themselves on being honourable men, should stoop so low as to make such works the guide of their consciences, and of the consciences of others. It is a sad day for old England that even one English clergyman should have learned from an apostate church to teach falsehood and practise treachery.

But it is worthy of especial note that while the Jesuit makes it easy for a servant to rob his master, or for a youth to commit sin, he has a very different code of morals and truth where the Church is concerned.

It is a deadly crime to deceive the Church. It is a deadly crime to conceal a sin, or even a failing, from the priest. Who authorised this double code of morals? Certainly not Scripture. Even the natural law of the heathen revolts against such double dealing.

When writing of the suppression of the Jesuits by the many nations who have revolted against their code of morals, we shall enter more fully into this subject. For the present we must limit ourselves to giving some extracts from the books which they have published. We have already shown that they teach disloyalty. The only loyalty which they allow to be practised is loyalty to the Pope, and even that is subjected to the will of the General of the Order. With all other authority they are openly or secretly at war. And this is what makes the Jesuit so dangerous to the state or country where he lives, and this is the reason why he has been expelled from so many Roman Catholic countries. In the remarkable life of Cardinal Manning, amongst so much that is noteworthy, there is nothing more so than the determined hand with which he kept down the Jesuits, and the fear which his otherwise outspoken biographer had of giving them the least offence. They rule by fear, but a day comes when men rise up against their excessive tyranny, and cast them out. History repeats itself. What the continental bishops of the 16th and 17th centuries did for the protection of the Church and their people, must be done in the 19th century.

In 1614, the French Parliament examined the treatise of the famous Jesuit Frances Suarez, published at Coimbra, in 1613, *permissu Superiorum* The *Arrêt du Parlement* described it as "tending to the subversion of States," and to "induce the subjects of kings and sovereign princes to make attempts on their sacred persons," and ordered it to be burnt by the public executioner. It contains such propositions as these:—"That the Pope has power to depose heretical and obstinate kings is one of the dogmas of the faith which has to be retained and believed:" "an excommunicated king may with impunity be killed by anyone." Servin, in one of his addresses to the Parliament, enumerates, as holding the same opinions on these subjects with Suarez, the names of

Bellarmine, Gretzer, Becan, Azorius, Bonarscius, Richeome, Keller, Lessius, Vasquez,—all of them Jesuits of note: to whom may be added Emmanuel Sà and Alphonsus Sà, Delrius, and Tanner. So highly, however, did Pope Paul V. approve of the work, that in September, 1614, he communicated to Suarez his approbation of its contents. The volume was re-issued in 1619, and again in 1655, thus demonstrating that the brief, alleged to have been issued by Acquaviva, prohibiting all discussion by members of the company on the two objectionable propositions noticed above, was written, as the Jesuit historian Jouvencius intimates, solely to allay the unpleasant controversy awakened in France, and was not intended to be a general instruction. It was simply a deception and a snare, and is, as is remarked by Mr. Cartwright, who brought it to light, "an illustration of the equivocation practised by the Order in its corporate capacity."

In 1652 the Jesuit Santarel taught "that the Pope can depose kings, not only for heresy, schism, and the like . . . but also for personal iniquity and uselessness; that he can depose the emperor and give his empire to another, if he does not defend the Church . . . . that, as St. Peter was given the power of punishing with temporal punishments *and even with death,* certain persons, for the correction and example of others, so to the Church and Chief

Pastor is given the power of punishing with temporal punishments princes, transgressors of divine and human laws, especially if the crime was heresy."

In 1665 and 1666 Alexander VII., in 1679 Innocent XI., and in 1690 Alexander VIII., successively condemned a large number of immoral propositions advanced by Jesuit writers, but they left altogether uncensured the maxims inculcating sedition, treason, and assassination, also contained in the works of the same authors.

On the 1st of January, 1631, the Archbishop of Paris published his condemnations of "some propositions from Ireland, and of two English books, the one by Edward Knott, whose real name is Matthias Wilson, Vice-Provincial of the Jesuits in England, and the other by John Floyde, Jesuit, under the false name of Daniel à Jesu."

On the 10th of February, 1631, a circular subscribed by the Archbishop of Paris and thirty-four bishops then in Paris, was sent to all the archbishops and bishops of France, declaring their condemnation of the same books, as maintaining "many schismatical and blasphemous maxims, which are most injurious to the sacrament of confirmation, and violate the authority of the Sovereign Pontiff."

On the 1st of April, 1641, the University of Paris condemned "La Somme des Pechés," written by Etienne Bauni, professor of moral theology, at Clermont, the

Jesuit College, and published by him at Paris in 1639, with the approbation of the provincial of the company. This sentence was soon after endorsed, on the 12th of April, 1642, by an assembly of clergy held at Mante, by the Archbishop of Toulouse, in which it was "resolved with one common voice, that the books of Father Bauni led souls to profligacy, corrupt good morals, violate natural equity and the law of nations, and excuse as light sins blasphemies, usuries, simonies, and several other sins more enormous."

On the 18th of February, 1655, the Archbishop of Malines published an order forbidding the faithful of his diocese to read the books of the Jesuit Caramuel, afterwards immortalised by Pascal, in "The Provincial Letters."

The parish priests of Rouen, about this time, found it necessary, for the sake of Christianity, to attempt to stem the increasing tide of Jesuit immoral teaching. On the 28th of August, and on the 26th of October, in the year 1656, they addressed a memorial to the Archbishop of Rouen, signed by twenty-eight of their number, complaining of the immoral doctrines taught publicly by the Jesuit fathers, Bauni, Hereau, Caussin, Brisacier, des Bois, Berard, and La Briere.

On the 14th of November, in the same year, the parish priests of Paris presented seventy-one propositions extracted from the published writings of

Caramuel, Mascarenhas, and Escobar, and on the 24th of November they laid before the General Assembly of the Clergy of France *a remonstrance*, from which we extract the following: "Will not the Church, Messeigneurs, disavow these rash men? Will she not testify publicly her heartfelt horror of them? Shall it be said that to be a Catholic a man must approve domestic robbery with Bauni; simony with Valentia; homicide to avoid a blow with Lessius; assassination for slander with Father Lamy; imposture and false accusations with Caramuel; that he must receive all the pernicious or extravagant decisions of Escobar as mysteries revealed by Jesus Christ; and that one is not to complain of them without being treated as a heretic?"

In 1665, the faculty of theology at Paris reported of a book published under the name of Amadeus Guimenæus by Matthew Moya, a Spanish Jesuit, Confessor to the Queen Mother of Spain, that "respect for decency prevented them from noticing the abominations which it contained on the subject of chastity."

Nor can it be said that these heavy charges against the Jesuits are mere "Protestant calumnies," they are simply Roman Catholic facts.

It is noteworthy, also, that English priests have again and again protested against the interference of the Jesuits in political affairs, have declared in plain and emphatic language that they would have enjoyed perfect religious freedom in England if the Jesuits had not tried persistently to stir up strife.

The great Roman Catholic historian, De Thou, has given the substance of a very important document, which appears to have been suppressed not long after its publication. It is a memorial presented to the reigning Pontiff, Clement VIII., by English Roman Catholic priests, remonstrating against the conduct of the Jesuits in England. In it they represented :—"That before the arrival of the Jesuits in England there had been profound peace and harmony among the Catholics . . . That up to that time charges of treason were unheard of; that capital laws against the Anglican priests, and those who harboured them, were not yet published; that the Jesuits, when they joined them as associates, though few in number, had swooped upon the labours of many years, and without toil had reaped what others had sown. That afterwards, when they perceived the danger to which the Catholics were exposed by their own conduct, they had quickly made off, and deserting the warfare of God, had betaken themselves to countries beyond the seas, away from the heat and dust of the conflict; and there, instead of being men devoted to religion, had become the vendors of kingdoms; had assailed chief magistrates in the bitterest terms; had disseminated letters about invading the kingdom with a foreign army, though it was forbidden by capital laws; had written and published volumes about the controverted succession to the throne. That the result was that Catholics, when dragged before the judgment seat, rarely were questioned about religion, always about the state; and almost everything said and done by the Jesuit fathers about the civil government was turned to the ruin of the accused. That in their seminaries their sole object was to entice into the Society any youth endowed with particular talent; that hence arose complaints and rivalries, since the pupils ever became divested of the old patriotic spirit, or were harassed by the Jesuits in divers ways, for refusing to join them. That Cardinal Borromeo, of holy memory, had perceived their mode of angling, and, disliking their ambition, had deprived them of the care of seminaries in the diocese of Milan, and committed it to the secular priests. That while they held sway in the Anglican Church, a wretched dole was grudgingly distributed among the needy and the prisoners, while the Jesuits themselves lived profusely; so that it became a proverb, that the Jesuits were distinguished by the vow of poverty, but the Catholic priests by poverty itself . . . That Catholics had suffered much in England from the time of Henry VIII., but never had they been beset by a heavier calamity than by this last conflict."

One William Watson, educated at Rheims, ordained a priest, and sent on the mission to England in 1586, and executed in 1603 for sharing in Raleigh's mysterious plot, into which, according to the report mentioned by Dodd, the Jesuits had inveigled him in order to get rid of a troublesome enemy, in his "Important Considerations," by the secular priests, printed A.D. 1601, says: "Whilst the said invasion (Spaniards' invasion, planned by Parsons) was thus talked of, and in preparation in Spain, a shorter course was thought of if it might have had success. Mr. Hesket was set on by the Jesuits, in 1592 or thereabouts, with Father Parsons' consent or knowledge, to have stirred up the Earl of Derby to rebellion against Her Highness. Not long after, good Father Holt, and others with him, persuaded an Irishman, one Patrick Collen (as he himself confessed) to attempt the laying of his violent and villainous hands upon Her Majesty. Shortly after, in the year 1593, that notable stratagem was plotted (the whole state knoweth by whom) for Doctor Lopez, the Queen's physician, to have poysoned her, for the which he was executed the year after . . . But we must turn again to Father Parsons, whose turnings and doublings are such as would trouble a right good hound to trace him. . . . .

Thirdly, we desire you, by the mercies of God, to take heed of Novelties and Jesuitism; for it is nothing but treachery, ambition, and a very vizard of most deep hypocrisie. When other kingdoms begin to loath them, why should you so far debase yourselves as to admire them?"

At the end of the pamphlet, after enumerating the designments of the Popes Pius V., Gregory XIII., and Sixtus V.; of the King of Spain; of the Jesuits, especially Cardinal Alan and Parsons, against the Crown and person of Elizabeth, he makes this memorable admission:—

"If we at home, all of us, both priests and people, had possessed our souls in meekness and humility, honoured Her Majesty, born with the infirmities of the state, suffered all things, and dealt as true Catholick priests; if all us (we say) had thus done, most assuredly the state would have loved us, or at least borne with us; where there is one Catholick there would have been ten; there had been no speeches amongst us of racks and tortures, nor any cause to have used them; for none were ever vexed that way, for simply that he was either priest or Catholic, but because they were suspected to have had their hands in some of the said most traitorous designments."

How many of the murders, and how many of the agrarian outrages which have disgraced Ireland, and reflected on the government of England, which has never dared to put them down with a stern hand, may be traced to the influence of Jesuit theology. When it is taught that it is not murder, in fact, that it is not sin to "remove tyrants," what is to prevent men who have been worked up to crime from committing it? And it is remarkable that no pope has ever denounced crime in Ireland, though many popes have specifically and openly encouraged it.

The exposure of the teaching of the Jesuits in the confessional by Pascal, in his famous "Provincial Letters," is well known to the historian. Pascal lived and died a Romanist, and devoted to his church, which he wished to save from a system which struck at the roots of all morality. But the public read of such incidents in the history of the past with a cold indifference, which contrasts strangely with the burning eagerness with which the controversy was pursued in the beginning.

We have already related an incident in which a Jesuit father was caught in his own trap. Another example of this retribution is given by Pascal as having happened in his time. Nor could this be an invention of an enemy, for the names, dates, and places are all given, and any discrepancy of statement would have been at once detected.

A certain John d'Alba was servant in the Jesuit college of Clermont; not being satisfied with the wages which he received, he stole some articles belonging to the fathers. He had learned from their theology that this was quite justifiable, but it was one thing to steal from "seculars," and quite another to steal from "fathers." The fathers in a moment of forgetfulness prosecuted him. When the culprit was brought before the judge he pleaded the teaching of the Jesuit father and casuist, Bauny.

But he pleaded in vain, the judge, M. de Montronge, declared that the doctrine was contrary to all law, human and divine, that the unhappy man should be flogged before the gates of the college, by the common hangman, and that the writings of the Jesuits should be burned publicly at the same time.

Such an arrangement, however, would have been too great an exposure for the fathers, so they contrived to stop the prosecution, and the servant escaped. There is evidence, however, that this affair, which was made public property, was one of several reasons which caused the expulsion of the Jesuits.

Even a cursory examination of the doctrines taught by the Jesuits will prove that their system is destructive of all law, human or divine. The continued existence of such a class of men is an amazing and inexplicable fact. But all the reproaches which have been heaped, and justly heaped, on the Church of Rome, pales before the accusation which must be brought against her, of supporting and encouraging a system which has been denounced again and again by the best and highest prelates in her own communion, by Catholic princes, and by Catholic people. Nay, even an infallible pope has denounced the Jesuit, and the system of the Jesuit as an unendurable evil.

The historian Mosheim says:—"There is scarcely any part of the Catholic world which does not offer for our inspection some conflict of the Jesuits with the magistrates, with other orders of monks, or with the bishops and other religious teachers."

It is impossible in these pages to give any detail of their conduct in carrying out their missions; but a sufficient estimate of it may be formed from the remarkable letter addressed to Innocent X., by Bishop Palafox, of Mexico, on the 8th of January, 1649. His character was so high that he was selected to occupy the post of Viceroy in Mexico, and eventually he was promoted to be Bishop of Osma, in Spain. He is described by Cretineau-Joli, the warm advocate of the Jesuits, as "A man full of apostolical gifts, possessing a bright intellect, and a heart overflowing with charity." But the Jesuits hated him because he would not allow them to rule his diocese.

In self-defence, he was obliged to forward to the Pope a formal remonstrance, in which he expressed himself very plainly regarding Jesuit proceedings, not only in his own case, but also in other instances of which he was cognisant. It is from this letter to

Pope Innocent X., dated 8th of January, 1649, that the following passages are cited :—

"What advantages can Ministers of State, great Lords and Princes, derive from the Jesuits sometimes serving them usefully in their Court, . . . when they see monks, under the pretext of the internal government of consciences, enter with so much pliability into the secrets of houses, which they thus govern as well as the souls, and thus pass scandalously and perniciously from things spiritual to things political, and from profane things to the most criminal? What other order, after having fallen from its first fervour, has by the writings and examples of some of its professors, carried so much laxity into the purity of the ancient morals of the church touching usury, the ecclesiastical precepts, those of the Decalogue, and generally, all the rules of the Christian life? Thus young men who have them as masters, being all filled with these maxims, these opinions, this doctrine, and these examples, become not only cowardly and effeminate, removed from all spirituality, and borne on to all the carnal pleasures, but there is even reason to fear that they have all their life an aversion, disgust, and horror, for all that is a little painful in the Church, and which leads to penitence and the mortification of the Cross. What order, most holy father, since the first foundation of monks and mendicants, has, like the Jesuits, practised banking in the Church of God, given out money at a profit, and held publicly, in their own houses, butchers' stalls and other shops for traffic, scandalous and unworthy of a religious order? What other has ever become bankrupt, and to the astonishment and scandal of seculars, filled almost all the world with their commercial dealings contracts on this by sea and land, and with their subject? The whole Church of China groans and publicly complains that it has not been instructed but seduced by the instructions given by the Jesuits touching the purity of our belief; that they have deprived it of all ecclesiastical jurisdiction; that they have concealed the Cross of the Saviour, and authorised all heathen customs! That they have rather corrupted than introduced those which are veritably Christian; that in making idolaters become Christians, they have made Christians become idolaters; that they have united God and Belial at the same table, in the same temple, at the same altars, and same sacrifices; and in fine, this nation beholds with inconceivable grief that under the mask of Christianity, they revere idols, or to speak better, that under the mask of Paganism they soil the purity of our holy religion. The bishops and ecclesiastics who, in the primitive Church, shed their blood in instructing peoples over all the earth, did they practise the methods which the Jesuits use to instruct these Neophytes? . . . Have all the holy order ever instructed the infidels in this way? . . . Have they ever exempted their Neophytes from the precepts of mortification, of fasting, and of the reception of the Holy Eucharist at least once a year? Have they ever permitted these same Neophytes not only to go into the temples where idols are worshipped, to assist at the abominable sacrifices offered to them; even to sacrifice to them, and thus to soil their souls by so horrible a crime? . . I am much deceived if the angel of darkness does not rejoice when he beholds, in temples raised to his honour, not only his old adorers, but also the baptised, the Neophytes, and sometimes those who profess to preach our holy faith, offering with these idolaters sacrifices at his altars, kneeling down, prostrating themselves, and giving him incense, thus communicating with them by external acts . . . which, since the Apostles' time, has never been suffered in the Catholic Church, with whatever pretext they try to cover this idolatry, by which, in directing internally their intention towards a cross which they carry secretly, they offer an external service to the idol of the demon."

CHAPTER XIV.

CONCLUSION.

I DO not conclude the present work without a very deep sense of personal responsibility, nor without a very clear knowledge of the danger to which I have exposed myself in writing it. It is always a serious matter to write history; but when the writing of the history of the past must so closely affect the history which we are all making at the present, then, indeed, truth and accuracy are of supreme importance.

No doubt I have omitted much which might have been said and said with advantage, but this omission has been the result of necessity, not of choice. To have said all that might have been said would have made it necessary to enlarge the work considerably, and this would have added to expenses, which are already difficult to meet. There is perhaps no more painful sign of the times than the difficulty in inducing the general public, and even some Christian people, to read any work which criticises Roman Catholic teaching. Witness the treatment which has been meted out to a recent biographer, not merely by his Roman Catholic brethren, but by the so-called Protestant press. One might suppose that Rome was and had always been the greatest benefactor to the people of England, instead of having been the cause of wrongs and sufferings which we should never forget, because by forgetting we risk the non-enforcement of even ordinary precautions against the renewal of such terrible evils. How are our children to be warned by the true history of the past if it is to be studiously concealed from them?

Again, a false charity has been the cause of much harm amongst those who as Christians should be eager, for the honour of their Lord, to protect the future of their country from the domination of an unchristian Church. Perhaps it may be added that a love of controversial sensationalism has had its share, and no small share, in producing this distaste for truth and solid facts. Those who seek truth, and truth only, will certainly hear all sides, but the side of strict truth is above all things the side which we should choose in matters of such supreme moment.

Again, there is no doubt that some of the usual Jesuit wiles have been played all too successfully on earnest Protestants. The question as to whether there are or are not Jesuits in disguise has been disputed with acrimony; acrimony always blinds to truth, and this is precisely what the Jesuit desires. In the face of history, which proves that Jesuits in disguise have been common and successful; and in the face of the fact that the Jesuits themselves, now become daring in England, have even given a list of those who have acted in this way, why should there be any doubt on the subject? But it should be remembered that the Jesuit in disguise is a Jesuit in disguise. Further, the Jesuit would be no Jesuit if he did not make the disguise suit times and circumstances. The plans which were carried out in the reign of Elizabeth of brave memory, or of James II., could not be carried out at the present day, as they would too easily be discovered.

We all live too much in public now to admit of men going about in multifarious disguises, however well these methods suited other times. I believe, and it should be remembered that I know Rome from the inside as well as from the outside, and this with no ordinary knowledge, that the danger to-day is from the relatives of Protestants who have become Romanists, and who have a power and influence which is unsuspected, and therefore a serious danger. In some families a mother has become a Romanist or a daughter has become a Romanist. The zeal of converts to Rome is proverbial. Family ties and affections are not easily loosened. What more natural than that the daughter should be influenced by the Romanist mother or the mother influenced by the Romanist daughter?

I do not speak without knowledge and painful

experience. The first object of these "converts" is the advancement of their Church. It is fashionable just now to be a Romanist. Rome is patronised in high quarters, and unhappily men and women who call themselves Christians are not always above the inducements of social advancement. They may be themselves persons of good social position, all the more, they desire, perhaps unconsciously, to maintain that position. They "wear their jewels still," they still wish to make the most of both worlds. On the platform they are perhaps strongly Protestant, but in private they listen to their Roman Catholic friends, and are influenced by them, and yet they may appear to be very pronounced Protestants, but those who are true and sincere converts from Rome to Christ must always suffer at their hands.

Rome smiles at their folly, while she uses it to her advantage. If Rome apprehends danger from one who has renounced her faith, and who exposes her tactics well and fearlessly, she at once tries to silence the voice which would condemn her effectually. It is easily done. The Romanist mother or daughter has only to wait her time, and insinuate that after all this brave protester against Rome is "a Jesuit in disguise," and the end is attained. Rome is a past master in duplicity and in understanding human nature, and how to work on the jealousy, pride, or other weaknesses of poor humanity.

If she can silence a tongue or a pen which has exposed her truthfully her end is gained, and it is all the more triumph to her if she can turn the arms of the enemy against the enemy. Rome has already described fully how successfully she worked in this way in former times, so that there is no excuse for ignorance.

There are two classes of English men and women to whom this work should appeal. Christian people should be aroused to save England from an unchristian power. Men who have even the least appreciation for intellectual and social freedom, should leave no effort unmade to save England from the dominion of a Church which has been everywhere the grave of thought and intellectual freedom.

This book will have been written in vain if it is not realised that there can be no religious freedom where Rome has power, if it is not realised that there can be no political or intellectual freedom where Rome has power.

We have said elsewhere that it is a mistake to suppose that the Jesuits are in some way different from the Roman Catholic Church. Would the Church of Rome have supported the Jesuits as she has done, if they were not Romanists of the Romanists? The fact is that Jesuitism is Romanism carried to its logical conclusion.

It would seem sometimes as if we were living

under the same social and moral conditions as those who lived before the Flood. They ate and drank, they married and gave in marriage, they mocked at those who warned them in the name of the Lord. But for all that, the Flood came and swept them all away. It is so pleasant to drift with the tide, it is so easy to be "popular," and to let troubles pass us by. That there will be a future retribution, either in this world or the next, for these despisers of prophetic warnings, is certain, but they live for the present, and they have their reward.

Sadder still is it for those who are truly called of God when they allow prejudice or self-interest to influence, if not warp their judgment, and who turn from those who, having had long experience of Rome, can best help them in the controversy. It is the object of Rome to divide those who are most earnest in opposing her, and unhappily she too often succeeds in attaining her end. Surely a careful study of the attempts of Rome, and especially of the Jesuits to divide Christian people, should be a sufficient warning. It is, after all, simply copying the worst characteristics of Rome when Christian people refuse to co-operate with each other because of trifling differences of doctrine or opinion. So it is also lamentable when differences arise as to the manner in which the holy war against the enemy of God and truth should be carried on; it weakens the hands, and chills the zeal of those who should maintain a united front against an always united enemy.

If Christians only united as Rome does, how soon would there be a change which would alter the whole face of society.

Again, even Christians often, perhaps unconsciously, are ashamed of a quiet, steady, but open profession of their detestation of teachings which are distinctly contrary to the Word of God. Rome is never either afraid or ashamed of her religion, and proclaims it on all occasions, and at all times and places. Protestants are doing the work of Rome by their indifference and want of courage. The outposts are being surrendered to the enemy. It is the first step, and an important step, in gaining an entrance to the citadel.

Even those who do not oppose Rome because she is unchristian, or who have persuaded themselves that she is Christian because they do not take the trouble to understand what she teaches, should pause ere they give her power to take away all our liberties. Rome is the grave of intellectual progress and of moral rectitude.

Mr. Cartwright, a calm and dispassionate writer on the Jesuits, says:—" Much has been said about the intellectual eminence of the Order, as shown in educational institutions, its scholastic efforts have uniformly been directed to substitute for the occasional irregularities attendant on a buoyant nature that monotony which accompanies stagnant life—the dead-level of mediocrity. Independence of character, of mind, of research, are objects hateful to the Society, which must be expelled, and in lieu of these it has evolved a system of pseudo-culture, studded with the counterfeits of science—playthings adapted to natures that are being carefully nursed to grow up with stunted strength. Accomplishments of a captivating order—talents of handy and specious character—have largely distinguished those trained in the schools of the Society; but in the long roll of Jesuit Fathers—men of undeniably busy and sedulous habits—it will hardly be possible to pick out one name, the bearer whereof admittedly takes rank amongst the great discoverers in the fields of science and of thought—amongst the men who have materially advanced the knowledge of mankind. A glance at the Ecclesiastical annals of the last centuries is enough to reveal the increasing sterility within the officially recognised area of the Latin Church.

"In the seventeenth century, the French clergy, in corporate declarations with their names appended thereto, over and over again protested against, and stigmatised as outrageous, the theological maxims propounded by Jesuit divines."

This system of moral theology leaves every man at the mercy of the confessor, so that between man and man there can be no social or business confidence. The confessor decides on the rectitude of contracts, and dictates the policy of the statesman. He decides the conduct of the husband to the wife, of the wife to the husband, of the employer towards the employed, of the servant to the master, and from his decisions there is no appeal. Nor is this iniquitous interference with the rights of humanity confined to the Jesuit. The moral theology of the Jesuit is approved by the universal Roman Catholic Church ; it is taught in every Roman Catholic college in the world. Rome is responsible for all the crimes which ever have been or ever may be committed by the Jesuit, for she has set the seal of her highest approval on his teaching. Even the present Pope, who is proclaimed, or proclaims himself, as one of the most learned and enlightened of his class, has, as we have shown elsewhere, bestowed the highest approval which pope can give on these men, and their soul destroying system. And are they to govern England, and are their pupils to be our legislators and rulers ? It seems so.

Perhaps there is no more remarkable statement in a remarkable book than that in which the writer declares when the religious orders were suppressed by the revolution in Italy, Pius IX. said that though he was bound publicly to condemn the suppression of monasteries, in his heart he could not but rejoice, for it was a blessing in disguise. Mr. Purcell says he asked Cardinal Manning in 1887 if this statement was well founded. The Cardinal replied that it truly represented the views of the Pope. What a commentary on the supposed sanctity of the religious orders of the Church of Rome, and what an exposure of the failings of infallibility. We find popes and cardinals very ready to interfere in the affairs of those with whom they have no concern, but very slow to attempt any reform in their own Church, no matter how necessary.

Further, Cardinal Manning declared that the success of the revolution in Italy was "*principally due to the laxity of morals in the clergy, and to defective education and religious training in the schools.*"

And yet we are asked to support monasteries and convents, and to endow colleges and other institutions with public money where precisely the same system is carried out. Has England been bewitched by Rome?

The Church which compelled Galileo to swear to what he knew to be a lie in order to obtain liberty to exist, has not changed. To-day, if Rome had the power, all scientific discussion would be baned and barred, and she would find some theological reason for forbidding the investigations of Röntgen, and discover heresy in the X rays. Rome flourishes best in darkness, and Rome knows it.

But grave as these matters are, what shall be said of the frightful heresies which she approves and encourages. If scientific research is discouraged, theological disquisitions are allowed which border on blasphemy.

Huber, in his admirable work, "Les Jesuites," calls attention to the heresy which teaches that the body of Mary is found in the sacrament with the body of Christ. This horrible, must we not say, blasphemy seems to have originated with Ignatius Loyola. Even so lately as the year 1851, Oswald, the professor of theology at Paderborn, taught in his *Mariologie dogmatique*, that priests, in reward for their virginity, received in the Communion not only the body of Christ, but also the flesh and the milk of Mary. Mgr. Malou, Bishop of Bruges, has taught that Mary wears a triple crown as the daughter of God the Father, the Mother of God the Son, and the spouse of God the Holy Ghost.

These are not mere mediæval theological pastimes or refinements; they are taught to-day as part of the deposit of faith, and approved by the Church as such. Much more might be said, but of what avail? The question of questions remains, Will Christian people support even by silent acquiescence a system which teaches blasphemy? Will they support by their indifference a system which places the forgiveness of sin in the hands of man, and deprives God of His chief attribute of mercy?

Will Englishmen, who pride themselves on their love of liberty, support a system which is based on the right to deprive all mankind of all liberty except what the "Church" permits? Will they vote for the pecuniary endowment of men who teach that rebellion against their lawful sovereign is so noble a virtue as to deserve the highest honours which the "Church" can pay? Every endowment, every pecuniary help which is given, whether it be large or small, national or private, will be used to teach the coming generation that the "Church" is above every power and every law, and that in order to be a faithful Romanist abject submission must be paid to every dictate of Rome in matters social and political as well as in matters of religion. It is time that this should be clearly understood, and it is time that when understood men and women who love their God, and who love their country, should have the courage of their opinions, rather we should say of their faith, and stay the plague which is destroying the land, and which, if it but spreads a little further, will make a desolation of England as it has made a desolation of every land and every clime where it has been fostered and encouraged.

APPENDIX I.

We give below extracts from two letters which throw a lurid light on the inside history of the Roman Catholic Church :—

The first letter is from Père la Chaise, confessor to Louis XIV., and is addressed to Father Peters, confessor to James II. of England, in 1688. It is copied from the seventh volume of the collection of manuscript papers selected from the library of Edward Harley, Earl of Oxford, and is entitled Father la Chaise's project for the extirpation of heretics, in a letter from him to Father Peters, 1688. The authenticity of this letter has been disputed, probably because it tells so strongly against Romanism.

Père la Chaise explains thus how he compelled his penitent, Louis IV., to sign the decree for the Revocation of the Edict of Nantes, which expelled from France her best and noblest sons, and inflicted a blow on that country, commercial and social, which she has never recovered. "It cost me many threats and promises, before I could bring it thus far, our King being a long time very unwilling. But at last I got him on the hip, for he had lain with his daughter-in-law, for which I would by no means give him absolution, till he had given me an instrument under his own hand and seal, to sacrifice all the heretics in one day. Now, as soon as I had my desired commission, I appointed the day when this should be done; and in the meantime made ready some thousands of letters to be sent into all parts of France in one post night."

But the father was baffled for the time. The Duke of Condé, whom he calls the "devil's instrument," got some idea of what was going on, and came to the rescue of the king. He succeeded in getting back the warrant from Père la Chaise, but the father was not so easily baffled. He says: "I soon gave an account of this affair to several Fathers of our Society, who promised to do their best to prevent the aforesaid prince's doing such another act, which was accordingly done; for, within six days after the damned action, he was poisoned, and well he deserved it. The King also did suffer too, but in another fashion, for disclosing the design unto the prince, and hearkening unto his counsel. And many a time since, when I have had him at confession, I have shook hell about his ears, and made him sigh, fear, and tremble, before I would give him absolution. Nay, more than that, I have made him beg for it on his knees before I would consent to absolve him."

In the end the plot was carried out, but the Jesuit confessor was obliged to content himself with the banishment of all the Huguenots, instead of a wholesale massacre.

APPENDIX II.

CARDINAL NEWMAN'S LETTER.

During the sitting of the Vatican Council the late Cardinal Newman wrote a confidential letter to his bishop, then Dr. Ullathorne. This letter was soon public property. It is well known that some of the best and most learned bishops of the Roman Catholic Church were strongly opposed to the proclamation of the new doctrine. But of what avail, when the Jesuits wished to take a step towards the accomplishment of their great object of establishing a universal monarchy with the White Pope nominally at the head and the Black Pope holding the reins.

This important letter was published in the London *Standard*, on the 7th of April. We give some brief extracts below:—

"Rome ought to be a name to lighten the heart at all times, and a council's proper office is, when some great heresy or other evil impends, to inspire hope and confidence in the faithful; but now we have the greatest meeting which ever has been, and that at Rome, infusing into us by the accredited organs of Rome and of its partisans, such as the *Civilta*, the *Armonia*, the *Universe* and the *Tablet*, little else than fear and dismay.

"Why should an aggressive, insolent faction be allowed to 'Make the heart of the just sad, whom the Lord hath not made sorrowful.' Why cannot we be alone when we have pursued peace and thought no evil?

"I assure you, my Lord, some of the truest minds are driven one way and another, and do not know where to rest their feet. One day, determining 'to give up all theology as a bad job' and recklessly to believe, henceforth, almost that the Pope is impeccable, at another tempted to 'believe all the worst which a book like Janus says,' others doubting about 'the capacity possessed by bishops drawn from all corners of the earth to judge what is fitting for European society,' and then, again angry with the Holy See for listening to the flattery of a clique of Jesuits, Redemptorists, and converts."

It proved a bolt from the blue. Newman had not yet learned not to put his trust in bishops, later he knew better. No wonder that Manning, the great promoter of papal infallibility, declared that his "spirit must be crushed." It need scarcely be said that the Jesuit organ in Rome, the *Civilta*, denounced Newman, and that M. Veuillot, the famous French ultramontane journalist, denounced him and all his works, in no measured language. Indeed, Newman had aggravated him past forgiveness for he had compared him to Murphy, who, later was made the victim of

Romanist rage and hatred for the crime of telling the truth.

At first Newman stoutly denied the authorship of the letter. Then, when absolute denial became impossible, he prevaricated, but finally neither prevarication nor denial were of the least avail and he was obliged to admit the authorship. It need scarcely be said that the publication of this letter did not advance his ecclesiastical prospects in Rome.

Note to page 258.—Cardinal Manning's biographer tells us that he tried to have himself called to the Upper House as a spiritual peer, and nearly succeeded through his influence with the Royal Family. The suggestion of the Jesuit Parsons that all parliamentary representatives should be approved by the Romanist bishops is already carried out in Ireland, where, with rare exceptions, none other need apply.

APPENDIX III.

From Hutton's "Life of Manning" *page* 257.

"The Salvation Army has a growing affinity with Catholicism, and its members, accustomed to an autocratic rule, might very well find in some future Archbishop of Westminster, the successor who will surely one day be needed, if the organisation is to be held together at all. Of course these soldiers and salvation lasses are far enough from being Catholics at present, but they have accepted fully the fundamental principle of Catholicism—obedience. There is here a promising field for the expansion of the Catholic Church, unless Catholics themselves shirk the opportunity."

AUTHORITIES CONSULTED.

LES JESUITES, par J. Huber, professeur a Munich ; traduit par Alfred Marchaud. 2 vols. Paris, Taudoy et Fischbacher.

THE POOR GENTLEMEN OF LIÉGE. M. Crétineau Joly. Shaw and Co.

THE JESUITS : THEIR CONSTITUTION AND TEACHING. W. C. Cartwright, M.P. J. Murray.

GERMAN SOCIETY AT THE CLOSE OF THE MIDDLE AGES. E. Belfort Bax. Swan, Sonnenschein and Co.

THE HISTORY OF THE JESUITS. G. B. Nicolini. Bell and Sons.

A HISTORICAL SKETCH OF THE CONFLICTS BETWEEN JESUITS AND SECULARS IN THE REIGN OF QUEEN ELIZABETH. Thomas Graves Law. David Nutt.

RECENT EVENTS AND A CLUE TO THEIR SOLUTION. Lord Robert Montagu. Hodder and Stoughton.

THE JUDGES OF FAITH. Thomas J. Jenkins. John Murphy and Co., U.S.A.

PARALLÈLE DE LA DOCTRINE DES PAIGENS AVEC CELLE DES JESUITES.

DEMONOLOGY AND WITCHCRAFT. Robert Brown. John Shaw and Co.

MAURESA ; OR, THE SPIRITUAL EXERCISES OF ST. IGNATIUS. Burns and Co.

MORAL THEOLOGY OF ST. ALPHONSUS LIGUORI.

A GLIMPSE OF THE GREAT SECRET SOCIETY. Macintosh.

THE CATHOLIC DOGMA. Müller. Benziger Bros., New York. U.S.A.

THE JESUITS. Overbury. Houlston and Wright.

THE JESUITS IN NORTH AMERICA IN THE SEVENTEENTH CENTURY. Francis Parkman. Macmilll n and Co.

LUTHER VINDICATED. C. H. Collette. Bernard Quaritch.

JESUITISM ANCIENT AND MODERN. M. de Pradt. Seroux and Constant-Chautpir, Paris.

BRITISH HISTORY AND PAPAL CLAIMS. James Paton. 2 vols. Hodder and Stoughton.

THE NOVELTIES OF ROMANISM. C. H. Collette. Religious Tract Society.

FAMILIAR EXPOSITION OF CATHOLIC DOCTRINE. Benziger Bros., New York.

CRIMINAL TRIALS: THE GUNPOWDER PLOT. Library of Entertaining Knowledge.

THE JESUITS; A HISTORY TOLD TO THE GERMAN PEOPLE. Theodore Griesinger. Allen and Co.

THE JESUITS. Paul von Hoenbraech.

CHEZ LEA LES JESUITES. Lucien Gleize. Dentu, Paris.

OUR COUNTRY. Strong, New York.

JESUITISME, ANCIEN ET MODERNE. De Pradt, Paris.

THE ROMAN-CATHOLIC CHURCH AND CHRISTIAN STATE Hergenrother.

HISTOIRE DES JESUITES. Guettée, Paris.

COMPENDIUM THEOLOGIÆ MORALIS. S. J. Gury, Ratisbon.

LES PROVINCIALES. Pascal, Paris.

CHURCH HISTORY, etc. Algoz.

Printed in the United States
149377LV00001B/12/A